# Reflected Values
# A Second Book of Assemblies

### Roy Blatchford

*'Do not confine your children to your own learning for they were born in a different time.'*

Hebrew Proverb

**Stanley Thornes (Publishers) Ltd.**

*for Luke Asa*

First published in 1996 by:
Stanley Thornes (Publishers) Ltd
Ellenborough House
Wellington Street
CHELTENHAM GL50 1YW
England

96  97  98  99  00  /  10  9  8  7  6  5  4  3  2  1

A catalogue record for this book is available from the British Library.

ISBN 0 7487 2312 9

Typeset by Northern Phototypesetting, Co Ltd., Bolton
Printed and bound in Great Britain by Redwood Books

# Contents

**Introduction**                                                  vi

**Turning Points**                                                 1
  1  The power of reading                       2
  2  The pleasure of reading                    3
  3  Stargazing                                 6
  4  Death in birth                             9
  5  Truths                                    11
  6  Great expectations                       12
  7  What am I doing here?                     15
  8  Reborn                                   18
  9  Daydreamer                               21
10  Brothers in arms                                     24

**Personal Values**                                               29
  1  Choice                                   30
  2  Sacred land                              32
  3  'No, you can't blame me at all'           35
  4  Love over gold                           37
  5  A gift of freedom                        40
  6  Injustice                                42
  7  Courage                                  45
  8  Selflessness                             48
  9  Sharing                                  50
10  Ageing                                               52

**Faith and Belief**                                              55
  1  Prisoners of conscience                  56
  2  Belief: who needs it today?              59
  3  Personal philosophies                    61
  4  The Creation                             66
  5  'I did survive'                          69
  6  Euthanasia                               71
  7  Dead friends and living friends          74
  8  A different way to say goodbye            76
  9  In search of the self                    79
10  The nation's soul                                   81

**The Twenty-First Century**                                      85
  1  Areas of darkness                        86
  2  Will robots rule?                        88

3  A perfect baby                                        91
4  Eating sushi                                          94
5  University challenge, AD 2020                          97
6  In place of schools                                    99
7  Learning to live with the city                        102
8  A sound of thunder                                    104
9  A silicon chip in your head                           108
10  Grand Tour: 2484                                     109

**Success and Failure**                                  113
1  Heroic failures                                       114
2  Grapes of wrath                                       116
3  The four-minute mile                                  118
4  The angel of the candy counter                        120
5  It was a very bad year … (1)                          123
6  It was a very bad year … (2)                          125
7  Humility                                              128
8  Capturing animals                                     130
9  The road not taken                                    133
10  If…                                                  135

**International Scenes**                                  139
1  Poverty as pornography                                140
2  Blood and belonging                                   142
3  Zlata's Diary                                         144
4  Refugees                                              146
5  Russia's railway children                            150
6  'God bless Africa'                                    152
7  The Terezín ghetto                                    155
8  An evil cradling                                      157
9  Barracuda breakfast                                   160
10  Midtown Manhattan                                    162

**The Human Being and Doing**                            165
1  Jailed for life                                       166
2  Room 101                                              169
3  As old as old could be                                172
4  Communication                                         174
5  Silence                                               177
6  Love                                                  180
7  Friends and enemies                                   182
8  What is a community?                                  185
9  Brain sex                                             187
10  Intelligences                                        190

**School Matters**                                       193
1  Reading books is not worth the effort                 194
2  Projects: 'Tarzan's easy'                             196
3  Reputations                                           199

 4 Stereotypes  201
 5 Value-added  204
 6 God in a test-tube  205
 7 Looking back  208
 8 Competition or co-operation?  211
 9 Passing exams: here are the answers  213
10 The best years of their lives  217

**Moral Mazes**  221
 1 Storytelling  222
 2 Death came to my front door  224
 3 Friendship  227
 4 Revenge  229
 5 Addictions  233
 6 Time  236
 7 Underclass or just unfortunates?  238
 8 Who not to treat?  240
 9 Being certain  242
10 Taking sides  244

**Index of authors**  248

**Acknowledgements**  250

# Introduction

## Using this collection

In common with its predecessor volume, *Reflected Values* works on the premise that it is possible to make most subjects relevant to any group within the 11–19 age range, given good preparation and delivery of the material. That said, certain readings included here are more challenging in language and subject-matter, and the presenter may wish to adapt or judiciously edit these.

The collection is simply organised around 9 core themes. Within each thematic section are 10 assemblies, organised to a common pattern: subject title; introduction; reading; reflections. Each assembly is planned to take around 15 minutes.

The *Readings* have been chosen first and foremost as a good read in any hands. If you use this book in no other way, you are guaranteed over 100 'stories' that have been tried and tested in secondary school assemblies.

The *Introduction* and *Reflections* provide a context for each reading. They have been drafted in a personal and colloquial style which the presenter can adapt to suit the audience and the topicality of the occasion. The use of questions offers an opportunity for students to reflect in silence either prior to or following a reading. Potential links between various readings are indicated in the text.

## The collective act of worship

Within the school setting a broad definition of worship makes sense. Something like this works well for pupils, parents, staff and governors alike:

*Worship has to do with worth and worthiness. It is the recognition, affirmation and celebration of the 'worth'ship of certain realities and values, held to be of central importance to the community which worships. The act of worshipping renews the meaning of these realities and values for the community, helping each of its members to grasp them personally. The community focuses on what it knows to be of great or supreme worth, hence worthy of preservation and promotion, and of its members' dedication.*

We cannot assume that our students constitute a body of worshippers. Our responsibility is to provide the *opportunity* for worship; individuals will respond and react at different levels and in different ways. Assemblies, thoughts-for-the-day, collective acts of worship, reflections – call them what you will – afford a much-needed alternative prospectus to that of the material values which dominate young people's contemporary culture.

In preparing assembly material each week, I try always to hold on to the spirit of the Hebrew proverb: 'Do not confine your children to your own learning for they were born in a different time'. At the same time, I hold fast to certain values and principles about a flourishing learning environment, values which are as vital today as they were to the young people my father taught in the early 1950s.

I remain optimistic that children in our schools today, if well taught rather than just left to learn, will shape a 21st century as dynamic and challenging as it will be compassionate and secure.

Roy Blatchford, Oxford 1995

# Turning Points

*The great advantage of not having children must be that you can go on believing that you are a nice person. Once you have children, you realise how wars start.*

Fay Weldon

*What we need in order to survive, and what we need in order to flourish are two different things.*

# 1 The power of reading

## Introduction

The golden key to so much learning is the skill of learning to read. In the following passage, Irish author Joe O'Connor writes about what first gave him an interest in books, reading and writing.

## Reading

### Reading with a pure heart

I've enjoyed books for as long as I can remember. I think this is because my first teacher took a dim view of the Montessori system. She was an elderly nun called Mother Lawrence. She wasn't too hot on plasticine, or on the putting of little plastic boxes into slightly bigger plastic boxes.

But she was very hot on reading. She taught us the alphabet as though it was the strangest compendium of magical symbols. The joy she brought to her teaching was absolutely infectious. Being able to read was the most important thing in the world, she would say, a person could do anything if only he or she could read. I was spellbound by her. There would often be tears of happiness in her eyes when she talked about the importance of books, what marvellous things were to be learned from books, what fabulous stories there were, how lucky we were that God had given us words and imaginations.

She taught us to read. And we were too young to be grateful. But Peter and Jane, in the dog-eared and battered Ladybird books that she would hand out to us, were nearly as real to me as my own family. She was a lovely gentle woman. I think about her a lot.

My parents were always wonderful about books too. There were always books in the house. My mother liked biographies, Irish history, all kinds of stuff. My father, Seán, was a very keen reader also. He was – still is – particularly fond of Tennyson's poetry. He used to read to me from *The Lady of Shallot* and the *Death of King Arthur*. I loved it when he did that. I still feel goose-pimples when I read the lines about the mystic hand 'clothed in samite' reaching out of the lake to grasp Excalibur.

In secondary school we had to read John Steinbeck's *The Pearl* and Hemingway's *The Old Man and the Sea*. The Steinbeck was particularly enthralling because it contained a brief description of a young woman undressing. The priest told us it was not a sin to read this page once, 'with a pure heart', but that if we read it over and over again – if we 'turned back to it, particularly when alone' – then that would be a sin.

He seemed to feel that reading was best done in large supervised groups, a bit like formation ballroom dancing or saying the rosary. He told us that the most dangerous parts of a book were invariably the bits to which you wanted to 'turn back when alone.'

As a writer, I have tried to remember this. I keep putting things into books that I want people to turn back to when alone. Later, in sixth year, I had a friend called Sarah Moore. She gave me a copy of Salinger's *The Catcher in the Rye*, which I adored. It made me want to write books myself. I began to try to write short stories around then, although I found it very difficult. I had another friend called Andrew Deignan who read a lot. He used to bring the most extraordinary books into school and lend them to me.

I read Flaubert's *Madame Bovary*, *The Trial* by Kafka, *The Kiss* by Chekhov, Joyce's *Dubliners*, Maupassant's short stories. And although other things in my life were tough enough when I was 17, I remember my last year in school with great happiness, the exquisite joy of discovering all these stories, the breathless excitement of taking the first steps towards making up stories of my own.

*Joe O'Connor*

## Reflections

\* 'Being able to read was the most important thing in the world, she would say, a person could do anything if only he or she could read.'

'He told us that the most dangerous parts of a book were invariably the bits to which you wanted to "turn back when alone." '

In these two quotations Joe O'Connor gives a personal view of reading and of the power of books. His views are worth reflecting on very carefully. They highlight the extent to which both in school and at home the written word has a vital part to play in our lives.

As we get older we become – with practice – more fluent and intelligent readers. We appreciate what a complex and rewarding skill reading actually is, and what horizons are opened up for us through an enjoyment of words and books.

The school library might be said to be the cornerstone of the school as a *learning* community.

(See also **Reading books is not worth the effort**, p. 194).

# 2 The pleasure of reading

## Introduction

This passage offers a glimpse into the reading history of the novelist Sue Townsend (creator of Adrian Mole) – from when she first learned to read through to her later passions for certain writers.

## Reading

*Secret passion between the covers*

I was eight before I could read. My teacher was a nasty drunken woman who looked like a dyspeptic badger. I'm 46 now and she is long dead, but my heart almost stops if I see anyone resembling her stomping along the pavement towards me.

I learnt to read during the three weeks I was away from school with a spectacular case of mumps. (Mumps *were* mumps in the Fifties.) My mother went to a rummage sale and came back with a pile of *William* books written by Richmal Crompton, a person I assumed to be a man. I looked at the illustrations and laughed, then I tried to read the captions underneath these delightful scratchy drawings. My mother helped me out and slowly and mysteriously the black squiggles turned into words which turned into sentences, which turned into stories. I could read.

There should have been a hundred-gun salute. The Red Arrows should have flown overhead. The night sky should have blazed with fireworks.

I joined the library thirsting after more *William* books. I read one a day and then two a day, then I ran out and fumbled along the library shelves pulling out books at random. Nothing was ever as good as William, but the die was cast. I was addicted to print.

Christmas came, and with it a stack of books in the Woolworth's classics series. They had serious red covers, and gilt lettering: *Treasure Island* and *Kidnapped*, R. D. Blackmore's *Lorna Doone, Heidi, Little Women*, Harriet Beecher Stowe's *Uncle Tom's Cabin*. In the front of each book there was a coloured illustration, and when I had read the last page I would turn back to the beginning and study this picture as closely as a Sotheby's expert, trying to extract more meaning and more pleasure. I've always felt a great sadness on finishing a book I've enjoyed. And a strong reluctance to actually close the book and put it on a shelf. I delay the moment of parting as other people might put off finishing a love affair.

During the junior school holidays, I would often read three books a day. The local librarian used to interrogate me on the contents, convinced that I was showing off, although there was nobody to impress in my immediate circle.

Most adults took my passion for books as a sign of derangement. 'Your brain will burst', was a common warning, one that I took seriously. When reading, I half expected my head to explode and hit the ceiling. It didn't put me off. Reading became the most important thing in my life. My favourite place to read was on my bed, lying on a pink cotton counterpane, and if I had a bag of sweets next to me, I was in heaven.

The first book I lost a night's sleep over was *Jane Eyre*. It was winter and our house wasn't heated – apart from a coal fire in the living room. I read in bed. My fingers and arms froze, my nails went blue. Frost formed on the inside of the window panes, but I could not put *Jane Eyre* down. I loved Jane. Snow fell, a few birds began to sing, my eyes drooped but I had to read on. I ate my porridge reading. I walked to school reading. I read in each lesson until the morning milk break. I finished the last page in the school cloakroom, surrounded by wet gabardine mackintoshes. I felt very lonely. I wanted to talk about *Jane Eyre*. There were so many references I didn't understand, but I made no attempt to talk about that or any other book.

Reading became a secret obsession: I would drop a book guiltily if anyone came into a room. I went nowhere without a book – the lavatory, a bus journey, walking to school.

I began to buy second-hand paperbacks from Leicester market. I soon realised that the orange-covered Penguins were an indication of quality. If I found a writer I liked, I would collect and read everything of theirs I could.

The first erotic book I read was about a Spanish bull-fighter. I don't recall the title or the author but I certainly remember the delicious anticipation it aroused in me. I couldn't wait to grow up and have a sexual experience. Though Spanish bull-fighters were thin on the ground in Leicester.

I left school one week before my fifteenth birthday and I remember what I was reading on my last day at school. The plays of Oscar Wilde. I took a biography of Ernest Hemingway with me to my first job. It was too large to fit in my narrow office drawer so I hid it inside a brown paper bag and shoved it *under* the desk. I didn't read it during the day, but its presence was a comfort.

I was an emotional reader. I laughed and cried over Dickens and Arnold Bennett, and Nevil Shute made me yearn for a faithful, plodding, Shute-type of man. I imagined us trekking across the Australian outback, finding a run-down hamlet, and then transforming it – together – until death or flood parted us.

When I was 16 I found a book that did truly change my life – *The Gambler* by Dostoevsky. Not his best book, but good enough for me at the time. I didn't know that Dostoevsky was a genius. I knew nothing about Russia, but I found something in *The Gambler* that comforted and satisfied me. I was annoyed by the Russian names and baffled by the references to historical events, but I liked the notion of duality; that good and evil co-exist inside every human being. I looked on the market stalls for more Dostoevsky but found nothing. I couldn't borrow more of his books from the library because I owed a fortune in library fines (I could never bear to take the books back). I realised that I would have to *buy* a book. Bookshops were intimidating places to me then. They were staffed by wizened old men who knew their stuff, and my big problem was that I didn't know how to pronounce Dostoevsky.

One day I was in a café and saw a man with a beard who was wearing a black polo-neck sweater. He was reading a book and smoking a French cigarette. I had *The Gambler* with me and I daringly crossed to this intellectual-looking stranger, showed him the book and asked him how to pronounce the author's name. He pronounced the name Dostoevsky carefully and we became friends. His name was Bob and he invited me back to his squalid cottage in the country. Over the next few years, Bob introduced me to Henry Miller, Kafka, Donleavy and Sean O'Casey. I would trek out to 'Mouse House', as I called it, at any hour of the day or night; Bob was always genial and welcoming, but was also, to my great sorrow, homosexual.

I married at 18, and in that year I discovered Graham Greene, John Steinbeck, George Eliot and the book review pages of the *Manchester Guardian*. I remember the first new hardback book I ever bought; it was Brendan Behan's *Hold Your Hour and Have Another*.

At 19 I had my first baby. My son was born prematurely and I was forced to leave him in hospital in an incubator while he gained weight. I found Evelyn Waugh's *Scoop* on the hospital trolley – a delightful compensation.

Being a very nosy person, I have always enjoyed reading diaries, letters and journals, especially Waugh's, Noël Coward's, Pepys's and Virginia Woolf's. Sylvia Plath's letters to and from her mother prove to me that she was programmed from an early age to take her own life. The standards she set herself were so impossibly high.

My favourite contemporary writers are Kingsley Amis, Paul Theroux, John Updike, Martin Amis, Iris Murdoch ... but I can't go on, there are so many. I seem to have spent my whole life reading.

*Sue Townsend*

## Reflections

* Sue Townsend's account of how she learned to read reminds us that there are many routes – in and out of school – to developing into an accomplished reader. She provides an interesting commentary on how reading can become a 'secret obsession', a very personal matter. She also tells us how important other people – teachers, parents, friends, librarians – can be in influencing and extending our reading habits.

* 'When I was 16 I found a book that did truly change my life.' This was a very personal choice – it would be different for everyone. But the power of literature to influence our lives is an underlying message in what Sue Townsend writes here. Enjoyment and inspiration come from reading. So too can an understanding of how we are as individuals. As the motto says: 'Good books are true friends.'

# 3 Stargazing

## Introduction

Sometimes we find ourselves in a situation that makes us think hard about who we are and what the purpose of our lives is. It is important that human beings do this. In this reading, American writer Garrison Keillor remembers such an occasion and the effect it had on him.

## Reading

*Laying on our backs looking up at the stars*

'We catched fish and talked, and we took a swim now and then to keep off sleepiness,' said Huckleberry Finn. 'It was kind of solemn, drifting down the big, still river, laying on our backs and looking up at the stars, and we didn't ever feel like talking loud, and it warn't often that we laughed – only a little kind of low chuckle. We had mighty good weather as a general thing, and nothing ever happened to us at all.'

Huck was a hippie, searching for freedom, and, long ago, most of the people I knew were too.

In 1970, in search of freedom and dignity and cheap rent, I moved out to a farmhouse on the rolling prairie in central Minnesota, near Freeport, where I planted a garden and wrote stories to support my wife and year-old son. Rent was eighty dollars a month. It got us a big square brick house with a porch that looked out on a peaceful barnyard, a granary, and machine sheds and corn cribs and silo, and the barn and feedlot where Norbert, the owner, kept his beef cattle.

Beyond the windbreak of red oak and spruce to the west and north lay 160 acres of his corn and oats. (I believed it was oats, but on the odd chance it might be wheat or barley, I didn't mention anything to Norbert about it being oats.) Our long two-rut driveway ran due north through the woods to where the gravel road made an L, where our mailbox stood, where you could stand and see for a couple miles in all directions, the green fields and the thick groves around the farmsites.

My pals in Minneapolis considered this a real paradise (so did we) and they often drove up and enjoyed a weekend of contemplating corn and associating with large animals. On the Fourth of July, 1971, we had twenty people come for a picnic in the yard, an Olympic egg toss and gunnysack race, a softball game with the side of the barn for a right-field fence, and that night we sat around the kitchen and made pizza and talked about the dismal future.

America was trapped in Vietnam, a tragedy, and how could it end if not in holocaust? We were pessimists; we needed fear to make us feel truly alive. We talked about death. We put on loud music and made lavish pizzas with fresh mushrooms and onions, zucchini, eggplant, garlic, green pepper, and drank beer and talked about the end of life on earth with a morbid piety that made a person sick, about racial hatred, pesticides, radiation, television, the stupidity of politicians, and whether Vietnam was the result of strategic mistakes or a reflection of evil in American culture. It was a conversation with concrete shoes.

I snuck out to the screen porch with my son and sat and listened to crickets, and my friend Greg Bitz sat with us and two others came out, tired of politics and talk, and we walked along the driveway out of the yard light and through the dark trees and sat down in a strip of alfalfa between the woods and the oats. ('What's that?' they said. 'Oats,' I replied.) And then we lay down on our backs and looked up at the sky full of stars.

\* \* \*

The sky was clear. Lying there, looking up at 180 degrees of billions of dazzling single brilliances, made us feel we had gone away and left the farm far behind.

As we usually see the sky, it is a backdrop, the sky over our house, the sky beyond the clotheslines, but lying down eliminates the horizon and rids us of that strange realistic perspective of the sky as a canopy centred over our heads, and we see the sky as what it is: everything known and unknown, the universe, the whole beach other than the grain of sand we live on. The sight of the sky was so stunning it made us drunk. I felt as if I could put one foot forward and walk away from the wall of ground at my back and hike out toward Andromeda. I didn't feel particularly American. Out there in the Milky Way and the world without end Amen, America was a tiny speck of a country, a nickel tossed into the Grand Canyon, and American culture the amount of the Pacific Ocean you bring home in your swimsuit. The President wasn't the President out there, the Constitution was only a paper, and what newspapers wrote about was sawdust and coffee grounds. The light I saw was from fires burning before America existed, when my ancestor John Crandall lived in the colony of Rhode Island. Looking out there, my son lying on my chest, I could imagine my grandchildren, and they were more real to me than Congress.

I imagined them strong and free, curious, sensual, indelibly cheerful and affectionate, open-handed – sympathetic to pain and misery and quick in charity, proud when insulted and modest if praised, fiercely loyal to friends, loving God and the beautiful world including our land, from the California coast to the North Dakota prairie to faraway Manhattan, loving music and our American language – when you look at the stars you don't think small. You don't hope your descendants will enjoy your mutual-fund portfolio, you imagine them as giants on the earth.

Between the tree line and my left elbow, a billion stars in the sky, each representing a billion we couldn't see. We lay in the grass, thinking about America and also a little bit about snakes and about spiders clambering from blade to blade who might rappel down into our mouths, and looked open-mouthed up at the heavens, and everything we said out loud seemed hilarious to us. Tiny us gazing up at the South Wall of the Unimaginable Everything and feeling an obligation to comment, and our most profound comments sounded like peas dropped in a big empty bucket. 'It makes you feel small, doesn't it.' *Plink*. 'I used to know the names of those.' *Plunk*. One more peabrain having to share the effect that the world is having on him. 'It's beautiful, isn't it ... I remember when I was a kid –' someone said and we laughed ourselves limp – Shut up, we said, laughing, we're sick of sensitive people, everything you see just reminds you of yourself! So stick it in your ear.

Perhaps in 1776 our ancestors, too, were rattled by current events and the unbeatable logic of despair and had to go out and lie in the weeds for a while and think: We hold these truths to be self-evident, that all men are created equal, that they are endowed by their Creator with certain unalienable Rights, that among these are Life, Liberty, and the Pursuit of Happiness.

Indoors, the news is second-hand, mostly bad, and even good people are drawn into a dreadful fascination with doom and demise; their faith in extinction gets stronger; they sit and tell stories that begin with The End. Outdoors, the news is usually miraculous. A fly flew in my mouth and went deep, forcing me to swallow, inducing a major life change for him, from fly to simple protein, and so shall we all be changed someday, but here under heaven our spirits are immense, we are so blessed. The stars in the sky, my friends in the grass, my son asleep on my chest, his hands clutching my shirt.

*Garrison Keillor*

# Reflections

* When the writer lies looking up at the stars it makes him reflect hard on what are the important things in life. He begins to think about both his ancestors and his grandchildren. The stars and the grandness of Nature all around remind him how insignificant humans are in the grand march of time:

'Tiny us gazing up at the South Wall of the Unimaginable Everything and feeling an obligation to comment, and our most profound comments sounded like peas dropped in a big empty bucket.'

'Indoors, the news is second-hand, mostly bad ... Outdoors, the news is usually miraculous.'

\*   At turning points in our lives – say, a decisive moment at which a new course of events or development begins – we are often thrown back on ourselves to ask questions about our purpose as humans being on this earth. Prayer and silent reflection will often meet a need at such moments.

# 4 Death in birth

## Introduction

The death of someone close to us can trigger all sorts of emotions. It can certainly make us look at life in a different way, as well as making us reflect on the sadness of a human no longer *being*.

The animal kingdom often has much to teach us. In the following story by the Irish writer Liam O'Flaherty, the theme of 'death in birth' is sensitively and compellingly handled.

## Reading

### The Cow's Death

The calf was still-born. It came from the womb tail first. When its red, unwieldy body dropped on the greensward it was dead. It lay with its head doubled about its neck in a clammy mass. The men stood about it and shook their heads in silence. The wife of the peasant who owned the cow sighed and said, 'It is God's will.' The cow moaned, mad with the pain of birth. Then she wheeled around cumbersomely, her hoofs driving into the soft earth beneath the weight of her body. She stooped over the calf and moaned, again smelling it. Then she licked the still body with her coarse tongue lovingly. The woman rubbed the cow's matted forehead, and there was a tear in her eye; for she too was a mother.

Then the cow, overcome once more with pain, moved away from the calf and stood with her head bent low, breathing heavily through her nostrils. The breath came in long pale columns, like sunbeams coming through the window of a darkened church. They drove her away to a corner of the field, and she stood wearily with her head over the fence, lashing her flanks with her tail restlessly.

They seized the calf and dragged it by the feet along the field to the fence, out through the fence into another field, then through another fence, then up the grassy slope that led to the edge of the cliff. They dropped it downwards into the sea. It lay in a pulped mass on the rocks. They rebuilt the gaps in the stone fences carefully and returned to the cow. The woman offered her a hot drink of oatmeal, but she refused it. They seized her and poured the drink down her throat, using a bull's horn as a funnel. The cow half swallowed the drink, half tossed it away with her champing mouth.

Then they went home, the woman still bemoaning the dead calf and apologizing to God for her sorrow. The peasant remained with the cow, watching until she should drop the afterbirth. He buried it under a mound of stones. He dug his heel in the ground, and, taking a handful of the brown earth, he made the sign of the cross on the cow's side. Then he too went home.

For a long time the cow stood leaning over the fence, until the pain lessened.

She turned around suddenly and lowed and tossed her head. She took a short run forward, the muscles of her legs creaking like new boots. She stopped again, seeing nothing about her in the field. Then she began to run around by the fence, putting her head over it here and there, lowing. She found nothing. Nothing answered her call. She became wilder as the sense of her loss became clearer to her consciousness. Her eyes became red around the rims and fierce like a bull's. She began to smell around on the ground, half running, half walking, stumbling clumsily among the tummocks of grass.

There was where she had lain in travail, on the side of a little slope, the grass compressed and faded by the weight of her body. There was where she had given birth, the ground trampled by many feet and torn here and there, with the brown earth showing through. Then she smelt where the calf had lain. There were wet stains on the grass. She looked around her fiercely, and then she put her nose to the ground and started to follow the trail where they had dragged the calf to the fence. At the fence she stopped and smelt a long time, wondering with her stupid brain whither the trail led. And then stupidly she pressed with her great bulk against the fence. The stones cut her breast, but she pressed harder in terror and the fence fell before her. She stumbled through the gap and cut her left thigh near the udder. She did not heed the pain, but pressed forward, smelling the trail and snorting.

Faster she went, and now and again she raised her head and lowed – a long, mournful low that ended in a fierce *crescendo*, like a squall of wind coming around a corner. At the second fence she paused again. Again she pressed against it, and again it fell before her. Going through the gap she got caught, and in the struggle to get through she cut both her sides along the flanks. The blood trickled through jaggedly, discolouring the white streak on the left flank.

She came at a run up the grassy slope to the cliff. She shuddered and jerked aside when she suddenly saw the sea and heard it rumbling distantly below – the waves seething on the rocks and the sea birds calling dismally with their noisome cackle. She smelt the air in wonder. Then she slowly advanced, inch by inch, trembling. When she reached the summit, where the grass ended in a gravel belt that dropped down to the sheer slope of rock, she rushed backwards and circled around wildly, lowing. Again she came up, and planting her feet carefully on the gravel, she looked down. The trail of her calf ended there. She could follow it no further. It was lost in the emptiness beyond that gravel ledge. She tried to smell the air, but nothing reached her nostrils but the salt smell of the sea. She moaned and her sides heaved with the outrush of her breath. Then she looked down, straining out her neck. She saw the body of her calf on the rocks below.

She uttered a joyful cry and ran backwards, seeking a path to descend. Up and down the summit of the cliff she went, smelling here and there, looking out over the edge, going on her knees and looking down and finding nowhere a path that led to the object on the rocks below. She came back again, her hind legs clashing as she ran, to the point where the body had been dropped over the precipice.

She strained out and tapped with her fore hoof, scratching the gravel and trying to descend, but there was nothing upon which she could place her feet – just a sheer drop of one hundred feet of cliff and her calf lay on the rocks below.

She stood stupidly looking at it a long time, without moving a muscle. Then she lowed, calling to her calf, but no answer came. She saw the water coming in with the tide, circling around the calf on the rocks. She lowed again, warning it.

Wave after wave came in, eddying around the body. She lowed again and tossed her head wildly as if she wanted to buffet the waves with her horns.

And then a great wave came towering in, and catching up the calf on its rest swept it from the rocks.

And the cow, uttering a loud bellow, jumped headlong down.

*Liam O'Flaherty*

## Reflections

\* As well as being a first-class piece of story telling, *The Cow's Death* does make us think hard about both birth and death, and the very powerful emotions these events give rise to. The cow–calf/mother–child bond comes through particularly powerfully.

We might also conclude that the farmers treated the cow rather callously, not giving it time to come to terms with the still-born calf. Perhaps this aspect of the story should serve to remind us just how important time is as a healer, especially when the trauma of death touches the life of someone we know.

We all need to remember the support – physical and emotional – we can give to a friend if they have to confront the tragedy of death.

# 5 Truths

## Introduction

It is important in our lives that we hold onto certain values and truths that guide our behaviour and dealings with other people. This is especially vital when we meet situations that threaten to overwhelm us and tempt us to desert what we know in our hearts and minds to be right.

The following reading is in two parts. First are some lines by the American poet Robert Frost; second is a short naval story.

## Reading

… why abandon a belief
Merely because it ceases to be true.
Cling to it long enough, and not a doubt
It will turn true again, for so it goes.
Most of the change we think we see in life
Is due to truths being in and out of favor.
As I sit here, and oftentimes, I wish
I could be monarch of a desert land
I could devote and dedicate forever
To the truths we keep coming back and back to.

*'The Black Cottage' by Robert Frost*

Two battleships assigned to the training squadron had been at sea on manoeuvres in heavy weather for several days. I was serving on the lead battleship and was on watch on the bridge as night fell. The visibility was poor with patchy fog, so the captain remained on the bridge keeping an eye on all activities.

Shortly after dark, the lookout on the wing of the bridge reported, 'Light, bearing on the starboard bow.'

'Is it steady or moving astern?' the captain called out.

Lookout replied, 'Steady, captain,' which meant we were on a dangerous collision course with that ship.

The captain then called to the signalman, 'Signal that ship: we are on a collision course, advise you change course 20 degrees.'

Back came a signal, 'Advisable for you to change course 20 degrees.'

The captain said, 'Send, I'm a captain, change course 20 degrees.'

'I'm a seaman second class,' came the reply. 'You had better change course 20 degrees.'

By that time, the captain was furious. He spat out, 'Send, I'm a battleship. Change course 20 degrees.'

Back came the flashing light, 'I'm a lighthouse.'

We changed course.

*Anon*

## Reflections

* These two passages, placed side-by-side, have much to say to us on the subject of how we deal with turning points in our lives.

  The poet Robert Frost warns us that we should be true to our own values – what we know is the difference between right and wrong – even and especially when passing fashions may challenge those values which have been lovingly passed onto us by our family, our teachers, our friends.

  'The truths we keep coming back and back to' – this is a line to remember and reflect upon.

  The naval story of course is an amusing incident that has a critical sting in the tale. Just as even the most senior naval commanders have to change direction sometimes, so we may have to adjust and interpret our principles when a particular situation arises.

  This does not mean that we forsake 'the truths we keep coming back and back to.' But it may mean applying them in different ways in different contexts. This is a difficult but important lesson for us all to learn – and we keep relearning it throughout our lives.

* And there are certain beliefs and natural laws that really should not be compromised. The famous film director Cecil B. deMille once said about his film *The Ten Commandments*: 'It is impossible for us to break the law. We can only break ourselves against the law.'

# 6 Great expectations

## Introduction

The following reading is the opening of Charles Dickens's famous novel (written in 1860) *Great Expectations*. The central character of the book is Pip and right at the beginning of Chapter One he is about to meet someone who will change his life forever. Enjoy Dickens's wonderful way with words.

# Reading

## *Great Expectations*

My father's family name being Pirrip, and my christian name Philip, my infant tongue could make of both names nothing longer or more explicit than Pip. So I called myself Pip, and came to be called Pip.

I give Pirrip as my father's family name, on the authority of his tombstone and my sister – Mrs. Joe Gargery, who married the blacksmith. As I never saw my father or my mother, and never saw any likeness of either of them (for their days were long before the days of photographs), my first fancies regarding what they were like, were unreasonably derived from their tombstones. The shape of the letters on my father's, gave me an odd idea that he was a square, stout, dark man, with curly black hair. From the character and turn of the inscription, '*Also Georgiana Wife of the Above*', I drew the childish conclusion that my mother was freckled and sickly. To five little stone lozenges, each about a foot and a half long, which were arranged in a neat row beside their grave, and were sacred to the memory of five little brothers of mine – who gave up trying to get a living exceedingly early in that universal struggle – I am indebted for a belief I religiously entertained that they had all been born on their backs with their hands in their trousers-pockets, and had never taken them out in this state of existence.

Ours was the marsh country, down by the river, within, as the river wound, twenty miles of the sea. My first most vivid and broad impression of the identity of things, seems to me to have been gained on a memorable raw afternoon towards evening. At such a time I found out for certain, that this bleak place overgrown with nettles was the churchyard and that Philip Pirrip, late of this parish, and also Georgina wife of the above, were dead and buried; and that Alexander, Bartholomew, Abraham, Tobias, and Roger, infant children of the aforesaid, were also dead and buried; and that the dark flat wilderness beyond the churchyard, intersected with dykes and mounds and gates, with scattered cattle feeding on it, was the marshes; and that the low leaden line beyond was the river; and that the distant savage lair from which the wind was rushing, was the sea; and that the small bundle of shivers growing afraid of it all and beginning to cry, was Pip.

'Hold your noise!' cried a terrible voice, as a man started up from among the graves at the side of the church porch. 'Keep still, you little devil, or I'll cut your throat!'

A fearful man, all in coarse grey, with a great iron on his leg. A man with no hat and with broken shoes, and with an old rag tied round his head. A man who had been soaked in water, and smothered in mud, and lamed by stones, and cut by flints, and stung by nettles, and torn by briars; who limped and shivered, and glared and growled; and whose teeth chattered in his head as he seized me by the chin.

'O! Don't cut my throat, sir,' I pleaded in terror. 'Pray don't do it, sir.'

'Tell us your name!' said the man. 'Quick!'

'Pip, sir.'

'Once more,' said the man, staring at me. 'Give it mouth!'

'Pip. Pip, sir.'

'Show us where you live,' said the man. 'Pint out the place!'

I pointed to where our village lay, on the flat in-shore among the alder-trees and pollards, a mile or more from the church.

The man, after looking at me for a moment, turned me upside down, and emptied my pockets. There was nothing in them but a piece of bread. When the church came to itself – for he was so sudden and strong that he made it go head over heels before me, and I saw the steeple under my feet – when the church came to itself, I say, I was seated on a high tombstone, trembling, while he ate the bread ravenously.

'You young dog,' said the man, licking his lips, 'what fat cheeks you ha' got.'

I believe they were fat, though I was at that time undersized, for my years, and not strong.

'Darn me if I couldn't eat 'em,' said the man, with a threatening shake of his head, 'and if I han't half a mind to't!'

I earnestly expressed my hope that he wouldn't, and held tighter to the tombstone on which he had put me; partly, to keep myself upon it; partly, to keep myself from crying.

'Now lookee here!' said the man. 'Where's your mother?'

'There, sir!' said I.

He started, made a short run, and stopped and looked over his shoulder.

'There, sir!' I timidly explained. 'Also Georgiana. That's my mother.'

'Oh!' said he, coming back. 'And is that your father alonger your mother?'

'Yes, sir,' said I; 'him too; late of this parish.'

'Ha!' he muttered then, considering. 'Who d'ye live with – supposin' you're kindly let to live, which I han't made up my mind about?'

'My sister, sir – Mrs. Joe Gargery – wife of Joe Gargery, the blacksmith, sir.'

'Blacksmith, eh?' said he. And looked down at his leg.

After darkly looking at his leg and at me several times, he came closer to my tombstone, took me by both arms, and tilted me back as far as he could hold me; so that his eyes looked most powerfully down into mine, and mine looked most helplessly up into his.

'Now lookee here,' he said, 'the question being whether you're to be let to live. You know what a file is?'

'Yes, sir.'

'And you know what wittles is?'

'Yes, sir.'

After each question he tilted me over a little more, so as to give me a greater sense of helplessness and danger.

'You get me a file.' He tilted me again. 'And you get me wittles.' He tilted me again. 'You bring 'em both to me.' He tilted me again. 'Or I'll have your heart and liver out.' He tilted me again.

I was dreadfully frightened, and so giddy that I clung to him with both hands, and said, 'If you would kindly please to let me keep upright, sir, perhaps I shouldn't be sick, and perhaps I could attend more.'

He gave me a most tremendous dip and roll, so that the church jumped over its own weather-cock. Then, he held me by the arms in an upright position on the top of the stone, and went on these fearful terms:

'You bring me, to-morrow morning early, that file and them wittles. You bring the lot to me, at that old Battery over yonder. You do it, and you never dare to say a word or dare to make a sign concerning your having seen such a person as me, or any person sum-ever, and you shall be let to live. You fail, or you go from my words in any partickler, no matter how small it is, and your heart and your liver shall be tore out, roasted and ate. Now, I ain't alone, as you may think I am. There's a young man hid with me, in comparison with which young man I am a Angel. That young man hears the words I speak. That young man has a secret way pecooliar to himself, of getting at a boy, and at his heart and at his liver. It is in wain for a boy to attempt to hide himself from that young man. A boy may lock his door, may be warm in bed, may tuck himself up, may draw the clothes over his head, may think himself comfortable and safe, but that young man will softly creep and creep his way to him and tear him open. I am keeping that young man from harming of you at the present moment, with great difficulty. I find it wery hard to hold that young man off of your inside. Now, what do you say?'

*Charles Dickens*

## Reflections

* Well – wouldn't you? – Pip *does* return to meet the escaped convict the follow-ing morning, and brings him food and the means of escape. If you read on you'll find that the desperate convict is quickly recaptured. But he never for-gets Pip's kindness, later leaving him a sum of money that gives Pip the 'great expectations' of the novel's title.

  Perhaps not in quite the same circumstances as Pip, but in our lives we are likely to meet individuals who do have a significant impact upon us. We may not know it at the time but later in life we may look back and recognise that the opinions or actions of a parent, a teacher, a friend, someone we'd never previously met, were decisive.

  Many turning points in our lives hinge upon chance encounters: love, adven-ture, job, hobby – very often these come upon us without our really knowing how.

* One teacher's advice to his pupils in the film *Dead Poets Society* was: 'Seize The Day.' By that he clearly meant: make the most of opportunities that come your way; they may not come again.

# 7 What am I doing here?

## Introduction

'Nobody made a greater mistake than he who did nothing because he could only do a little.'

*Edmund Burke*

We may frequently look around us at a problem – local, national, international – and shrug our shoulders. We feel as individuals that we can't make a difference because the problem is just too big. Pat Kerr, while still a British Airways stewardess, began to work as a part-time volunteer at an overcrowded city-centre orphanage in Dhaka, the capital of Bangladesh, which she had flown into and out of many, many times.

Here is the introduction to the book about her experiences, followed by an extract from a fax she sent to friends back home in England.

# Reading

## *'What am I doing here?'*

Walking in mud, slimy and high above my knees. When my toes felt something solid that my feet could rest on for a second I was both relieved and horrified. For all I knew, I could have been balancing on a corpse. It was better not to think too much and to wade on towards the boat. We were on a flooded mudflat, just after the cyclone of April 1991, and I'd seen the photographs of the hundreds of bodies washed up on this coast.

No one quite knows the exact population of Bangladesh – partly because the registration of births is a little casual – but it is somewhere between 120 million and 150 million. The habitable landmass is roughly the size of Wales. This poor, new, under-funded and misunderstood nation was simply experiencing the latest tragedy in a recent history of flood, famine, war, pestilence and indifference, and there wasn't even a way to afford simple human dignity to those who survived. It wasn't up to me, or the team of which I was part, to ponder these horrors as we tried to reach an area of damp – not dry – land where people might want our basic first-aid skills, supplies and advice.

Most experts believe that at least 150,000 people died in the spring cyclone of 1991.

Entire villages and communities had been obliterated, fragile mud-constructed houses were blown apart, crop fields were flooded and basic services like village telephones, electricity links and decent drinking water had gone. Drugs were needed to cope with the sort of infections that set in so fast in conditions like this, and aid agencies all over the world were rushing relief into the area.

So what was I doing here wading in mud?

### *Extract from fax to friends*

Last week we got a team together and went to Chittagong with supplies such as medicines, food for distribution and for staff, gas cylinders for cooking, four huge barrels of water, kerosene lamps, kerosene. We even took one of those concrete bases for a local style latrine. The first day I visited many of the other agencies and government offices to see exactly where medical teams were still needed – co-ordination and liaison has obviously been rather haphazard. Everyone agreed that the coastal areas had been neglected, so we drove as far as we could into the coastal area and met the local relief co-ordinator, who suggested we walked the supplies into an area called Sadhanpur. This we did, and on our return to Chittagong, I had a message that the government's relief co-ordinator wanted to see me. He said he wanted us to go to a place called Chanua which is on the coast next to Kutibdie Island, as they had not received any medical help. He would arrange for us to be taken in by the American task force by helicopter.

We had a list of goods and their weights, and I was on the phone to several people that evening (you can make local calls within Chittagong – it's the lines out that have been destroyed). Early the next morning, I went to the task force meeting and the American Colonel in charge of the area said he was sure he could get us in and that we should bring our truck to the airport. I went to see the Managing Director of Glaxo, to pick up provisions, leaving everyone with allocated jobs. On return, things were extremely chaotic, with nothing really ready, but then we got a message that the helicopter was ready to leave the military airport. We pelted to the military airport which was some distance away, and as we finally turned in, the truck got one of its tyres mired. All the goods, many articles of which were very heavy, had to be unloaded, taken on the Pajero to the helicopter lift site. By then I was in a real state, but luckily the helicopter's programme for that day was running behind, and we finally got everything ready. Although I had been given a list of things needed, we were now told that we had too much stuff for one helicopter, so I said we could leave the sacks of dry food, mollasses and some of the water behind. Four Bangladeshi doctors who knew the area were also travelling but they went in the first helicopter. Unfortunately, this left no-one in our plane who actually knew what the drop site looked like! We loaded as much as we could into the helicopter and the crew said they would make sure to bring the rest of the stuff by coming back for it. You can guess what happened. We landed, and I unloaded everything, only to discover it was the wrong place. Everything was reloaded and off we went again. This time, I checked before I unloaded – just as well, since it was once more the wrong place! Third time lucky! I spotted the doctors so we landed, unloaded, and sent the helicopters back for the rest of 'our team' and goods.

We had it all carried to a building that was still standing and had a look round at the awful devastation. There were a few buildings left standing and we had to start by digging a latrine. We all slept in the same room as our supplies and got up at 5.30 to put up a tent, sort the medicines etc., and by 7am there was a long queue so we started seeing people in our tent clinic. The nurses we took with us are very experienced at dealing with the diseases that are the aftermath of such a disaster – mostly we saw diarrhoea, dysentery, skin problems and wounds. This area must have been pretty rough before the cyclone as many of the people who came with diarrhoea also had other, longer term illnesses. Many of the children were very malnourished and we made some food and milk (we took in about two sacks full of dried milk in tins with us) to give them. We also gave out a lot of vitamins, especially vitamin A, as there were a lot of children with eye problems. The first day we treated 194 people. As we saw each person, we marked the cuticle of one thumb with a felt tip pen so we knew who we had treated. After a night in a hot crowded room with two snorers, one sleep talker, several thousand flies and mosquitos and a rat who thought I might be lonely and crept under my pillow, we got up and opened the clinic at 6am. We were already running short of number of medicines, so the following day I returned to the city by sea to arrange for a further supply. A US navy landing craft brought in food, so I hitched a lift back! Actually getting onto the boat was not without problems. The mud was up to my knees and as a large number of bodies had been washed up on this area, I had difficulty not yelping every time my foot touched something hard deep in the mud. We waded out to the boat, everything wet and soggy as the water was choppy. As luck would have it, we hit a storm on the way, so had to stop in the middle of the bay until it was over. Finally back in Chittagong, I travelled back to Dhaka to sort things out. One of the first things I did was to photocopy a load of labels that the Cholera Hospital have with diagrams showing the sun rising, at midday etc. These are given out to illiterate people with a tick beside the position of the sun which is the time of day they should take their medicine. As the women of Chanua are mostly illiterate and many need to take more than one medicine, we will pin these to their medicine packets so they know when to take each one.'

By the 30th June we had treated 7,366 people – quite a feat, I am sure you will all agree. The Relief Centre is staffed and supplied from Sreepur on a weekly basis, and it will be kept open while the urgent need exists. The response from the UK sponsors has been tremendous, and it has enabled us to send extra money designated especially for this disaster – as ever, thank you all very much.

*Pat Kerr*

## Reflections

* According to VSO (Voluntary Service Overseas) Bangladesh is currently one of the poorest countries in the world: 85% of the people are living below the poverty line, half the babies are born with malnutrition, and life expectancy is 30 years shorter than in the West due to basic levels of health care and treatment. Nevertheless, the Bangladeshi people have a great determination to improve their lives.
Pat Kerr is just one individual who recognised that, despite the enormous problems, she could make a difference, even if only a small one for the children she worked with.
We live in an age when people talk a lot about caring – for the environment, for the elderly, for refugees – but often do not seem to do very much.

* Pat Kerr's words in a Prologue to her book are worth our reflecting upon:

'Being involved in a project that has totally dominated my life for over ten years has been a great privilege. Almost everybody is happier when engaged in an undertaking they see as greater than themselves, whether it's building up a business, bringing up a family or working for a charity. Having been happy and consistently average throughout school and adult life I saw an opportunity and decided to get out there and do something.'

'We're all involved with each other and with our increasingly fragile environment and we haven't time to wait for saints or politicians to sort the world out for us.'

# 8 Reborn

## Introduction

What must it feel like to be released from prison after a sentence of fifteen years? How do you think someone adjusts to a society which has moved on and changed irreversibly while they've been shut away? In particular, what must it feel like when you've been released because you were wrongly imprisoned in the first place?

Here is Gerry Conlon's account. He was one of the so-called Guildford Four, imprisoned with three other men in 1975 for the bombing of a pub by an IRA terrorist gang. The reference to Guiseppe is to his father, who died in prison.

# Reading

## *'Reborn!'*

ITN had arranged a reception party at the Holiday Inn near Swiss Cottage, London, I gave them their exclusive interview – which they well deserved, just for getting my ma and sisters over from Belfast so they could be there for the greatest day of my life.

The reception didn't go well for me. I was beginning to feel deflated as my high wore off. I'd not slept properly for two nights and the flow of adrenalin that had kept me going was beginning to pack up. People were coming up to me wanting to shake my hand, asking me the same questions over and over again. I tried to be polite, but I could feel the strain.

Soon I began to notice there were two big men hanging around me. They always seemed to be somewhere near by. When I went to the toilet, one of them, a big Scotsman, followed me inside. In the lift, I had the two of them with me.

'Hey, who are youse?'

'We're just here to make sure nobody bothers you, don't take no notice.'

I was shown to my room. The two big men walked along the corridor just behind us and positioned themselves outside the doors of the room. They were security guards, hired by ITN. Whoever had the bright idea of getting them in can't have had much imagination, can't have thought how I would see it. To my mind the only difference between these two and a couple of screws were the clothes.

I couldn't get comfortable in the hotel room. I'd spent the evening talking to my family but it wasn't late when I got ready for bed. I knew I was tired, but sleep would not come. As I lay in the dark I thought first about the other innocent people I'd left behind: Paddy Joe Hill, Gerry Hunter, Johnny Walker, Dicky McIlkenny, Hughie Callaghan, Billy Power. I thought about the scores of other prisoners, Irish political prisoners, English prisoners, Palestinian and black, cockneys, con-men and fraudsters, men from every kind of background who'd given me their friendship over the years. I thought of how we made food-boats and tea-boats on the wing, cooked and played cards, shared hooch and tobacco, argued and joked.

Suddenly I felt utterly lonely. I wanted to go to the window and call out to the next room for some contact. But this wasn't D Wing at the Scrubs. It was the Holiday Inn, and I didn't even know the people in the next rooms. It had been my greatest fear, ever since I knew I would be coming out. After fifteen years inside, would I be able to communicate with the outside?

It was five in the morning when I went along to my mother's room and sat on her bed. I tried to tell her how I felt, how miserable I was in this place. I started to cry, saying it was no better than a prison, and these media people had me held hostage. All I waned to do was get out. All this time I kept thinking about my father and how he must be feeling. How he knew that this day would come. His prophesy that his death would result in us clearing his name, because without a doubt his death triggered off people's consciences, setting off a whole chain reaction.

I talked about all this with my mother and Aunt Bridget. All the emotions I held in check for years came bursting out. All the things I'd never been able to say to them while I was in prison. We were all in tears, a cloud burst – it was the first real conversation we'd had since 1974. I remember my Aunt Bridget saying, 'Guiseppe up in heaven will be smiling today, 'cos he knows it's through him that all this has come about. Now we've got to get his name cleared.'

My head was spinning with all this – thoughts of my father, suddenly being out of prison, suddenly being a free man again. There were only two places I didn't want to be – back in prison or at the Holiday Inn. I just had to get away, to find myself. I knew I would have to readjust, and I didn't feel this was the way to start off. I just needed common sense and people who knew me, who could reassure and help me. My family were readjusting to me as I was to them. So I just rang Gareth Peirce and said, 'Come and get me out of here. They're treating me like a prisoner.'

And Gareth came within fifteen minutes and took me away to her house.

Most long-term prisoners who have a known release date set about preparing for it, and the authorities help them. There are special courses, shopping trips, exercises in handling money again. I had none of this. I was just reborn into the world.

The most frightening thing about this new life – which was also the most exciting thing about it – is choice. When I walked out of the Holiday Inn I had exercised choice. But now I faced an incredible range of strange choices: the choice of clothes, of entertainment, of music, of drinks in the pub. I had a big problem with menus. I'd never seen menus before and didn't know how to cope with them. I didn't know what half the things on them *were*. They all seemed to be in French or Italian and I hadn't a clue what I was supposed to be ordering. So I used to ask for chips.

My eyes almost popped out when I saw the electronic goods shops in Tottenham Court Road – CDs, videos, personal stereos, portable phones, computers, things which the rest of the world took for granted, but which didn't exist in 1974. I thought back to Haslett's in Belfast, as I'd known it. I'd thought then it was like an Aladdin's cave, but this was space age. I'd jumped ahead a decade and a half in one leap and I couldn't believe what I saw.

This also affected how I handled myself with people. I had gone away as a kid, an absolute menace. I came out more mature, but I still wasn't sure whether I could communicate with people in a meaningful way. I needed time to work out where I was in this new world, and how a man like me should talk to it. I had to deal with people in shops, with officials, with bus conductors. I had to learn to cross the road. I had to begin to make relationships with friends and family that were fifteen years older than when I last saw them. I had the enormous worry of sorting out how I was going to relate to women in this new world.

Being a 'celebrity' has made it harder of course. My face was all over the news and the papers in that first week or so, and I had to cope with complete strangers coming up to me and wanting to talk. Prison is a world of no strangers. You know and are known by everybody.

When I was home in Belfast I went for a drink with a friend of mine and I was telling him how I was finding being recognized in the street a bit daunting. He said to me, 'It shouldn't bother you. This is where you come from. Have a look around you, where you were born, born into abject poverty. You own the keys to one half of the city, the reason being the nationalist people and ordinary Catholic people in the North have known nothing but being attacked by the police in 1969, internment, the dirty protests, the hunger strikes, kids being killed by plastic bullets. People in the North have known nothing but heartache until the release of the Guildford Four. You have no ideals, are not a member of any political organization, or the IRA, but you represent an enormous victory to all these people.'

Now, seven months after my release, I am still buttonholed in the streets. I have realized in this way that my case really is the cause for concern that I imagined and hoped it would be. I feel honoured by that.

People ask me what I will do with the rest of my life. What a question! I say I will travel, get to know the world which I've spent all my adult life excluded from. Beyond that, the future awaits. But I am certain of one thing. I don't want to spend the rest of my life being known only as one of the Guildford Four.

*Gerry Conlon*

## Reflections

\*    The book from which this is taken is titled *Proved Innocent*. A film was made of the events and retitled *In the Name of the Father*, highlighting how strongly Gerry Conlon felt about the wrongful imprisonment of his father and, of course, his subsequent death in prison.

But apart from the deeply felt family issues in this extract, what emerges is the tremendous sense of rebirth – a feeling most of us must find it almost impossible to imagine. How might each of us cope with such a dramatic change in our personal circumstances?

Gerry Conlon's emotions at this turning point in his life are worth reflecting on. So too are his words: 'The most frightening thing about this new life – which was the most exciting thing about it – is choice.'

(See also **An evil cradling**, p. 157)

# 9 Daydreamer

## Introduction

What might it be like to have an altogether different view of the world from the one you currently have? Perhaps you have asked yourself the question – if I could be reincarnated, in what form or as what person would I come back to earth? Would I choose to be male or female, Chinese or American, human or animal? And how might I see the world differently?

In the novel *Metamorphosis* by Franz Kafka, the opening page describes a boy waking up one morning to find himself turned into an insect.

What's your reaction to this extract from a novel titled *The Daydreamer?* It is about a 10-year-old boy named Peter who has a powerful imagination. Kate is his younger sister.

# Reading

## *The Daydreamer*

There was nothing Peter liked better on a winter's afternoon when he came home from school than to kick off his shoes and lie down beside William Cat in front of the living-room fire. He liked to get right down to William's level, and to put his face up close to the cat's and see how extraordinary it really was, how beautifully non-human, with spikes of black hair sprouting in a globe from a tiny face beneath the fur, and the white whiskers with their slight downwards curve, and the eyebrow hairs shooting up like radio antennae, and the pale green eyes with their upright slits, like doors ajar into a world Peter could never enter. As soon as he came close to the cat, the deep rumbling purr would begin, so low and strong that the floor vibrated. Peter knew he was welcome.

It was just one such afternoon, a Tuesday as it happened, four o'clock and already the light fading, curtains drawn and lights on, when Peter eased himself on to the carpet where William lay before a bright fire whose flames were curling round a fat elm log. Down the chimney came the moan of the freezing wind as it whipped across the rooftops. Peter had sprinted from the bus stop with Kate to keep warm. Now he was safely indoors with his old friend who was pretending to be younger than his years by rolling on to his back and letting his front paws flop helplessly. He wanted his chest tickled. As Peter began to move his fingers lightly through the fur, the rumbling noise grew louder, so loud that every bone in the old cat's body rattled. And then, William stretched out a paw to Peter's fingers and tried to draw them up higher. Peter let the cat guide his hand.

'Do you want me to tickle your chin?' he murmured. But no. The cat wanted to be touched right at the base of his throat. Peter felt something hard there. It moved from side to side when he touched it. Something had got trapped in the fur. Peter propped himself on an elbow in order to investigate. He parted the fur. At first he thought he was looking at a piece of jewellery, a little silver tag. But there was no chain, and as he poked and peered he saw that it was not metal at all, but polished bone, oval and flattened in the centre, and most curiously of all, that it was attached to William Cat's skin. The piece of bone fitted well between his forefinger and thumb. He tightened his grip and gave a tug. William Cat's purr grew even louder. Peter pulled again, downwards, and this time he felt something give.

Looking down through the fur, and parting it with the tips of his fingers, he saw that he had opened up a small slit in the cat's skin. It was as if he were holding the handle of a zip. Again he pulled, and now there was a dark opening two inches long. William Cat's purr was coming from in there. Perhaps, Peter thought, I'll see his heart beating. A paw was gently pushing against his fingers again. William Cat wanted him to go on.

And this is what he did. He unzipped the whole cat from throat to tail. Peter wanted to part the skin to peep inside. But he did not wish to appear nosey. He was just about to call out to Kate when there was a movement, a stirring inside the cat, and from the opening in the fur there came a faint pink glow which grew brighter. And suddenly, out of William Cat climbed a, well, a thing, a creature. But Peter was not certain that it was really there to touch, for it seemed to be made entirely of light. And while it did not have whiskers or a tail, or a purr, or even fur, or four legs, everything about it seemed to say 'cat'. It was the very essence of the word, the heart of the idea. It was a quiet, slinky, curvy fold of pink and purple light, and it was climbing out of the cat.

'You must be William's spirit,' Peter said aloud. 'Or are you a ghost?'

The light made no sound, but it understood. It seemed to say, without actually speaking the words, that it was both these things, and much more besides.

When it was clear of the cat, which continued to lie on its back on the carpet in front of the fire, the cat spirit drifted into the air, and floated up to Peter's shoulder where it settled. Peter was not frightened. He felt the glow of the spirit on his cheek. And then the light drifted behind his head, out of sight. He felt it touch his neck and a warm shudder ran down his back. The cat spirit took hold of something knobbly at the top of his spine and drew it down, right down his back, and as his own body opened up, he felt the cool air of the room tickle the warmth of his insides.

It was the oddest thing, to climb out of your body, just step out of it and leave it lying on the carpet like a shirt you had just taken off. Peter saw his own glow, which was purple and purest white. The two spirits hovered in the air facing each other. And then Peter suddenly knew what he wanted to do, what he had to do. He floated towards William Cat and hovered. The body stood open, like a door, and it looked so inviting, so welcoming. He dropped down and stepped inside. How fine it was, to dress yourself as a cat. It was not squelchy, as he thought all insides must be. It was dry and warm. He lay on his back and slipped his arms into William's front legs. Then he wiggled his legs into William's back legs. His head fitted perfectly inside the cat's head. He glanced across at his own body just in time to see William Cat's spirit disappear inside.

Using his paws, Peter was able to zip himself up easily. He stood, and took a few steps. What a delight, to walk on four soft white paws. He could see his whiskers springing out from the side of his face, and he felt his tail curling behind him. His tread was light, and his fur was like the most comfortable of old woollen jumpers. As his pleasure in being a cat grew, his heart swelled, and a tingling sensation deep in his throat became so strong that he could actually hear himself. Peter was purring. He was Peter Cat, and over there, was William Boy.

The boy stood up and stretched. Then, without a word to the cat at his feet, he skipped out of the room.

'Mum', Peter heard his old body call out from the kitchen. 'I'm hungry. What's for supper?'

*Ian McEwan*

# Reflections

* On one level, yes, this is a story about daydreaming, about letting the imagination run wild. Peter does just this to recover from a winter's day at school.

But he is also fascinated by just what it is that makes a cat tick. As the story unfolds Peter has the opportunity to view the world through the cat's eyes and mind – to see how adults like his mum deal with enquiring pets!

*The Daydreamer* is a powerful collection of tales that make us pause and reflect on how narrow our own human view of the world is. Standing in someone *else*'s shoes – just for a few moments – can be quite illuminating.

\*   On the subject of finding out all about what makes cats tick, the poem 'The Secret in the Cat' by May Swenson opens with the lines:

'I took my cat apart
to see what made him purr.
Like an electric clock
or like the snore

of a warming kettle,
something fizzled and sizzled in him.
Was he a soft car,
the engine bubbling sound?

Was there a wire beneath his fur,
or humming throttle?
I undid his throat.
Within was no stir.'

# 10 Brothers in arms

## Introduction

When we face a difficult situation which requires action it is often tempting to take the easy decision to do nothing. In the following extract from the first chapter of John Grisham's novel (also a film) *The Client*, taking the difficult decision leads to a series of events that changes two brothers' lives. Mark is 11, Ricky is 8, and they live with their mother on a caravan site. As this passage opens the boys are sitting in the wood sharing a quiet cigarette.

## Reading

*Brothers in arms*

Ricky heard the car first. There was a low, rushing sound coming from the dirt road. Then Mark heard it, and they stopped smoking. 'Just sit still,' Mark said softly. They did not move.

A long black, shiny Lincoln appeared over the slight hill and eased toward them. The weeds in the road were as high as the front bumper. Mark dropped his cigarette to the ground and covered it with his shoe. Ricky did the same.

The car slowed almost to a stop as it neared the clearing, then circled around, touching the tree limbs as it moved slowly. It stopped and faced the road. The boys were directly behind it and hidden from view. Mark slid off the log and crawled through the weeds to a row of brush at the edge of the clearing. Ricky followed. The rear of the Lincoln was thirty feet away. They watched it carefully. It had Louisiana license plates.

'What's he doing?' Ricky whispered.

Mark peeked through the weeds. 'Shhhhh!' He had heard stories around the trailer park of teenagers using these woods to meet girls and smoke pot, but this car did not belong to a teenager. The engine quit, and the car just sat there in the weeds for a minute. Then the door opened, and the driver stepped into the weeds and looked around. He was a chubby man in a black suit. His head was fat and round and without hair except for neat rows above the ears and a black-and-gray beard. He stumbled to the rear of the car, fumbled with the keys, and finally opened the trunk. He removed a water hose, stuck one end into the exhaust pipe, and ran the other end through a crack in the left rear window. He closed the trunk, looked around again as if he were expecting to be watched, then disappeared into the car.

The engine started.

'Wow,' Mark said softly, staring blankly at the car.

'What's he doing?' Ricky asked.

'He's trying to kill himself.'

Ricky raised his head a few inches for a better view. 'I don't understand, Mark.'

'Keep down. You see the hose, right? The fumes from the tail pipe go into the car, and it kills him.'

'You mean suicide?'

'Right. I saw a guy do it like this in a movie once.'

They leaned closer to the weeds and stared at the hose running from the pipe to the window. The engine idled smoothly.

'Why does he want to kill himself?' Ricky asked.

'How am I supposed to know? But we gotta do something.'

'Yeah, let's get the hell outta here.'

'No. Just be still a minute.'

'I'm leaving, Mark. You can watch him die if you want to, but I'm gone.'

Mark grabbed his brother's shoulder and forced him lower. Ricky's breathing was heavy and they were both sweating. The sun hid behind a cloud.

'How long does it take?' Ricky asked, his voice quivering.

'Not very long.' Mark released his brother and eased onto all fours. 'You stay here, okay. If you move, I'll kick your tail.'

'What're you doing, Mark?'

'Just stay here. I mean it.' Mark lowered his thin body almost to the ground and crawled on elbows and knees through the weeds toward the car. The grass was dry and at least two feet tall. He knew the man couldn't hear him, but he worried about the movement of the weeds. He stayed directly behind the car and slid snake-like on his belly until he was in the shadow of the trunk. He reached and carefully eased the hose from the tail pipe, and dropped it to the ground. He retraced his trail with a bit more speed, and seconds later was crouched next to Ricky, watching and waiting in the heavier grass and brush under the outermost limbs of the tree. He knew that if they were spotted, they could dart past the tree and down their trail and be gone before the chubby man could catch them.

They waited. Five minutes passed, though it seemed like an hour.

'You think he's dead?' Ricky whispered, his voice dry and weak.

'I don't know.'

Suddenly the door opened, and the man stepped out. He was crying and mumbling, and he staggered to the rear of the car, where he saw the hose in the grass, and cursed it as he shoved it back into the tail pipe. He held a bottle of whiskey and looked around wildly at the trees, then stumbled back into the car. He mumbled to himself as he slammed the door.

The boys watched in horror.

'He's crazy as hell,' Mark said faintly.

'Lets get out of here,' Ricky said.

'We can't! If he kills himself, and we saw it or knew about it, then we could get in all kinds of trouble.'

Ricky raised his head as if to retreat. 'Then we won't tell anybody. Come on, Mark!'

Mark grabbed his shoulder again and forced him to the ground. 'Just stay down! We're not leaving until I say we're leaving!'

Ricky closed his eyes tightly and started crying. Mark shook his head in disgust but didn't take his eyes off the car. Little brothers were more trouble than they were worth. 'Stop it,' he growled through clenched teeth.

'I'm scared.'

'Fine. Just don't move, okay. Do you hear me? Don't move. And stop the crying.' Mark was back on his elbows, deep in the weeds and preparing to ease through the tall grass once more.

'Just let him die, Mark,' Ricky whispered between sobs.

Mark glared at him over his shoulder and eased toward the car, which was still running. He crawled along his same trail of lightly trampled grass so slowly and carefully that even Ricky, with dry eyes now, could barely see him. Ricky watched the driver's door, waiting for it to fly open and the crazy man to lunge out and kill Mark. He perched on his toes in a sprinters stance for a quick getaway through the woods. He saw Mark emerge under the rear bumper, place a hand for balance on the taillight, and slowly ease the hose from the tail pipe. The grass crackled softly and the weeds shook a little and Mark was next to him again, panting and sweating and, oddly, smiling to himself.

They sat on their legs like two insects under the brush, and watched the car.

'What if he comes out again?' Ricky asked. 'What if he sees us?'

'He can't see us. But if he starts this way, just follow me. We'll be gone before he can take a step.'

'Why don't we go now?'

Mark stared at him fiercely. 'I'm trying to save his life, okay? Maybe, just maybe, he'll see that this is not working, and maybe he'll decide he should wait or something. Why is that so hard to understand?'

'Because he's crazy. If he'll kill himself, then he'll kill us. Why is that so hard to understand?'

Mark shook his head in frustration, and suddenly the door opened again. The man rolled out of the car growling and talking to himself, and stomped through the grass to the rear. He grabbed the end of the hose, stared at it as if it just wouldn't behave, and looked slowly around the small clearing. He was breathing heavily and perspiring. He looked at the trees, and the boys eased to the ground.

He looked down, and froze as if he suddenly understood. The grass was slightly trampled around the rear of the car and he knelt as if to inspect it, but then crammed the hose back into the tail pipe instead and hurried back to his door. If someone was watching from the trees, he seemed not to care. He just wanted to hurry up and die.

The two heads rose together above the brush, but just a few inches. They peeked through the weeds for a minute. Ricky was ready to run, but Mark was thinking.

'Mark, please, let's go,' Ricky pleaded. 'He almost saw us. What if he's got a gun or something?'

'If he had a gun, he'd use it on himself.'

*John Grisham*

# Reflections

* It's worth reading this popular American novel to find out what happens next. It is, we must remind ourselves, glorious fiction.

  That said, Mark recognises that he has a duty to stop the man killing himself, even though he knows it's likely to be a risky adventure. His younger brother is less certain and tries to persuade him otherwise.

  Events don't turn out happily for the boys and their mother – that is the plot of the novel. But behind this fictional situation lies the question of choosing to take the difficult decision in a serious situation. How might each of *us* react when confronted by something that requires a strong, but maybe unpopular decision?

  When you next come face to face with a problem, you might reflect on Mark's presence of mind here. Of course we would all need to think very carefully before doing anything dramatic that might lead to anyone being harmed; equally, it is important to take prompt decisions in certain circumstances, perhaps taking action ourselves or summoning further assistance.

* The words of the politician Edmund Burke come to mind here: 'Nobody made a greater mistake than he who did nothing because he could only do a little.'

# Personal Values

*You ought to believe something in life, believe that thing so fervently that you will stand up with it till the end of your days … We have a power, a power as old as the insights of Jesus of Nazareth and as modern as the techniques of Mahatma Gandhi.*

Martin Luther King

*As long as you feel you are serving others, you do the job well. When you are concerned only with helping yourself, you do it less well – a law as inexorable as gravity.*

# 1 Choice

## Introduction

One of the most successful television producers of the past decade has been Phil Redmond, creator of both *Grange Hill* and *Brookside*. He takes his responsibilities to his audience very seriously. His personal values are in evidence in his television output.

In the following passage he talks about what *choice* means to him as a maker of television programmes which often tackle controversial topics. He also focuses on the much-debated subject of the freedom of the press and the electronic media.

## Reading

### *The Limits of Broadcast Language*

My own experiences as a programme maker have led me more and more to believe and respect the audience's ability and desire to control their own viewing. Make their own choices. I have come more and more to believe in the concept of Watersheds and timesharing on television. Different programmes for different audiences at different times. It is right that programme makers should adhere to the generally accepted social mores. Before 7.00pm there will obviously be more young people and children able to view. The numbers will drop throughout the evening and by nine or ten o'clock it is generally acceptable that the audience will be predominantly adult. Before 10.00pm therefore, I think broadcasters have a responsibility for the control of viewing – whether live or by access to video recorders.

No one group should try and dismiss this broad consensus, nor try and inflict its own cultural taste on everyone else. Neither should the rule be unbreakable. If a movie starts at 9.00pm and does not finish until 11.00pm – the total content should be suitable for a pre-ten o'clock viewing. Similarly, if the context demands, the use of a four-letter word pre-nine o'clock should not be viewed as a capital offence.

As technology develops the capacity to deliver more and more television – so its audience will become more and more sophisticated. It is already far more sophisticated than many practitioners – because quite simply, audiences participate more often than practitioners. A practitioner may make one programme a week – an audience will watch over thirty.

More and more attention and marketing resources will have to go in to 'selling' individual programmes. We will have to be much clearer with our descriptions of programmes to enable our consumers to make choices that fit with their own desires. Their own interpretations of taste and decency. If they do not watch, they will not and why should they?

I do believe greater information about programme content could help preempt a lot of the pseudo concern about taste and decency. From a young boy growing up on a council estate, attending a comprehensive school and later studying sociology at University as a mature student – it surprised, and often amused me, that most of society's cultural arbiters belong to a minority cultural elite divorced from the day-to-day life experiences of the majority of the population. The daily factual readers and the readers of the daily comics.

We live, always have lived and probably always will live in a pluralistic democracy where the plurality of choice and opinion is perceived as a civil right. A pluralist society that views tolerance as a primary goal and one which engenders different cultural values. Yet in such a society how can a middle-to-upper class public school Oxbridge-educated public servant share the same interpretation of taste and decency as a working class inner-city sink school unemployment statistic? What may seem shocking in the House of Lords may appear commonplace on a council housing estate.

One group will find it 'intolerable' for people to wilfully collect state benefit rather than work, while the other will find it 'disgusting' that someone can make a quick buck through insider trading. However, while they will not share a common vocabulary, they will share a common sentiment. Each will think the other is just 'like the rest of them – out for themselves'.

Therefore, with such a diversity of cultural values it is important to have guidelines in a mass marketing industry like television, radio, or the press, but it is also important for any such guidelines to embrace two important principles. The ability to challenge accepted social mores, and the latitude to make mistakes.

Programme makers must also acknowledge these principles. They must respect the generally held consensus to protect certain values, yet at the same time they must be free to challenge their continual validity. In doing so, there are bound to be mistakes. Someone at some stage is going to take a step too far. But we must respect the right to do so.

John F. Kennedy once said that there can be no progress without dissent. We are constantly witnessing that around the globe. We must always allow people to challenge accepted custom, practice and social niceties. The reassurance is that such challenges will only succeed if there is a general consensus to support them. If there is not, they will fade through the lack of credibility to sustain them.

With the ability to make mistakes as we should paraphrase JFK's remark about dissent. There can be no progress without cock-ups. Like swearing and blasphemy, everyone gets something wrong sometime. Mistakes are another part of human development. Failed attempts from which we learn alternatives. The reassurance here is the same one of credibility. To err is human. To err repeatedly is perversion.

Above all, any guidelines should embrace the democratic right to the plurality of choice and cultural expression. It is these principles that should guide us in any of life's multiple codes.

*Phil Redmond*

# Reflections

* On discussing what ought and ought not to be on television, Phil Redmond clearly sees the need for some sort of guidelines. But he reminds us that

people in society have different views about what is acceptable or not acceptable. Therefore, viewers as well as programme makers have responsibilities; for example, parents can turn the television off if they feel a particular programme is not suitable for their children.

He also argues that choice and freedom of expression are important in a free society. That very choice brings with it both individual rights and responsibilities to those around us.

\* There are two other ideas in the passage worth reflecting upon:

- 'John F. Kennedy (former president of the United States) once said there can be no progress without dissent.'

- 'To err is human. To err repeatedly is perversion.'

# 2 Sacred land

## Introduction

One of the most powerful statements ever made about the preciousness of our natural environment was made by Chief Seattle to the President of the United States in 1854. He made the statement at a time when native American tribes were being driven from their land as settlers moved westwards across the Great Plains of the USA in the mid-nineteenth century.

What follows is lucid, unambiguous and poetic. Chief Seattle's personal values are not in doubt.

## Reading

### Chief Seattle to the President of the United States (1854)

*Seattle, c. 1784–1866, Chief of the Dwamish, Suquamish and allied Indian tribes; Franklin Pierce, President of the United States. This letter was presumably written with the help of an amanuensis. Seattle ceded his lands in Washington State by the Treaty of Point Elliot, signed on 22 January 1855. He was anxious that the new settlement should not be named after him, as he believed that after his death his spirit would be disturbed every time human lips uttered the syllables of his name; accordingly he used to solicit gifts from whites as a kind of tax to recompense himself in advance for his oft-broken sleep of eternity.*

How can you buy or sell the sky, the warmth of the land? The idea is strange to us.

If we do not own the freshness of the air and the sparkle of the water, how can you buy them?

Every part of this earth is sacred to my people.

Every shining pine needle, every sandy shore, every mist in the dark woods, every clearing and humming insect is holy in the memory and experience of my people. The sap which courses through the trees carried the memories of the red man.

The white man's dead forget the country of their birth when they go to walk among the stars. Our dead never forget this beautiful earth, for it is the mother of the red man.

We are part of the earth and it is part of us. The perfumed flowers are our sisters; the deer, the horse, the great eagle, these are our brothers.

The rocky crests, the juices in the meadows, the body heat of the pony, and man – all belong to the same family.

So, when the Great Chief in Washington sends word that he wishes to buy our land, he asks much of us. The Great Chief sends word he will reserve us a place so that we can live comfortably to ourselves.

He will be our father and we will be his children. So we will consider your offer to buy our land.

But it will not be easy. For this land is sacred to us.

This shining water that moves in the streams and rivers is not just water but the blood of our ancestors.

If we sell you land, you must remember that it is sacred, and you must teach your children that it is sacred and that each ghostly reflection in the clear water of the lakes tells of events and memories in the life of my people.

The water's murmur is the voice of my father's father.

The rivers are our brothers, they quench our thirst. The rivers carry our canoes, and feed our children. If we sell you our land, you must remember, and teach your children, that the rivers are our brothers, and yours, and you must henceforth give the rivers the kindness you would give any brother.

We know that the white man does not understand our ways. One portion of land is the same to him as the next, for he is a stranger who comes in the night and takes from the land whatever he needs.

The earth is not his brother, but his enemy, and when he has conquered it, he moves on.

He leaves his father's graves behind, and he does not care. He kidnaps the earth from his children, and he does not care.

His father's grave and his children's birthright, are forgotten. He treats his mother, the earth, and his brother, the sky, as things to be bought, plundered, sold like sheep or bright beads.

His appetite will devour the earth and leave behind only a desert.

I do not know. Our ways are different from your ways.

The sight of your cities pains the eyes of the red man. But perhaps it is because the red man is a savage and does not understand.

There is no quiet place in the white man's cities. No place to hear the unfurling of leaves in spring, or the rustle of an insect's wings.

But perhaps it is because I am a savage and do not understand.

The clatter only seems to insult the ears. And what is there to life if a man cannot hear the lonely cry of the whippoorwill or the arguments of the frogs around a pond at night? I am a red man and do not understand.

The Indian prefers the soft sound of the wind darting over the face of a pond, and the smell of the wind itself, cleaned by a midday rain, or scented with the pinon pine.

The air is precious to the red man, for all things share the same breath – the beast, the tree, the man, they all share the same breath.

The white man does not seem to notice the air he breathes. Like a man dying for many days, he is numb to the stench.

But if we sell you our land, you must remember that the air is precious to us, that the air shares its spirit with all the life it supports. The wind that gave our grandfather his first breath also receives his last sigh.

And if we sell you our land, you must keep it apart and sacred, as a place where even the white man can go to taste the wind that is sweetened by the meadow's flowers.

So we will consider your offer to buy our land. If we decide to accept, I will make one condition: the white man must treat the beasts of this land as his brother.

I am a savage and I do not understand any other way.

I have seen a thousand rotting buffaloes on the prairie, left by the white man who shot them from a passing train.

I am a savage and I do not understand how the smoking iron horse can be more important than the buffalo that we kill only to stay alive.

What is man without the beasts? If all the beasts were gone, man would die from a great loneliness of spirit.

For whatever happens to the beasts, soon happens to man. All things are connected.

You must teach your children that the ground beneath their feet is the ashes of your grandfathers. So that they will respect the land, tell your children that the earth is rich with the lives of our kin.

Teach your children what we have taught our children, that the earth is our mother.

Whatever befalls the earth befalls the sons of the earth. If men spit upon the ground, they spit upon themselves.

This we know: the earth does not belong to man; man belongs to the earth. This we know.

All things are connected like the blood which unites one family. All things are connected.

Whatever befalls the earth befalls the sons of the earth. Man did not weave the web of life: he is merely a strand in it. Whatever he does to the web, he does to himself.

Even the white man, whose God walks and talks with him as friend to friend, cannot be exempt from the common destiny.

We may be brothers after all.

We shall see.

One thing we know, which the white man may one day discover – our God is the same God.

You may think now that you own Him as you wish to own our land; but you cannot. He is the God of man, and His compassion is equal for the red man and the white.

This earth is precious to Him, and to harm the earth is to heap contempt on its Creator.

The whites too shall pass; perhaps sooner than all other tribes. Contaminate your bed, and you will one night suffocate in your own waste.

But in your perishing you will shine brightly, fired by the strength of the God who brought you to this land and for some special purpose gave you dominion over this land and over the red man.

That destiny is a mystery to us, for we do not understand when the buffalo are all slaughtered, the wild horses are tamed, the secret corners of the forest heavy with scent of many men, and the view of the ripe hills blotted by talking wires.

Where is the thicket? Gone.

Where is the eagle? Gone.

The end of living and the beginning of survival.

## Reflections

*   There are some thought-provoking questions and statements here about what 'progress' has done and continues to do to our environment:

    'Contaminate your bed, and you will one night suffocate in your own waste.'

    'The end of living and the beginning of survival.'

*   There is also in Chief Seattle's words a repeated sense of wonder: wonder and awe about the natural environment that has supported his tribes for generations; wonder that the white man can want to destroy:

    'There is no quiet place in the white man's cities. No place to hear the unfurling of leaves in Spring, or the rustle of an insect's wings.'

    There is of course added potency when he says, ironically, 'I am a savage and I do not understand any other way.'

*   His words are a reminder to us to stand up for what we believe to be right, and to remember that all human beings need to live in harmony with their environment if humanity is to *flourish* as well as survive.

# 3 'No, you can't blame me at all'

## Introduction

How often do we find ourselves shifting blame onto someone else when something goes wrong? The boss blaming her secretary, the shop-keeper blaming the delivery man, brother blaming sister, friend blaming friend, the speeding motorist blaming the fallen cyclist!

Listen to the following song lyrics about the death of a boxer. As it's being read, see if you can decide who killed Davey Moore?

## Reading

*Who Killed Davey Moore?*

Who killed Davey Moore,
Why an' what's the reason for?

'Not I,' says the referee,

'Don't point your finger at me.
I could've stopped it in the eighth
An' maybe kept him from his fate,
But the crowd would've booed, I'm sure,
At not gettin' their money's worth.
It's too bad he had to go,
But there was a pressure on me too, you know.
It wasn't me that made him fall.
No, you can't blame me at all.'

Who killed Davey Moore,
Why an' what's the reason for?

'Not us,' says the angry crowd,
Whose screams filled the arena loud.
'It's too bad he died that night
But we just like to see a fight.
We didn't mean for him t' meet his death,
We just meant to see some sweat,
There ain't nothing wrong in that.
It wasn't us that made him fall.
No, you can't blame us at all.'

Who killed Davey Moore,
Why an' what's the reason for?

'Not me,' says his manager,
Puffing on a big cigar.
'It's hard to say, it's hard to tell,
I always thought that he was well.
It's too bad for his wife an' kids he's dead,
But if he was sick, he should've said.
It wasn't me that made him fall.
No, you can't blame me at all.'

Who killed Davey Moore,
Why an' what's the reason for?

'Not me,' says the gambling man,
With his ticket stub still in his hand.
'It wasn't me that knocked him down,
My hands never touched him none.
I didn't commit no ugly sin,
Anyway, I put money on him to win.
It wasn't me that made him fall.
No, you can't blame me at all.'

Who killed Davey Moore,
Why an' what's the reason for?

'Not me,' says the boxing writer,
Pounding print on his old typewriter,

Sayin', 'Boxing ain't to blame,
There's just as much danger in a football game.'
Sayin', 'Fist fighting is here to stay,
It's just the old American way.
It wasn't me that made him fall.
No, you can't blame me at all.'

Who killed Davey Moore,
Why an' what's the reason for?

'Not me,' says the man whose fists
Laid him low in a cloud of mist,
Who came here from Cuba's door
Where boxing ain't allowed no more.
'I hit him, yes, it's true,
But that's what I am paid to do.
Don't say "murder," don't say "kill."
It was destiny, it was God's will.'

Who killed Davey Moore,
Why an' what's the reason for?

*Bob Dylan*

## Reflections

\*    Originally written as an angry protest song following the death of boxer
Davey Moore in the 1960s, the words ask not only who killed him but was
there any reason in his death? Each person in turn says it was nothing to do
with them; they were only doing their job – the referee, the crowd, the manager, the gambler, the journalist, the opponent himself. All of them seek to shift
the blame.
Perhaps we might conclude that they were all in some way involved in the
boxer's tragic death in the ring. Or we might say 'that's sport – there are
risks.' Or perhaps we might accept it was destiny or God's will.

\*    When something goes wrong – badly wrong – yes, of course it is important to
ask why. It is equally important to learn to accept responsibility for our
actions and not try to shuffle blame on to someone else. Davey Moore's tale is
one to reflect on when we next catch ourselves saying 'No, you can't blame
me at all.'

# 4 Love over gold

## Introduction

How important is material wealth to us? How do we compare its value with say,
friendship, love, good health? What are our own deep personal values? What
*really* matters to us most?

The following passage is taken from the celebrated nineteenth-century novel *Silas Marner* by George Eliot. Silas Marner is a weaver living in the small village of Raveloe. He is known by his neighbours to be a miser, always counting the gold that lies hidden beneath the loom in his cottage. Then one day his precious gold is stolen – only to be replaced, as we shall hear, by an unexpected arrival.

There is reference in the passage to Silas's 'catalepsy', a sort of epileptic trance he experiences from time to time.

# Reading

*Love over gold*

During the last few weeks, since he had lost his money, he had contracted the habit of opening his door, and looking out from time to time, as if he thought that his money might be somehow coming back to him, or that some trace, some news of it, might be mysteriously on the road, and be caught by the listening ear or the straining eye. It was chiefly at night, when he was not occupied in his loom, that he fell into this repetition of an act for which he could have assigned no definite purpose, and which can hardly be understood except by those who have undergone a bewildering separation from a supremely loved object. In the evening twilight and later whenever the night was not dark, Silas looked out on that narrow prospect round the Stone-pits, listening and gazing, not with hope, but with mere yearning and unrest.

This morning he had been told by some of his neighbours that it was New Year's Eve, and that he must sit up and hear the old year rung out and the new rung in, because that was good luck, and might bring his money back again. This was only a friendly Raveloe-way of jesting with the half-crazy oddities of a miser, but it had perhaps helped to throw Silas into a more than usually excited state. Since the on-coming of twilight he had opened his door again and again, though only to shut it immediately at seeing all distance veiled by the falling snow. But the last time he opened it the snow had ceased, and the clouds were parting here and there. He stood and listened, and gazed for a long while – there was really something on the road coming towards him then, but he caught no sign of it; and the stillness and the wide trackless snow seemed to narrow his solitude, and touched his yearning with the chill of despair. He went in again, and put his right hand on the latch of the door to close it – but he did not close it: he was arrested, as he had been already since his loss, by the invisible wand of catalepsy, and stood like a graven image, with wide but sightless eyes, holding open his door, powerless to resist either the good or evil that might enter there.

When Marner's sensibility returned, he continued the action which had been arrested, and closed his door, unaware of the chasm in his consciousness, unaware of any intermediate change, except that the light had grown dim, and that he was chilled and faint. He thought he had been too long standing at the door and looking out. Turning towards the hearth, where the two logs had fallen apart, and sent forth only a red uncertain glimmer, he seated himself on his fireside chair, and was stooping to push his logs together, when, to his blurred vision, it seemed as if there were gold on the floor in front of the hearth. Gold! – his own gold – brought back to him as mysteriously as it had been taken away! He felt his heart begin to beat violently, and for a few moments he was unable to stretch out his hand and grasp the restored treasure. The heap of gold seemed to glow and get larger beneath his agitated gaze. He leaned forward at last, and stretched forth his hand; but instead of the hard coin with the familiar resisting outline, his fingers encountered soft warm curls. In utter amazement, Silas fell on his knees and bent his head low to examine the marvel: it was a sleeping child – a round, fair thing, with soft yellow rings all over its head. Could this be his little sister come back to him in a dream – his little sister whom he had carried about in his arms for a year before she died, when he was a small boy without shoes or stockings? That was the first thought that darted across Silas's blank wonderment. *Was* it a dream? He rose to his feet again, pushed his logs together and, throwing on some dried leaves and sticks, raised a flame; but the flame did not disperse the vision – it only lit up more distinctly the little round form of the child and its shabby clothing. It was very much like his little sister. Silas sank into his chair powerless, under the double presence of an inexplicable surprise and a hurrying influx of memories. How and when had the child come in without his knowledge?

But there was a cry on the hearth: the child had awaked, and Marner stooped to lift it on his knee. It clung round his neck, and burst louder and louder into that mingling of inarticulate cries with 'mammy' by which little children express the bewilderment of waking. Silas pressed it to him, and almost unconsciously uttered sounds of hushing tenderness, while he bethought himself that some of his porridge, which had got cool by the dying fire, would do to feed the child with if it were only warmed up a little.

He had plenty to do through the next hour. The porridge, sweetened with some dry brown sugar from an old store which he had refrained from using for himself, stopped the cries of the little one, and made her lift her blue eyes with a wide gaze at Silas, as he put the spoon into her mouth. Presently she slipped from his knee and began to toddle about, but with a pretty stagger that made Silas jump up and follow her lest she should fall against anything that would hurt her. But she only fell in a sitting posture on the ground, and began to pull at her boots, looking up at him with a crying face as if the boots hurt her. He took her on his knee again, but it was some time before it occurred to Silas's dull bachelor mind that the wet boots were the grievance, pressing on her warm ankles. He got them off with difficulty, and baby was at once happily occupied with the primary mystery of her own toes, inviting Silas, with much chuckling, to consider the mystery too. But the wet boots had at last suggested to Silas that the child had been walking on the snow, and this roused him from his entire oblivion of any ordinary means by which it could have entered or been brought into his house. Under the prompting of this new idea, and without waiting to form conjectures, he raised the child in his arms, and went to the door. As soon as he had opened it, there was the cry of 'mammy' again, which Silas had not heard since the child's first hungry waking. Bending forward, he could just discern the marks made by the little feet on the virgin snow, and he followed their track to the furze bushes. 'Mammy!' the little one cried again and again, stretching itself forward so as almost to escape from Silas's arms, before he himself was aware that there was something more than the bush before him – that there was a human body, with the head sunk low in the furze, and half-covered with the shaken snow.

*George Eliot*

## Reflections

\* For years before this episode in the novel happens, Silas Marner has been
known by others to be a miser and a recluse. With the unexpected arrival of
the girl Eppie – whom Silas adopts – life begins to change for him. No longer
is material wealth the be-all and end-all for him. Eppie draws Silas out into
the community and he begins to value friendship and human ties as much as
he once did his gold.
It is a powerful tale about human *values* – what ultimately matters to someone
in their life. It might help us reflect on what matters to us – is it material
wealth, friendship, a loving family, a healthy environment? Perhaps it is some
or all of these at different points in our lives?

\* 'A child, more than all other gifts
That earth can offer to declining man,
Brings hope with it, and forward-looking thoughts.'

*'Michael', William Wordsworth*

# 5 A gift of freedom

## Introduction

One of the time-honoured questions by parents is: Which is the more important?
Nature or nurture? In other words, are personality, character, behaviour, attitudes shaped by what we inherit from our parents in our gene pool? Or are they
shaped by our environment and those around us? Or is it a chancy mixture of
nature and nurture?

The following poem is all about the freedoms we should enjoy as we grow up
and, in some ways, grow away from our parental influences. It is titled *To an
English Friend in Africa* and is written by Ben Okri who comes from Nigeria.

## Reading

*To an English Friend in Africa*

Be grateful for the freedom
To see other dreams.
Bless your loneliness as much as you drank
Of your former companionships.
All that you are experiencing now
Will become moods of future joys
So bless it all.
Do not think your way superior
To another's
Do not venture to judge
But see things with fresh and open eyes
Do not condemn

But praise when you can
And when you can't be silent.

Time now is a gift for you
A gift of freedom
To think and remember and understand
The ever perplexing past
And to re-create yourself anew
In order to transform time.

Live while you are alive.
Learn the ways of silence and wisdom
Learn to act, learn a new speech
Learn to be what you are in the seed of your spirit
Learn to free yourself from all the things
That have moulded you
And which limit your secret and undiscovered road.

Remember that all things which happen
To you are raw materials
Endlessly fertile
Endlessly yielding of thoughts that could change
Your life and go on doing so for ever.

Never forget to pray and be thankful
For all things good or bad on the rich road;
For everything is changeable
So long as you live while you are alive.

Fear not, but be full of light and love;
Fear not, but be alert and receptive;
Fear not, but act decisively when you should;
Fear not, but know when to stop;
Fear not, for you are loved by me;
Fear not, for death is not the real error,
But life – magically – is.

Be joyful in your silence
Be strong in your patience
Do not try to wrestle with the universe
But be sometimes like water or air
Sometimes like fire
And constant like the earth.

Live slowly, think slowly, for time is a mystery.
Never forget that love
Requires always that you be
The greatest person you are capable of being,
Self-regenerating, strong and gentle –
Your own hero and star.

Love demands the best in us

To always and in time overcome the worst
And lowest in our souls.
Love the world wisely.
It is love alone that is the greatest weapon
And the deepest and hardest secret.

So fear not, my friend.
The darkness is gentler than you think.
Be grateful for the manifold
Dreams of creation
And the many ways of the unnumbered peoples.

Be grateful for life as you live it.
And may a wonderful light
Always guide you on the unfolding road.

*Ben Okri*

## Reflections

\*   Ben Okri sets forth here the values of freedom and love which he holds dear.
    He also reminds the friend to whom he has written the poem that tolerance of
    other people's way of life is important:

    'praise when you can
    And when you can't be silent.'

\*   There are many exhortations in the poem to live life to the full and to hold fast
    to those values which you have grown up with and thus cherish. Yet there is
    also the recognition that each of us has to make our own way in life and shape
    our own values out of both our nature and our nurture. The following words
    are worth careful reflection:

    'Learn to free yourself from all the things
    That have moulded you
    And which limit your secret and undiscovered road.'

# 6 Injustice

## Introduction

If freedom is one of the cornerstones of a democratic and healthy society, then
injustice is something we should all oppose – wherever we meet it.

The following powerful words come from Paul Hill, a man who was imprisoned for crimes he did not commit. Naturally he has some provocative thoughts
about justice and injustice in Britain today.

# Reading

## *Prisoners on the outside*

I know what democracy is. Democracy is living in a society where you have free thought, equality, the right to choose to do whatever you want within the parameters of what's normal in society. And being afforded the mechanisms to educate yourself, to feed your family.

My name's Paul Hill. For 15 years I was imprisoned for crimes, horrendous crimes – the worst ever committed on the British mainland. In 1989 the establishment conceded grudgingly that I was *innocent*! Then, in a Belfast Court of Appeal, I was finally able to clear my name of another murder, of a British soldier. I have never experienced democracy. But I don't believe that most people in the United Kingdom have either.

I was born in a West Belfast Catholic ghetto. There was nothing democratic about where we lived. But there was still good respect for law and order within the community. We could play in the street till midnight. Mugging was unheard of. When I was very small, in the 1960s, I remember my family watching the news when Harold Wilson got in. My father said: 'Take no notice – it doesn't apply to us.'

From my own experience of being part of a community in Northern Ireland that never really identified with democracy, I can identify with a young guy in Moss Side in Manchester who never felt part of a democratic process. We've created another whole social class who are young people who have never been employed. They may have no respect for law and order at all, because as far as they were concerned, law and order never gave them any respect: they've got very low self-esteem.

We are told by politicians that democracy is the be-all and end-all. Apply it! Apply it to these people in West Belfast, to the blacks in Brixton, to the Asians in Southall by taking them in and making them a part of society. If you are not *made* inclusive, you will never be. In West Belfast, people asked for their basic demographic rights and they got beaten off the streets. If society doesn't embrace everyone within it equally and fairly, the exclusion of those people is going to undermine the whole of our stability.

One day in Winchester prison, I was taken downstairs and locked in a white room, completely bare apart from the statutory nine-inch window. And after a while I realised that they were starving all the senses. I also learnt later from reading that under normal prison conditions the brain is damaged irreversibly after 12 years. And in order to accelerate this process, they give you these massive doses of solitary confinement. And I thought – what kind of society wants to do this to someone?

Had they taken me to prison, put me in a cell and left me completely alone for 15 years, I would have been a wreck. But they gave me constant stimulation because I was moved 54 times – between 35 or 36 different prisons. So I was meeting new people, and I was meeting people I'd met before, and there was always something stimulating going on.

And I thought for a long time that they were doing this to keep me healthy! I really did! They were doing it to try and break me down, to disorientate me. I'd be at Parkhurst, and I'd be getting a visit tomorrow morning. I'd be moved tonight and I'd be in Hull, and my mother would be travelling to the Isle of Wight. I've left prison and seen my mother standing outside as I was being driven 250 miles the other way!

They did that to me and hundreds of other young men, who were in for ridiculous things in relation to what I was in prison for. There's no need to treat those people like that. If you treat people like that and then throw them back on society, you'll have angry, embittered young men going out there. These young men came out, their families have broken up – probably their mother's the only person in the house, maybe with three or four other kids. What's that kid going to do? Straight back to crime.

Prison is only a microcosm of society at large: the same rules apply. If you treat people uncaringly, you will create brutalised, desperate people. It's the same inside as out.

Most people in prison don't tend to say they are innocent when they are, because prisons are a very macho environment. It's actually the opposite: people tend to say they did more than they did because of the environment they are in. It was common knowledge in Wormwood Scrubs, among black prisoners, who had killed PC Blakelock – and it wasn't the people who were in for killing PC Blakelock. It was common knowledge to every long-term prisoner in Parkhurst Prison, who had killed the young man at Yew Tree Farm for which three people were serving life imprisonment. And if every long-term prisoner in Parkhurst was in possession of his name, then so was the security officer and so were the police.

Once you are through the court system there's no real benefit to the system to find you innocent, and there's no real benefit to the police to find the guilty people. We not only have innocent people in prison, but we have people who have committed murders still on the streets.

When I first came out of prison there were moments when I would have liked to see those police officers go to prison for the same period that I did. But on reflection, I have no wish to see very junior police officers being held accountable for the actions of senior officers.

There comes a point when anger is a healthy thing. When I was in prison no matter what they could do to me physically, they couldn't make me mentally guilty. Anger is a motivating force. But hatred destroys the individual. So I was angry but I never really hated the people who were doing this to me. I certainly dislike them, but I knew if I continuously hated these people, I would be eaten away inside. So I stayed as angry as I possibly could, and it gave me a sense of righteousness and an indignation towards these people. And I was lucky, I survived.

If you treat people well and give them something to live for, so that they have a zest for life, they're going to behave well. And that applies to all of us: the working class in West Belfast, Catholic and Protestant; the women in Holloway Prison, the blacks in Moss Side, the unemployed up and down the land. We should treat these people as human beings, not as people who we prey upon, not as people who the police force see as a direct threat to them, not as people the establishment would view as something other than themselves.

Only then will we have a democracy which we all want to join.

*Paul Hill*

# Reflections

* Paul Hill throws into sharp focus some of the worrying flaws in any democracy; his comments that innocent people are in prison while murderers are still on our streets are a further reminder to us that justice and injustice need to be fought for and against by everyone in society.

  But he is also saying that injustice leads to people feeling excluded and that those people then turn against what is good in our society.

  How can we remedy this state of affairs? Paul Hill's own suggestion is: 'If you treat people well and give them something to live for, so that they have a zest for life, they're going to behave well.'

  Is this view optimistic, realistic? His own experiences as someone wrongfully imprisoned are certainly to be listened to carefully. What can we – in our own lives – learn from him about the importance of treating others with justice, and about the difference between anger and hatred?

(See also **Reborn**, p. 18)

# 7 Courage

## Introduction

Are there times when the ends justify the means? The Suffragettes in the early years of the twentieth century clearly thought so. Many were prepared to go to prison and go on hunger strike in order to draw attention to their fight for women's rights – and the vote for women, which eventually came in 1928.

Being prepared to suffer and – in some cases – die for your cause often demands acts of great courage. The following is taken from the novel *A Question of Courage* and is a fictionalised account of one suffragette's imprisonment in Holloway Gaol. Emily is the central character and she has been imprisoned together with a friend Louise.

## Reading

### A Question of Courage

Courage! Where was it now with the terrible blank door no more than a seam in the wall? The fact that there was no handle brought a black despair which muffled her so close she felt she must suffocate; she opened her mouth gasping for air. The walls closed in. The high ceiling was surely inches nearer? Above the door a recessed gas jet shed thin light. The panic was unbearable, cutting out thought, hope, air ... With her head swimming, Emily forced herself to look round the cell, mechanically naming the objects she saw in a desperate attempt to regain control of herself.

'Bed-boards, shelves, mattress, bedding, wooden spoon, yellow soap, hairbrush, comb, tin mug, watercan, wash basin, slop pail ...' She compelled herself to list them all, thankful to find breathing easier, the iron bands relaxing. From a small barred window too high to see through, came a weak shaft of sunlight. In her trembling fear it seemed a single link with hope. Out there, beyond the stone walls and endless locked doors, was real life and one day she would join it again.

'Not finished yet, 13? Where's your pint?' The wardress, a bony woman with a widow's peak and cheese-grater voice, spoke sharply.

Emily slowly got up from her knees and the floor she had been scrubbing. The cell walls were curving like sea waves and she was forced to clutch at the corner shelf to stop herself from falling.

'Supper not touched nor cleared away? Slovenly habits, 13. You'd best look sharp about it or you'll get no gruel.' It was customary to have plate and pint mug clean and shining, ready on the little cloth for breakfast, so there was more than a hint of kindliness in being given this second chance. But Emily shook her head. 'Stubborn, eh? You'll do yourself no good. Eat and drink a morsel or you know what'll happen.'

Emily closed her eyes, wanting no contact for fear her resolution might weaken. Two nights and a day since she had taken food or drink. An eternity. The scummy cocoa in her mug tempted like the best of Mam's tea. Would she ever hold out? She must ... must ...

'Can't stand here all day. If you insist on this foolishness, you know what you'll get.' With this dark threat the wardress slammed out into the landing, turning the key on hope with a cold rattle of metal.

Weak and ashamed, Emily slumped on the stool and sobbed. Her head ached and there was a furious rushing noise in her ears. Tears channelled on to her parched lips, their wet saltiness stinging the cracked skin. Oh sod it ... sod all of them, those blown-up barrels of self-important parliamentary muck! She'd not give in. There was still enough moisture in her to make tears, so she wasn't going to die just yet. But there was the day to get through and another and another. Louise had said they would be out in a week, but there was the torment of Hell to go through before then. Don't look into that pit. One thing at a time. Scrub the floor, then get on with sewing that shirt. The liquid in the mug pulled with all the power of a whirlpool. She stretched out longing hands, held it, brought it nearer, then with a cry hurled the contents over the freshly washed floor.

It began with a single buzz, more of a whisper than anything. A musty reek of ageing herbs came from the knotty pillow under Emily's head. She opened her eyes into a darkness where the pains in her body were magnified into a gigantic all-over toothache. The buzz came again, louder this time, soaring and swooping.

Silence.

Mouth dry and cracked as the Sahara Desert, tongue swollen. There was a crystal-clear spring coming out of the mountainside, pouring over rocks, bubbling with little splashes between pebbles that glinted in the fresh sunlit air. Someone had spread a white cloth embroidered with cherries and apples, but they were changing from stitches into perfect fruit and behind was a tureen, blue and white china, the lid removed, allowing the steam smelling of rich garlic gravy to drift round her head.

With a jerk she was thumped into wakefulness. What was it? Another thud and another! The grey square filtered a little light and now she could see it, a humble bee crashing with desperate urgency against the glass pane. Like herself, a prisoner. She covered her head, trying to blot out sight and sound, but it went on and on until it occupied the whole of her head. She lumbered out of bed, her limbs obeying from a great distance. On the shelf beside her soap and brush was a paper bag which held cotton and thimble. She tipped them out, then with heavy stumbling caution stood on the stool. Careful ... slide it nearer, nearer! The bee took off, skimming her head, circling the cell, then back again, drawn by the light, only to crash fruitlessly again and again and again. Her desperation increased with each attempt to put it in the bag, but she would not kill a living thing trapped like herself in this airless fetid coffin. Yet she couldn't stand the sound, not one single minute longer. The stool was no good, she needed them to stand on. Her shoe would serve. It was heavy enough. Gathering the last shreds of her strength, she hammered with all her might at the barred window, not caring about the punishment to follow. It was tougher than she expected, but she would not give it. One more blow ... another ... With a sharp crack and the tinkle of falling glass, the bee winged away into freedom.

They were coming. The sound of footsteps mingled with the rattle of keys and opening doors. Voices echoed along the landing. Curses. Someone cried: 'Have pity!' In bed, Emily covered her head with the blanket. Shrieks now, and a single high-pitched scream of an animal in terror. A human animal. How was she to stand it? Perhaps it was only part of the nightmares that troubled sleep and spread out into the endless days. If only Louise was here. The touch of her hand. A warming, strengthening smile. But the last of Louise had been that hurried kiss before they were separated in the Bow Street cells.

'Number 13!'

It was no dream. The doctor speaking to her was the one who had examined her when she first entered Holloway.

'Listen carefully to what I have to say. Food has been brought for you and I give you a last chance to take it of your own free will.' He beckoned to a wardress standing behind.

Emily saw the glass of water and bowl of thin milky gruel. Everything else receded. Her thirst was a huge all-embracing drive. She shut her eyes tight, gripping the bedclothes.

'Very well. I have no other course than to compel you to take food.'

Her eyes still tightly closed, Emily felt the bedding stripped off and she was roughly pulled to her feet. A chair had been brought into the cell and she was made to sit down.

'Open your eyes, 13.'

He was holding a long tube made from two lengths of rubber joined by a glass junction. 'You still have a choice. This must pass into your stomach. It is easier by mouth.'

Emily clenched her teeth.

'Very well!' He signalled to the group of wardresses. Two came and held her shoulders, two more leaned on her legs, another grasped her head. As the doctor approached, Emily saw hairs sprouting from his nose, and the large pores of his skin. Then there was nothing but the agony of the tube being forced up her nostril.

In spite of herself she yelled out; begging for mercy, but there was no escape. The tube pressed down her throat into her stomach with a burning tearing sensation that stretched to the end of her breastbone. She stared up with wide anguished eyes and saw the doctor raise the funnel end and pour a brownish liquid into it.

She must suffocate! Her distended stomach heaved. Pain tore throat and nose, searing tender membrane. There was thunder in her head and a waterfall in her ears. No more ... no more ... no more ... But the pain increased in ferocity as the tube was withdrawn, as if a hand were wrenching out the back of her nose and throat. Her body in revolt, she retched, spraying herself and her captors with vomit.

*Marjorie Darke*

## Reflections

* Evidently the novelist Marjorie Darke intends to bring home to us just how violent the business of hunger-strikes became for prisoners and warders alike. But she also skilfully explores the inner courage of the character Emily.

* We may not in our own lives ever face such extreme circumstances, but tales of the Suffragettes are a powerful reminder of the need sometimes to take courageous actions in order to achieve certain goals.

    Courage is one of those personal qualities that can be seen as both powerful and destructive. Being fool-hardy and over-adventurous can lead to disaster. On the other hand, knowing your own strengths and harnessing your courage in the right direction will always be valued by those around you.

# 8 Selflessness

## Introduction

One of our most basic human instincts is for self-survival. In moments of extreme hardship or in everyday situations we are often inclined to put ourselves before others. There may of course be exceptions to this: the mother who risks her own life to save her drowning son or the doctor treating casualties of a bomb blast. Nonetheless, it is difficult not to think of the self first.

The following passage is a fictional account of Captain Scott's famous Antarctic exploration in 1912, in which his team found they had just been beaten to the South Pole by the Norwegian Amundsen. Their return from the Pole ended in their deaths. The reading is in two parts and is told through the eyes of Captain Oates.

## Reading

*'The Birthday Boys'*

(i) The trip to the Pole

Our high spirits lasted all of two days, mostly on account of the smooth surfaces and calm weather. Four in the tent had been cramped enough, five was a squeeze and cooking for five took longer than for four, but it didn't matter when the sun was so warm we could stand about outside the tent in perfect comfort.

Then the weather turned bad and we got amongst sastrugi and had to take off our skis and pull on foot – Bowers, of course, was without his the whole time. Scott got into a frightful dither over whether or not we should dump our skis altogether, and no sooner had he made up his mind and we'd done as he ordered and had struggled on another fearful two miles or so, than the surface improved and he had us plodding back to retrieve them. I think we were all weaker than we let on – I know I was – and we simply couldn't afford to be indecisive and fritter away our meagre resources of energy on such manoeuvres. Cold was one thing, and hunger another, and we'd grown callous to both these forms of torture, but it was simply more than flesh could stand when exhaustion was added to the catalogue of pain. Then it mattered terribly that it took an extra half hour to get the food into our stomachs.

Scott, poor devil, seemed genuinely perplexed at this setback. 'I must admit,' he confessed, 'it hadn't occurred to me that cooking for one more would add thirty minutes to preparation time.' For a moment he seemed cast down. Then he said, 'However, I'm sure we'll get used to it.'

In his ruthlessness of purpose he resembled Napoleon, who, when the Alps stood in the way of his armies, cried out, 'There shall be no Alps.' For Scott there was no such word as impossible, or if there was it was listed in a dictionary for fools. In the dreadful circumstances in which we found ourselves, half-starved and almost always frozen, our muscles trembling from the strain of dragging those infernal sledges, I expect his was the only way. To have faltered at this late stage would have been like pulling in one's horse while it was leaping. He spared no one, not even himself, and he drove us on by the sheer force of his will. And then Birdie spotted that black flag.

(ii) On the return journey

I think it's my birthday tomorrow. Last night I showed Bill my left foot. He blenched. Scott saw it too.

'It's all up for me, isn't it?' I asked. 'How will it finish? I shouldn't want to end screaming.'

'Nonsense,' said Bill, 'you'll pull through.'

'Stop it,' Scott shouted, 'tell him the truth.'

Poor old Bill pulled a face. One could tell he wanted death to come like a thief in the night.

'I want the morphia,' I said. I knew we had thirty tablets apiece.

'No,' he said. 'It's against my principles.'

'I order you to hand them over Bill,' Scott said. 'I order you to give every man the means to choose his own time to die.'

There was such a struggle over it that I lost heart. I lay in my bag, hands, feet, nose, hip, rotting to hell. Dozing, I plodded towards the Pole again, towards that blue dish atop the cairn. This time I saw dog prints in the snow.

Bill gave me the morphia, five tablets washed down with tea.

'Pray God I won't wake in the morning,' I said, and sleepily shook hands with Birdie.

What dreams I had! I think the approach of death is possibly heralded by a firework display of days gone by. My mother came to me, bossy, competent, convinced she could nurse my dead feet into life. 'No, Mother,' I said, 'they've gone beyond recall.'

And then she embraced me, and I thought it was her tears that rolled down my cheeks until the pain in my legs jerked me into consciousness, and I realised it was my own eyes that spilled with grief.

I could hear Birdie snoring. There was a little chink of daylight poking through the canvas above Bill's head. In that moment before I struggled upright it came to me that my greatest sin had been that of idleness. I had wasted my days.

Birdie woke when I struggled out of my bag. I put my fingers to my lips, enjoining silence. I wanted to kiss him good-bye, but I was too shy.

'I'm just going outside,' I said, 'and may be some time.'

*Beryl Bainbridge*

## Reflections

* On their return journey, their morale low and weather conditions deteriorating, members of the team died one by one. Captain Oates's memorable final words – 'I'm just going outside and may be some time' – indicate the self-sacrifice he made in the hope that some of his friends would make it back to base. They didn't. But his personal action has long been talked about as an act of selflessness amongst explorers.

* Our own everyday lives do contain moments when we could put others first, ourselves second, from time to time. Actions *do* speak louder than words.

# 9 Sharing

## Introduction

In any community there will be people who are naturally more generous than others. But something which many great religious leaders have always taught is that there *is* generosity of spirit and action in us all – we just sometimes need the circumstances to show that generous side of our nature.

Listen to the following simple tale about *sharing*.

## Reading

### A traditional tale

Once upon a time and long ago, a weary soldier was marching along the road on the way to rejoin his unit. As night had begun to fall, he decided to take shelter in a small village. He knocked on the door of a cottage and an aged crone came out. 'Go away, you'll get nothing here', she quavered, 'we haven't had any food for days.' So he went next door and a bent old man came out. 'Go away, you'll get nothing here', he croaked, we haven't had any food for weeks.' So he went next door and a little boy came out. 'Go away, you'll get nothing here', he piped, 'Mother says we haven't had any food for months.'

'Ask your mother', said the soldier, 'if at least I can borrow her big black cooking pot.' This was agreeable at any rate, so the soldier carried the pot to the village green, filled it with water from the river, and put seven large stones in the bottom of it which he had picked from the river bed. Then he lit a fire under it. The villagers peeped out from behind their curtains in a fever of curiosity. Whatever was he doing?

The little boy was the most feverishly curious of all, so plucking up his courage he walked over and stood beside the soldier and watched. 'Whatever are you doing?', he asked eventually. 'Making stone soup', replied the soldier. 'What, just with stones? That won't be very interesting! I'll get you a spoonful of salt and some herbs from the garden. He's making stone soup!', shouted the little boy so that the whole village could hear. 'That won't be very interesting!', quavered the aged crone, 'here are two old carrots you can put in if you like.' 'That won't be very interesting!', croaked the bent old man, 'here's some cabbage leaves and an onion you can put in as well if you like.'

One by one all the villagers began putting their bits and pieces into the big black pot, a turnip here, a few potatoes there, a couple of leeks, a handful of dried beans, even an old chicken that hadn't laid an egg for as long as anyone could remember. Thank you very much', said the soldier, 'but there's far too much for me here, you'll all have to help me out.' Thank you very much', replied the villagers, 'indeed we will', and they happily shared every last morsel together.

Everyone agreed that stone soup was the best soup they had ever tasted.

*Retold by Francis Kinsman*

# Reflections

* The traditional tale is self-explanatory. It reminds us that we do have it in us to share – but we may sometimes need prompting. We might then just surprise ourselves and others around us.
  Communities of people need to share – material goods, ideas, friendship – so that they flourish and become better places for everyone in them.

* *Jesus Feeds the Five Thousand*

[30]The apostles gathered round Jesus and reported to him all they had done and taught. [31]Then, because so many people were coming and going that they did not even have a chance to eat, he said to them, 'Come with me by yourselves to a quiet place and get some rest.'

[32]So they went away by themselves in a boat to a solitary place. [33]But many who saw them leaving recognised them and ran on foot from all the towns and got there ahead of them. [34]When Jesus landed and saw a large crowd, he had compassion on them, because they were like sheep without a shepherd. So he began teaching them many things.

[35]By this time it was late in the day, so his disciples came to him. 'This is a remote place,' they said, 'and it's already very late.'[36] 'Send the people away so that they can go to the surrounding countryside and villages and buy themselves something to eat.'

<sup>37</sup> But he answered, 'You give them something to eat.'

They said to him, 'That would take eight months of a man's wages! Are we to go and spend that much on bread and give it to them to eat?'

<sup>38</sup> 'How many loaves do you have?' he asked. 'Go and see.'

When they found out, they said, 'Five – and two fish.'

<sup>39</sup> Then Jesus directed them to have all the people sit down in groups on the green grass. <sup>40</sup> So they sat down in groups of hundreds and fifties. <sup>41</sup> Taking the five loaves and the two fish and looking up to heaven, he gave thanks and broke the loaves. Then he gave them to his disciples to set before the people. He also divided the two fish among them all. <sup>42</sup> They all ate and were satisfied, <sup>43</sup> and the disciples picked up twelve basketfuls of broken pieces of bread and fish. <sup>44</sup> The number of the men who had eaten was five thousand.

*Mark 6, 30–44 Gideons (p. 136)*

# 10 Ageing

## Introduction

How do you see and look at an old person you meet for the first time? Do you have certain expectations about what they might say to you, about their attitudes and opinions? Do you think you afford them the respect they deserve? Do you ever – for just a moment – think, yes, she or he was my age once?

Listen to the following poem. It was written by someone living in an old people's home. She was unable to speak although the nurses saw her writing from time to time. The piece was found in her locker after her death.

## Reading

*Ageing*

What do you see nurses
    what do you see?
Are you thinking
    when you are looking at me
A crabbit old woman,
    not very wise.
Uncertain of habit
    with far-away eyes,
Who dribbles her food
    and makes no reply,
When you say in a loud voice
    'I do wish you'd try'
Who seems not to notice
    the things that you do,
And forever is losing
    a stocking or shoe.

Who unresisting or not
    lets you do as you will
With bathing and feeding
    the long day to fill,
Is that what you're thinking,
    is that what you see?

Then open your eyes nurse,
    you are not looking at me,
I'll tell you who I am,
    as I sit here so still;
As I use at your bidding,
    as I eat at your will.

I'm a small child of ten
    with a Father and Mother,
Brothers and sisters who
    love one another,
A young girl of sixteen,
    with wings on her feet,
Dreaming that soon now
    a lover she'll meet:
A bride soon at twenty,
    my heart gives a leap,
Remembering the vows
    that I promised to keep:
At twenty-five now
    I have young of my own
Who need me to build
    a secure happy home.
A woman of thirty,
    My young now grow fast,
Bound to each other
    with ties that should last.
At forty my young sons
    now grown and will all be gone
But my man stays beside me
    to see I don't mourn.

At fifty once more
    babies play round my knee,
Again we know children
    my loved one and me.
Dark days are upon me,
    my husband is dead,
I look at the future
    I shudder with dread,
For my young are all busy
    rearing young of their own,
And I think of the years

and the love I have known,
I'm an old woman now
  and nature is cruel,
'Tis her jest to make
  old age look like a fool.
The body it crumbles,
  grace and vigour depart,
There now is a stone
  where once I had a heart:
But inside this old carcase
  a young girl still swells.
And now and again
  my battered heart swells,
I remember the joys,
  I remember the pain,
And I'm loving and living
  life over again,
I think of the years
  all too few – gone too fast.
And accept the stark fact
  that nothing can last.

So open your eyes nurses,
  open and see,
Not a crabbit old woman,
  Look closer – see ME.

*Anon*

## Reflections

*   Winston Churchill once remarked that a true test of a civilisation was how it treated its prisoners. Britain has an increasingly ageing population and we might say now that how society treats old people will be the real test of its humanity. Kate's moving poem roundly reminds us that we should not judge old people merely by their outward appearances; their inner life is every bit as vibrant as that of the young person.

*   An important aspect of living in the community is the mutual respect of young and old alike, each valuing the other for what it has to offer by way of energy and wisdom. As medical technology advances, diets improve and we all live longer, an interesting question emerges: 'How old is *old* nowadays? To the 75-year-old man in excellent health someone 'old' needs perhaps to be 85!

# Faith and Belief

*Two frogs lived on a dairy farm and fell into a churn of milk. The sides were too steep for them to climb out and, after swimming around for some time, one of them gave up the struggle and drowned.*

*The other worked his feet to the rhythm of 'With Allah's Help, With Allah's Help, With Allah's Help.'*

*In the morning he was discovered exceedingly tired but perched safely on a mound of soft butter.*

*Happiness is not wanting anything.*

Buddhism

# 1 Prisoners of conscience

## Introduction

What is a prisoner of conscience? A prisoner of conscience is a man, woman or child detained anywhere for their beliefs, colour, sex, ethnic origin, language or religion, who has neither used nor supported violence.

Terry Waite, a man working for the Church of England in the Middle East to help free hostages, suddenly found himself a prisoner of conscience. His imprisonment lasted nearly five years. Here are his words of thanks just after he arrived back in England (in 1991).

## Reading

### *A guard came with a postcard*

'Ladies and gentlemen I think you can imagine that after 1,763 days in chains it's an overwhelming experience to come back and receive your greetings.

From the bottom of my heart thank you for turning out on such an awful day, but a typically English day and thank you so much for your welcome.

This is an emotional day for me, it's a day when thanks are due to many people.

First of all to the Secretary General of the United Nations and his envoy for their hard and persistent work to seek a resolution to the problem of all hostages who are detained in the Middle East.

Also it has been a particular pleasure for me to meet a moment or two ago my old boss, Lord Runcie, who I am glad to say is looking as fit and as well as ever and who I know has kept all of us close to his heart and prayers and his active work in the last years.

And it has been also a particular pleasure to meet the new Archbishop of Canterbury, someone whom I have met previously on a couple of occasions and who I know also has worked so hard and will continue to work so hard until this problem is resolved.

And to all the Lambeth staff, they're a small staff but they are keen, good people. And I must pay a personal tribute to the late John Lyttle who worked so hard for our release and unfortunately died before he could see this and other happy days.

It was also my pleasure a moment or two ago to meet the Foreign Secretary, who's had in these last years the unenviable job of trying to walk on eggshells in a territory that is indeed difficult and dangerous.

And also it's been my pleasure and privilege to meet members of his staff both in Damascus and again on the plane. I extend to them my gratitude and thanks.

And of course what could a home-coming be of this kind without the RAF.

And I can tell you one thing that when I left Hizbollah yesterday afternoon they did their best to kit me out with a sweater and a pair of trousers but they couldn't find a pair of shoes my size.

But when I got to Cyprus late at night all I had to say to the RAF was, 'Can you find a pair of size fourteens?' and within half an hour they contacted the Navy and provided me with two barges. Thanks to the RAF.

I think more especially, and I must say this, many, many people, both here in this country and around the world, have kept the name and the cause of hostages alive.

They have kept that alive in their prayers, in their thoughts and in their actions, and the presence here today of so many people is indicative not only of your concern for western hostages but your concern for justice, for peace and for truth throughout the world.

I'll tell you a small story which I told in Damascus. I was kept in total and complete isolation for four years. I saw no one and spoke to no one apart from a cursory word with my guards when they brought me food.

And one day out of the blue a guard came with a postcard. It was a postcard showing a stained glass window from Bedford showing John Bunyan in jail.

And I looked at that card and I thought, 'My word Bunyan you're a lucky fellow. You've got a window out of which you can look, see the sky and here am I in a dark room. You've got pen and ink, you can write but here am I, I've got nothing and you've got your own clothes and a table and a chair'.

And I turned the card over and there was a message from someone whom I didn't know simply saying, 'We remember, we shall not forget. We shall continue to pray for you and to work for all people who are detained around the world'.

I can tell you, that thought, that sent me back to the marvellous work of agencies like Amnesty International and their letter-writing campaigns and I would say never despise those simple actions.

Something, somewhere will get through to the people you are concerned about as it got though to my fellows eventually.

The occasion today would not be complete without a word of special thanks and affection to the World Service of the BBC.

For four years again one had nothing and then out of the blue a small radio appeared. Just a cheap set and I said, 'Thank God I'm in the Middle East where the World Service can be received on the medium wave for virtually 24 hours a day'.

In the last 12 months the World Service helped to keep us alive both spiritually, through the work of the religious department, and mentally, through the variety of cultural and new programmes that are broadcast with such excellence.

Thank you World Service. Thank you very much.

My family of course, who have had the unenviable task of having to face so many difficulties. I am proud of them and I am proud of my friends and those whom I love and care for and look forward to seeing soon.

Today also I remember that yesterday afternoon I left my prison with Tom Sutherland and we left behind Terry Anderson.

Fortunately yesterday, for the first time, after we had made a special plea to our guards, his chain was released and he was at least able to walk around the room in which we were confined.

My captors assured me yesterday that in a few days time Joseph Cicippio and Alann Steen, the two American hostages, will be released.

They also assured me that Terry Anderson, a journalist of whom the journalistic profession can be justly proud, will be released by the end of this month.

I trust the Hizbollah and those who hold these men will honour that commitment that they made to us.

We furthermore asked about the German hostages and we were not able to get as definite a response concerning their case.

We, however, were told that it was hoped that they would be freed by the end of the year. We would hope that that certainly is the case.

And on this day, it would not be right for me to leave this podium without remembering all those, and all those in particular in the Middle East, who are held captive.

It is wrong to hold people in such a way. It is self-defeating and those who do it fall well below civilised standards of behaviour, no matter who they are, no matter what nationality or what organisation they belong to.

We have lived in these last years through the appalling sufferings of the people of Lebanon.

We have been in the midst of shelling. We have seen people die and killed in most brutal ways.

We know that the people of Lebanon have suffered greatly and those from whom I have just come can be assured that we in the Church, for our part, will not rest until all are freed and there is justice and peace brought to people who deserve a better deal.

One again my gratitude to you, my thanks to you, and I hope that I shall have the opportunity at a later day of speaking in greater detail and perhaps a little more personally.

Thank you very much.'

*Terry Waite*

# Reflections

*   At such an emotional moment Terry Waite is naturally anxious to thank the many people who were active in securing his release. He is equally keen that his audience should remember that other hostages are still in captivity and should not be forgotten, and that justice and peace continually need to be worked for in the troubled Middle Eastern countries. As a Church of England envoy he sees the role of the Church as quite central.

*   What also comes through Terry Waite's sincere votes of thanks is his faith in God and the profound belief that, during all his time in captivity, he had not been forgotten by the outside world. He mentions John Bunyan, the 17th century English preacher who wrote the famous book *The Pilgrim's Progress* (1678) and was imprisoned from 1660 to 1672 for his own outspoken views – an original prisoner of conscience!

    And he draws particular attention to the postcard he received and the work of *Amnesty International*, an organisation that organises letter-writing and other campaigns to free prisoners of conscience.

    Perhaps Terry Waite might conclude that it was his inner faith – faith in himself – and his faith in others in the outside world that enabled him to survive his ordeal.

* Amnesty International
  5 Roberts Place
  London EC1R OEJ

  (See also **An evil cradling**, p. 157)

# 2 Belief: who needs it today?

## Introduction

In previous centuries the Church of England provided one of the cornerstones of community life. Relatively few people attend church regularly these days, though of course many churches, mosques, synagogues, shrines and temples are well attended by dedicated followers of different faiths.

If people don't attend church, does it mean they don't have religious beliefs? Indeed, is a spiritual belief of some kind necessary for us in this technological age which often pretends to have the answer to most human problems?

Listen carefully to the following contrasting views. What is *your* verdict?

## Reading

*Belief: who needs it today?*

Referring to the story of the nativity in his Christmas letter to the Canterbury diocese, the Archbishop of Canterbury, Dr George Carey, expressed his astonishment that not everyone believes it.

'It is also amazing that unbelief is the first reaction of most intelligent people,' he wrote. 'Yes, it is easy to be sceptical of such a tale, but is it beyond the scope of God to do it? Of course not; it is in fact all of a piece with his love expressed in the risk of salvation.'

Nevertheless, only one in ten adults in this country now shares the archbishop's confidence to the extent that he or she goes to church regularly on Sunday – although many more will undoubtedly put in an appearance over Christmas. What, if anything, does everyone else believe? Is a spiritual belief of some kind necessary for us, or is it unnatural?

According to a recent survey by the European Values Group, 54 per cent of Britons claimed to be 'religious' and 71 per cent said they believed in God.

People's definitions of these concepts obviously vary enormously, and vast numbers are becoming interested in 'New Age' organisations, which attempt to explore spiritual and philosophical questions – why are we here? what happens to us after death? – from non-Christian viewpoints.

Sigmund Freud, who was a fervent atheist, believed that religious ideas are 'illusions, fulfilments of the oldest, strongest and most urgent wishes of mankind'. He argued that religion was 'a collective neurosis', an unconscious distortion of our perception of reality which we need in order to live reasonably comfortably.

But Carl Jung, writing a generation later, said Freud's views were based on the 'rationalistic materialism of the scientific views current in the late nineteenth century', and ascribed a more positive function to religion. 'Among all my patients in the second half of life [over 35], there has not been one whose problem in the last resort was not that of finding a religious outlook on life,' he wrote.

Later psychologists, notably Erich Fromm, have maintained that everyone has some sort of 'religion', in the sense of something that gives them an object of devotion and a framework of reference.

The Rev Brendan Callaghan SJ, principal of Heythrop College, London, and lecturer in the psychology of religion, agrees with this. 'The weight of psychological evidence supports the view that belief is natural to man. I would say that the capacity for belief in something that transcends oneself is part of being human. Somebody who doesn't exercise that capacity is missing out on an aspect of being human ... and is therefore less full than they might be.'

Belief need not be religious in the conventional sense. But for Fromm and others, the key question is whether the belief adopted is sufficiently big to challenge the individual to grow.

Fr Callaghan said: 'The life of creative artist, or a life devoted to a political cause, could be big enough, while devotion to a football team is unlikely to satisfy this human need. Even a religion, in the conventional sense, could be so cut down to "safe" size that it would not be big enough.'

Dr Eileen Barker, lecturer in the sociology of religion at the London School of Economics, said people 'cannot live without any beliefs', although they often do not know, at a conscious level, what their beliefs are. 'Most people don't have clear sets of belief, but different beliefs which they draw on in different situations.'

Peter Byrne, lecturer in the philosophy of religion at King's College, London, said: 'I would hazard that while, over the centuries, the forms of religious belief alter – sometimes very radically, and there is now a wider variety of them – the underlying need to use some kind of religious symbols has remained unchanged.' One reason for the decline in church-going, he suggested, is the fact that 'Christian symbolism – the cross, the Passion, the Trinity – no longer moves people in the same way'.

This accounts, perhaps, for much of the attraction of new religious movements and 'New Age' ideas.

Liz Puttick, senior editor at Aquarian Press, argues that people are increasingly disenchanted with the 'handed-down dogmas' or orthodox religion, but are looking nevertheless for 'a deeper significance in life, beyond materialistic goals and worldly success'.

New Age philosophies, many of them rooted in eastern spirituality and meditation, are concerned with self-knowledge and a search for 'the inner god', the 'inner divine essence'. 'Eastern religion is much more in tune with scientific empiricism,' Ms Puttick said. 'You are given a technique, and the whole idea is that you find out for yourself. The process is what is important.'

Fr Callaghan said: 'One of the difficulties for faith and belief is that we live in a culture that tends to use scientific criteria for proof. But in other aspects of our lives – for instance, when we take a marriage vow – we do not look for that same degree of proof.'

He said one danger of the 'Newtonian culture' was that it created 'a real materialism'. It could also lead people to be attracted to extreme 'fundamentalist' forms of religion because they were looking for the same 'power of certainty' in religion that they found in science.

Dr Barker, who specialises in the study of new religious movements, such as the Moonies, emphasised the dangers of rigid belief.

'The psychological discomfort of ambiguity and lack of knowledge has to be balanced by the danger of certainty. Anyone who claims to know the absolute truth – even if your absolute truth is that there are no absolute truths – is potentially dangerous, because they are not open to the inevitable exceptions and complications: they can't adjust.'

Different people, quite clearly, need different degrees of certainty and different amounts of structure in the beliefs they adopt.

Fr Callaghan said this 'seemed to relate to their experience of security, or lack of it, in their early life'. Belief systems should offer a combination of 'security, challenge and space', which people should be able to take up in differing proportions according to their needs, he said.

But even if we still turn to religious belief partly for security, it is a mistake to assume that possessing a firm belief will necessarily help us at times of crisis.

Michael Stewart, at the Centre for Crisis Psychology, in Skipton, North Yorkshire, said: 'A rigidly-held belief can sometimes be obstructive, and prevent people from asking for the help they need.

'Possessing a belief-system may initially con them and make them think that everything is all right. But there is nothing that can spare people from the grief, the sorrow, the wilderness that you enter when something really terrible happens.'

*Diana Hinds*

## Reflections

\*   There are several interesting comments here worth reflecting on. Which of these do you find persuasive?

'Belief is natural to man'.

'Most people don't have clear sets of belief, but different beliefs which they draw on in different situations.'

'People are increasingly disenchanted with the "handed-down dogmas" of orthodox religion.'

'We live in a culture that tends to use scientific criteria for proof.'

\*   There certainly seems to be a degree of agreement amongst the sources quoted that some kind of belief is an important part of being human. What is important is that each of us explores, as we grow as human beings, a religion or belief system whose values we feel comfortable with and which may guide how we live our lives.

# 3 Personal philosophies

## Introduction

A key part of our developing as a human being is thinking about what gives life its purpose. For each person the answer will be different.

The following eight people were asked the question 'What are your most deeply-held beliefs, and why do you hold them?'

# Reading

1 **Ludovic Kennedy, writer and broadcaster:** 'Basically I am a liberal humanist. I agree with Alexander Pope that the 'the proper study of mankind is man', and I also agree with John Keats that the only important things in life are 'the holiness of the heart's affections and the truth of imagination'.

'As a rule of thumb to live by, I would say, 'do unto others as you would hope they would do unto you'. I would also agree with the biblical sentiment 'judge not, and ye shall not be judged'.

'My objection to so many so-called Christians is that some are the most intolerant people I know. These are the people who call for the return of the rope and the lash. Throughout history, and particularly today, I believe religion has been inclined, on balance, to do more harm than good.

'Dostoyevsky once said: 'nothing human is alien to me'. In one's relationships, I believe one must always try to understand the opposing point of view and why other people act as they do.

'I haven't the faintest notion why we are here, and I doubt if anyone else has either. But I am full of wonder and awe at the mystery of creation and I am totally happy to live with a sense of mystery. I look at the natural wonders of the world – the sea, which I adore, and the mountains – and that line from the Psalms, 'I will lift up mine eyes unto the hills, from whence cometh my help', seems very true to me.

'I don't believe anything happens after death: one dies, and that's that. I can't think of anything worse than knowing I was going to meet people I've tried to avoid all my life. All that is left of us is what we manage to leave behind: we live on, such as we deserve, in the hearts and minds of those who have loved us.'

2 **Jean Byers, Headteacher at Highworth School for Girls, Ashford, Kent:** 'Loyalty is the first and foremost of my beliefs. I give loyalty and I expect to receive it, and if it isn't there then I am not interested in the person or their opinions. I admire loyalty in others: to a person, a cause or a belief.

'I believe in moving forward, in positive action and thought. I do not look down, I look up. I believe there is a positive side to all situations and that is what I look for.

'I believe passionately that men and women have the same capability. We have a long way to go in society before everyone else believes this and we must not give up trying to show this is so – not in a domineering way but just by being capable.

'My parents encouraged me to go to church as a child, and I am a confirmed member of the Church of England. My Christian principles, I believe, come across in my job in connection with school assemblies, which always end with a Christian prayer; but I am not the sort of person to stand up in a pulpit and shout about my religion.

'I know I believe that life is the most precious thing. In discussion with my daughter, we concluded that our most valued beliefs could be hidden because they are personal, precious and private. Do we really know what our most deeply-held beliefs are, or are they so well hidden that we can't find words to express them – even though our way of life and attitudes are governed by them?

'I asked family and colleagues what they felt were my beliefs and was told: rights of the individual, hard work, putting others first, don't look back, the establishment, high standards.'

3 **Dr Richard Dawkins, zoologist and author of** *The Blind Watchmaker*: 'I believe whatever is supported by evidence. I do not believe something because of faith or revelation, or because of tradition.

'In atlases, you can see maps of the distribution of religious beliefs. What that implies is that religious belief depends on geography and history, on where you were born. But important beliefs about the universe cannot depend on where you happen to be born. Facts about the cosmos are the same in Pakistan and Norway.

'Let us take an example. Nobody knows why the dinosaurs became extinct. There are various theories: some people believe that a meteorite struck the earth; some believe that there was a virus plague; some believe that the mammals drove the dinosaurs extinct, or that a drastic change of climate did. But imagine a map of the distribution of such beliefs. Can you imagine anything more silly than a map of the world with shaded areas where everyone believes the meteor theory, or the virus theory?

'Science doesn't work like that. Scientific beliefs are based on evidence, not on something arbitrary like tradition. A scientist would not say, 'I believe the meteor theory because my parents and grandparents did before me', yet that is the main reason why religious people hold a particular set of beliefs. Nor would a scientist ever say, 'I believe the meteor theory because it has been privately revealed to me that it is true'.

'Any scientist who said such a thing would be laughed out of court. So would any scientist who said, 'I believe the meteor theory because I just believe it and that's all there is to it', yet that is exactly what faith means.

'It might indeed be comforting to believe in a god, but just because something is comforting, that doesn't make it true. Truth means scientific truth.'

4 **Dave Nellist, politician:** 'The thing that moves me most is injustice. At the moment I deal a lot with the insecurity and suffering that arises from unemployment, and yet my job takes me into often splendid surroundings.

'Being an MP has opened a lot of doors for me: I have seen inside the great universities, spoken in public schools such as Eton, and even been inside big hotels like the Savoy. Then I go back home to Coventry to thousands of constituents who are no less deserving than the people in these splendid surroundings, but who are confined to a secondary role because of capitalism and the collapse of society: in many cases, they are poorly housed, they have no holidays, they are existing rather than living. It is that regular contact that keeps a sense of injustice burning inside me.

'I have tried, in my nine years in this job, to take up a number of campaigns to ameliorate these conditions. One thing that has been reinforced in me, and is probably my most strongly-held belief, is that I am not going to live long enough to solve all these problems. Although brought up a Methodist, I have no religious

faith. What makes me a socialist is the realisation that society has to be fundamentally transformed, so that the kind of people I represent can have a decent
life. It is not that the individuals currently in charge are evil, but that the system
they preside over is wrong and unjust.

'I often meet people involved in different struggles and campaigns, and it is
easy for them to get disheartened.

'I have an advantage in that I move around so much that I generally see someone who is having a success: that keeps me going, and reinforces my belief that
there are plenty of people out there capable of changing things themselves.'


5 **The Rev Gary Dowsey, Roman Catholic parish priest in Norwich:** 'My
deeply-held beliefs centre on a person. That person is Jesus Christ. There is, for
me, a very important moment in St John's gospel when a number of Jesus's followers begin to walk away from him, unable to accept his teachings. Jesus turns
to his closest friends, his disciples, and says: 'Are you going to walk away too?'
Peter replies: 'Lord, to whom should we go? You have the message of eternal
life.'

'In those words, I find my profession of faith. Jesus alone has the message of
eternal life. God has come to us as a person, Jesus, to show us the way to live; to
open our eyes and hearts to what is true about ourselves and each other; and
most of all, to take the fear out of death.

'Such convictions come to me through forming a relationship with Jesus Christ
through prayer, the scriptures, the Church and the witness and love of countless
other Christians.

'If you allow Jesus Christ to be the driving force in your life, you do indeed live
it to the full. My beliefs are practical and liveable. I am called by Jesus to build –
through my daily life, my decisions, my choices, my words and my actions – a
kingdom of justice, love and peace.

'Without my faith, my life would be very empty: it would have no purpose, no
fun, no challenge and no end. If you see faith as a relationship, as I do, then there
are bound to be doubts at times, depending on what you are going through in
your life.

'Questioning is an important part of a living faith. My beliefs centre on God,
whose love I can never totally comprehend. But God is not at a distance: he has
become flesh, in Jesus, so that we can get to know him as a friend.'


6 **Margaret Drabble, novelist:** 'I deeply distrust most forms of belief. Certainties
do far more damage than uncertainties. The most deeply-held beliefs kill the
most people.

'As human history and evolution edge forward we should learn that the certainty of one generation is at best, the laughing stock and at worst, the murderer
of the next. This goes for all religions, all cultures and all faiths. We live in a
deeply relativist world, where we must learn to be more aware of the nature of
change.

'If I have a belief, it is that we cannot rest on any certainty. Of course, I have
negative beliefs – that cruelty is the worst thing we can do, that the death penalty
is one of the worst crimes any state can ever commit against its citizens. My posi-

tive beliefs – that there is a light of goodness in every man and woman, that we are born free and equal and create our own chains, that we have a right to liberty, good health and happiness – seem pitiful little candles.

'I stick to the view that possibly the best we can do is to do no harm. I hope this position is sufficiently feeble: it may lack heroism, but it does not kill. I am greatly in favour of feeble positions.'

7 **Professor Akbar Ahmed, anthropologist and Iqbal Visiting Fellow at Cambridge University:** 'My most deeply felt beliefs rest in the divine message that humanity is one, regardless of race and religion.

'In accordance with the Koran, I believe that the essence of humanity is contained in the notions of *adl* [balance] and *ahsan* [compassion], and I believe in the equality of all people, whether men or women, rich or poor. I also believe, from the Koran, that we must work softly and tread the earth gently, that we must not speak in loud voices and that we must care for the weak among us.

'On a sociological level, the most important focus for my beliefs is the family, whose members must all be treated with dignity, compassion and affection. If I can generate these things in a family situation, then it reflects on my world-view in my dealings with people outside the home. The Holy Prophet Muhammad – the best example of a caring and pious human being – is a very important model for me.

'I sometimes really wonder at the events of my own life, which have taken me right across the globe from remote and inaccessible parts of Pakistan to the universities of Harvard and Cambridge. The bewildering range of human activity and interaction makes me wonder at the complexity and richness of life and reinforces my belief that there are patterns in our lives of which we are only faintly aware.

'This reinforces my belief in a divine creator. I am convinced that there are benevolent forces which I am not aware of, and I have complete faith in them. This is what helps me in times of pain and despair: it soothes and calms me. If I didn't have this anchor of belief, I wouldn't be able to make sense of what is happening. My Muslim faith is the one constant thread that ties the chronology of my life together.'

8 **Professor Arnold Wolfendale FRS, Astronomer Royal and Professor of Physics at Durham University:** 'At the sociological level, I believe that mankind is still evolving and is becoming more sensible and more humane – despite the dramatic backward lurches that occur from time to time. At the religious level, like many other people, I believe in God, despite the absence of positive proof. My own work in the astronomical field, which of course has to do with the enormity of the universe, leads me to feel that there must be some purpose in it all.

'My faith provides me with that purpose. As concerns revelation, I am a Christian – I suppose for the reasons of upbringing and tradition – but my belief in God is stronger than my belief in Christianity. I suspect that Christianity, like everything else, is evolving.

'I have difficulty with many aspects of Christianity – one might call them "technicalities" of biblical description. Miracles, for instance, are a problem for me, and I suspect the descriptions of many of them were meant in a metaphorical rather than a literal way.

'But I feel that the uncertainties of my Christian belief are outweighed by the undoubted value of the faith in providing a firm bedrock for humanity by way of its emphasis on family life, friendship and compassion. Without my faith, I would not have a frame of reference on which to hang a number of attitudes. Science does not give me that frame of reference: I find it a fascinating subject, but rather cold and impersonal.'

## Reflections

* Clearly our own backgrounds and family influences will shape our personal response to the question, 'What are your most deeply-held beliefs, and why do you hold them?' And that response will to some extent change with the years as we meet new experiences and enjoy new relationships.
For some people their religious faith will be at the heart of their belief system. For others, the cornerstone of their values will lie elsewhere; for example, according to novelist Margaret Drabble, 'there is a light of goodness in every man and woman, that we are born free and equal and create our own chains.' In contrast, for Dr Richard Dawkins, 'truth means scientific truth.'

* The question – 'What gives life purpose?' – becomes more and more relevant and complex as we move through childhood and adulthood. It is a question that has pre-occupied philosophers and humankind since time began. It remains an important personal question for each and every one of us.

# 4 The Creation

## Introduction

Since the beginning of humankind different cultures have accounted for the creation of the world in contrasting ways. Each has its own unique tale to tell but what is also interesting to note is what parts they have in common. As the following American Indian myth is being read, it is worth trying to think about any other creation story you are familiar with; that in Genesis in the Christian Bible may be a familiar starting-point.

## Reading

### The Creation of Man

*One dark and starry night a group of American Indians sat huddled round a fire. Suddenly the oldest warrior stood up. His face was as old and as brown as the earth, and round his shoulders he wore a brightly-coloured blanket. He began to tell the story about the beginning of the world ...*

'When Coyote, the desert dog, finished making the world, he took the wind, which was shaped like a sea-shell, and turned it upside down to form the sky. He put bright colours at the five corners of the world and a rainbow sprang up over-head and divided the night from the day. Then he sat back on his haunches and howled – and the sun and moon began to move across the sky.

Coyote planted the plains with trees and ponds, and mountains and rivers, and he made all the animals.

'Last and best of all, I shall make *Man*,' Coyote thought aloud. But the animals heard him and wanted to help. So they all sat down in a circle in the forest: Coyote, Grizzly Bear, Lion, Honey Bear, Deer, Sheep, Beaver, Owl and Mouse.

'You can make Man whatever shape you like,' said Lion, 'but I think he should have sharp teeth for tearing meat, and long claws, too.'

'Like yours?' asked Coyote.

'Well, yes. Like mine,' said Lion. 'He will need fur, of course. And a big, loud, roaring voice'

'Like yours?' asked Coyote.

'Like mine,' said Lion.

'Nobody wants a voice like yours,' Grizzly interrupted. 'You frighten everyone away. Man must be able to walk on his back legs and creep up on things and hug them in his arms until they're squashed flat.'

'Like you do?' asked Coyote.

'Well, yes. Like I do,' replied Grizzly.

Deer, who trembled nervously and kept glancing over her shoulder, said: 'What's all this about tearing meat and squashing things? It isn't nice. Man has to be able to know when he's in danger and run away quickly. He should have ears like sea-shells to hear every tiny sound. And eyes like the Moon, which sees everything. Oh, and antlers, of course. He will need antlers.'

'Like yours?' asked Coyote.

'Well, yes. Like mine,' said Deer.

'Like *yours*?' scoffed Sheep. 'What good are antlers? Long, spiky things that get caught in every branch and bush! How is Man going to be able to *butt* things? Now if he had horns on either side of his head …'

'Like yours?' asked Coyote.

Sheep only sniffed. He did not like being interrupted.

Then Beaver stood up and said: 'You are forgetting the most important thing of all – Man's *tail*. Long thin tails are all right for swatting flies, I suppose. But Man must have a broad, flat tail. How else can he build dams in the river?'

'Like yours?' asked Coyote.

'Nobody builds dams like *mine*,' said the Beaver, in a very boastful way.

'Man sounds far too *big*,' squeaked Mouse. 'He would be better being small.'

'You're all out of your wits-wits-woo!' hooted Owl. 'What about wings? If you want Man to be the best animal of all, he must be able to fly. He *must have wings*!'

'Like yours?' asked Coyote.

'Is that all you can say?' Owl complained. 'Don't you have any ideas?'

Coyote jumped to his feet and prowled to the centre of the circle. 'You silly animals! I don't know what I was thinking about when I made you! You all want Man to look exactly like you!'

'And I suppose Man should be just like *you*, Coyote,' growled Honey Bear.

'Then how could anyone tell us apart?' replied Coyote. 'Everyone would point at me and say, "There goes Man". And they would point at Man and say, "There goes Coyote". No, no. Man must be *different*.'

'But with a tail!' shouted Beaver. 'And wings!' hooted Owl. 'And antlers!' bayed Deer. 'And horns!' baaed Sheep, 'And a roar!' roared Grizzly. 'And be very small,' squeaked Mouse. But nobody heard him. They were too busy fighting.

Biting and butting and clawing and chewing, the animals fought each other across the forest floor while Coyote stood by and shook his head. Fur and feathers and hooves and horns flew all over the place.

Coyote picked them up, and putting them together again he made all sorts of new, peculiar animals – like the camel and the giraffe.

Soon all the animals lay in an exhausted heap, too tired to fight any more. 'I think I may have the answer,' said Coyote at last.

The animals blinked at him, and some of them snarled. But Coyote spoke to them all the same.

'Bear was right to say that Man should walk on his back legs. That means he can reach into the trees. And Deer was right to say that Man should have sharp ears and good eyes. But if Man had wings he would bump his head on the sky. The only part of a bird that he needs is Eagle's long claws. I think I'll call them fingers.

'And Lion was right when he said that Man should have a big voice. But he needs a little voice, too, so that he's not too frightening. I think Man should be smooth like Fish, who has no fur to make him hot and itchy. But most important of all,' said Coyote finally, 'Man must be more clever and cunning than *any* of you!'

'Like you are,' muttered all the animals.

'Well, yes, thank you.' said Coyote. 'Like I am.' There was a lot of angry growling and hissing and the animals began to shout: 'Sit down Coyote! Nobody likes your silly ideas!'

'Well,' said Coyote patiently. 'Let's have a competition. We'll each make a model of Man out of mud. Tomorrow we can look at all the models and decide which is the best.'

So all the animals rushed away to fetch water and make mud. Owl made a model with wings. Deer made a model with large ears and wide eyes. Beaver made a model with a broad, flat tail. Mouse made a very small model. But Coyote made Man.

The sun went down before any of them could finish their models. So they went to sleep on the forest floor. All except Coyote.

He fetched water from the river and poured it over all the other models. Beaver's mud tail was washed away. Deer's mud antlers were washed away. Owl's mud wings were washed away.

Coyote blew into the nose of his model of Man made of mud. And when the other animals woke up, they found that there was a new animal in the forest. His name was Man.'

*With these words the old warrior sat down, wrapping his blanket round him. As the glow from the fire died down, he sat as silent as the earth staring into the darkness. And in the distance the cry of the coyote floated across the plains.*

*American Indian myth*

# Reflections

\* Why have human beings always wanted to explain their own creation? Why does each culture seek to explain the creation of the world in its own particular way? Perhaps the answer lies deep in ourselves as human beings – the need to know something for certain, especially when it relates to how *we* came to be on the planet. Perhaps the answer goes to the heart of our need for some kind of faith and belief in all our lives?

\* In this myth the American Indians were clearly seeking to draw a distinction between humans and the animal world:

'Man must be more clever and cunning than *any* of you!'

And as people who lived in close harmony with their natural environment, maybe their creation myth is also trying to say something about how the human and animal kingdoms should seek to live alongside one another.

(See also **Sacred land**, p. 30)

# 5 I did survive

## Introduction

Most of us – we trust – will not in our lifetimes come into contact with the kind of inhuman brutality that was experienced by millions of Jews in the Nazi concentration camps of the 1930s and 1940s. Many of the camp survivors have written of their experiences. Amidst the scenes of horror and degradation what often shines through their stories is the sheer will to survive that so many showed. That inner belief in the future – no matter how dreadful the past and present – kept body and soul fighting on.

Listen to the following, very poignant true story, titled *The Dance*.

## Reading

*The Dance*

The sun broke through the heavy grey clouds for a moment and disappeared again. It was playing hide and seek, illuminating for seconds one spot, then another in the big room with the wooden bunks.

There were masses of them standing in rows, one on top of the other, leaving an empty square space in the middle.

On each bunk a human bundle was lying – motionless. Some were in crouched positions, others stretched out.

Looking more closely, one could see they were breathing. They seemed to be in a dreamless, heavy slumber.

The sun rays, now stronger, continued their game. The light seemed to disturb the sleepers. They started moving their bodies, turning and twisting in their narrow, restricted places, as they were unable to sit upright.

Now some eyelids moved, closed again, reopened. Eyes wandered round from one shelf to another, up to the ceiling, down to the square-shaped space and finally to the huge window from where the light came.

Only those in the row next to the window could look out of it. The view astonished them. Yellow fields and green meadows spread out in the distance. A tree stood nearby. Its branches almost touched the window.

Now nearly all the bundles started showing signs of life. From each bunk they were staring, making an effort to take in their surroundings, trying to count how many they were. Fifty? – sixty faces, united by the same fate?

To reach the floor or the empty space, where one could stand erect, most of them had to climb down from their bunks like monkeys.

Not a sound was heard. They didn't try to communicate. They just stared at each other, fixedly and inert.

What had happened to them?

Where did they come from?

Why this extreme apathy, as if nothing mattered anymore?

They were half naked or in rags, their heads shaven. All were young girls or women.

One of these ghostlike figures moved into the empty space. She stood there for a moment, naked and erect, her eyes closed. In her left hand she was dragging some rags – probably her clothes. She bent down, made a bundle of the rags and took them into her arms. She hugged the bundle to her breasts as if it were a baby. Slowly she started moving from one side to the other, gently rocking it – the instinctive movement of mothers. Her face was not empty anymore – it expressed all the joy, the ecstasy of a mother holding her infant in her arms. She stood on her toes and then began to dance in the confined space.

Her eyes were closed. She was in a trance – dreaming perhaps. With the most radiant smile on her lips she danced in ecstasy – and then her expression changed. Somebody seemed to tear her child from her arms. She struggled, trying with all her strength to keep her baby. But brutal force was stronger and she had to yield.

The struggle for the possession of her child was expressed in all the movements of her body. She whirled frantically round and round and round – a white face in agony – till she collapsed exhausted.

She was nothing now but a naked body on the floor.

Her eyes opened to look around her and down at her empty arms.

And so too the prisoners lived once more. They had watched the dancing woman, followed her minutest movements. Her pain, sorrow and despair were theirs. Like her they had lost their loved ones in the extermination camp. They had seen the chimneys burning day and night without interruption. The continuous smoke had obscured the sky and the sun and the past. It had annihilated all feelings and transformed them into beings, who still existed, but didn't live any more.

As in a mirror they had seen themselves reflected in the dance. A storm with terrific almost supernatural force invaded and brought back the dead life to them. Their faces were distorted and their bodies twisted. A kind of wailing like animals in pain broke the deadly silence, but even the wailing was subdued – a whisper. There was hatred in their eyes for her who had stirred their feelings and aroused emotions, forgotten long ago.

But all that was only a fleeting moment and again they were drained of pity and hope.

But one girl kept on staring at the dancer on the floor. Like all the others her eyes had followed her – hypnotised.

She crawled now slowly towards the body on the floor. For a moment she hesitated. Then she stretched out her arm and put it round the motionless figure lying before her. She breathed in deeply as if relieved to be able to feel again. Her hand moved towards the head of the dancer and rested there. The two are now lying side by side, united, cheek against cheek, removed from the others.

The women around them didn't stir. They continued looking with their expressionless eyes at the two figures in the square. Not a sound was heard.

The sun shone through the window at the motionless bodies on the wooden bunks. The world turned round mechanically. But almost imperceptibly something had changed.

*Elro*

## Reflections

*   This story comes from a short collection written by a survivor of the Auschwitz concentration camp; her own mother was gassed there. In very simple language she describes the 'beings, who still existed, but didn't live any more.' Yet the actions of the dancer and the girl who moves to lie beside her offer a kind of desperate hope that a future beyond the camps is possible. The final words of the story echo round us, even today: 'The world turned round mechanically. But almost imperceptibly something had changed.'

*   Millions of Jews were killed in the concentration camps. Steven Spielberg's film *Schindler's List* is a powerful study of this period in 20th century history. We trust we shall never see its like again. At the same time we should reflect on the power that humans possess within themselves to have an inner faith that keeps them going in even the most terrible conditions. Perhaps that sense of an inner faith is one of the defining characteristics of what it is to be a human being.

(See also **The Terezín ghetto**, p. 155)

# 6 Euthanasia

## Introduction

A subject that challenges many people's religious views and belief in the sanctity of life is euthanasia – or mercy killing. Euthanasia has become one of *the* moral dilemmas of our times. Why? Because advances in medical technology mean that people suffering from chronic illness and disability are living longer and in less (though not necessarily without) pain.

In the pro-euthanasia camp are those who argue that we have the right to end our life if we feel the quality of life is worthless. In the anti-euthanasia camp are those who consider life sacred and that a humane society should not allow someone to die if medicine and technology can keep them alive.

What are your thoughts?

Listen to the following three accounts in favour of euthanasia. Clearly they present only *one* side of the argument.

# Reading

## *My life is so lonely – the chronically ill man*

*Peter Raynor, 61, is managing director of his own travel firm in Wetherby, Yorkshire. He has twice been married and lives alone in Harrogate. He was diagnosed as having multiple sclerosis 26 years ago. Recently he consulted lawyers to draw up an advance directive, or 'living will'.*

The times when I enjoyed life are long gone. I am partially sighted, doubly incontinent and I cannot wash, dress or feed myself. I haven't stood up alone since 1981, can't turn over in bed and I am seldom free from pain. If I were a dog or a cat, I would have been put down long ago.

I have contemplated suicide many times, but it is not a matter of choice, it is simply a question of ability. And even if someone offered to help me, I would have to refuse. I would be implicating them in a criminal offence.

I consider myself fortunate that my deterioration has been slow, so I have been able to continue working to a greater or lesser extent. But when my first marriage ended in divorce in 1983 and my second was annulled in 1988, it took a lot out of me. By that point, I was able to be present at work only in a consultative capacity.

My assistant at work, Jane, is the only person I have ever met who has done things for me unselfishly. I've asked her to live with me, but she is much younger and cannot make that kind of commitment. I suppose it is selfish of me to suggest it – but mine is such a lonely life.

I know my chances of remission at this stage of the disease are extremely remote and I am still deteriorating. That is why, last year, I signed an advance directive. It states that, in specific circumstances listed in the document, I do not wish to be kept alive by medical technology. The document has no legal status, but my doctor and solicitor have copies, so at least there is written proof of my wishes, should the time come when I am unable to express them.

I get so angry with these Pro Life people, I would like to take one person from that movement, and sit them in my wheelchair, blindfolded, their hands tied, and refuse them the chance to go to the toilet. A few weeks of that and I feel sure they would no longer speak with the same conviction.

\* \* \*

## *His pain was too much for him to bear – the doctor*

*Dr Stephen Henderson Smith worked for the Missionary Society in China during the Second World War and as a doctor in the Belgian Congo before returning to Britain in 1956 to become a GP in Huddersfield. He retired in 1992.*

A doctor's job is to relieve suffering, and that is something which can never be done by procrastination. Why should one allow nature to take its long and painful course when you have the means to help people immediately?

One of my first patients, an elderly man, had pneumonia which, in 1942 when the supply of antibiotics was inadequate and penicillin wasn't available, was considered a terminal illness. He begged me to help him die. His pain was too much for him to bear. I struggled for days with my conscience and, eventually, I gave him a dose of morphine that was just over the usual limit. I remember thinking, if death occurs, so be it. I wanted to release him.

Ten years ago a man I had never seen before came into my surgery just as I was about to leave and asked to be seen as a private patient. He was in his late seventies and had bronchitis and emphysema. Every breath he took was agony. He told me that he wanted to end his life.

I said that I couldn't risk the legal complications, but he was so desirous of a way out of his pain and suffering that he begged me, 'If you can't do it, at least tell me how many of my tablets I should take to be sure of death'. I wrote '30' on a piece of paper.

The following week I read in the local paper that he had died. For some time I felt very nervous that I would be arrested. People knew my views on euthanasia. A doctor who raises his head above the parapet is asking for trouble.

The medical establishment's attitude to ending life is the same as a century ago. Radical change is needed. There should of course be adequate legal safeguards, and I would also like to see a religious service with hymns and the person in question surrounded by loved ones before being taken into a side room for a lethal injection. Suicide is a lonely and miserable end to someone's life. Why should an individual feel forced to take that option?

I live alone now and my purpose for living is my children and grandchildren.

I dread them having to put me in a nursing home and draining all their resources while I wait for a telegram from the Queen. What kind of a life would that be for them? And what kind of an end would that be for me? Lonely and miserable.

* * *

## I sat holding his hand until he was dead – the spouse

*Ruth is a 70-year-old former teacher. Five years ago she helped her husband, an academic, to die.*

My husband was a social anthropologist. He retired in 1983, but continued to be a very active man. Then, seven years into his retirement, he was found to be suffering from multiple sclerosis. It is unusual to develop the condition over the age of 60 and he was 69. He refused to give in to it, sleeping upstairs although he often had to drag his feet over every step.

But while he fought physically, psychologically he became angry, bitter and frightened. Then a serious infection robbed him completely of his mobility. He could not even roll over in bed and became incontinent. The doctors did all they could but it was clear that he would never recover the use of his body.

Then he began to have trouble with his eyes. It was bad enough being unable to walk over and take a book from the shelf; to face the prospect of being unable to read it was the final straw. If it had been a question of dying in six months' time, he said he might have been able to cope, but he knew he might go on living for years. The situation was intolerable for him and he attempted to commit suicide by suffocation with a plastic bag. But because of his condition, this was too difficult for him.

It was then that I realised I could not allow someone with whom I had lived for 40 years, whom I loved, to set off on such a journey alone. I told him if he was absolutely sure he wanted to end his life, then I would be there to ensure it happened. He said: 'Please don't feel you have to, but that would be wonderful.'

In the following days, the years seemed to fall away from his face and his bitterness and anger disappeared. There had been a good deal of strain in our marriage because of his illness, but in those last days we were very much together. I had to make sure there was no one in the house and he told me not to call for help too soon afterwards because the emergency services might be able to resuscitate him. I found in myself a residue of strength, which I suppose we all have. I wasn't crying – this was too important for that. I sat holding his hand until he was dead. I then sat with him through the night. It was a time of thought and a great many memories, I was glad he wasn't going to suffer any more, that he had escaped. I told the police I had come downstairs in the morning and found him dead.

We have three children and I told them, and my husband's close friends and family, exactly what had happened. I didn't want them thinking that he had committed suicide in a state of despair. They knew the option he had taken was right for him. He had been a member of the Voluntary Euthanasia Society and firmly believed that everyone should be able to choose when to die.

The memory of his courage at the end of his life is far from ghastly. Not a day goes by without me thinking of him.

*Elizabeth Udall*

## Reflections

* Are you persuaded by any of these arguments or, given the sacredness of human life, would you think it always wrong to allow someone to speed up their own death?

  This is a subject which is going to become more and more an issue for everyone in a society with an increasingly ageing population. Those who make our laws – and we who vote for governments – need to address this moral dilemma which goes to the heart of our belief in the specialness of human life. And for those with strong religious convictions euthanasia continues to appear in direct opposition to deeply-held views that human life cannot be treated in this way.

  Meanwhile, in the American state of Oregon, a Death with Dignity Act has now been passed, making it legal for doctors to prescribe a lethal dose of drugs.

(See also **Who not to treat?** p. 240)

# 7 Dead friends and living friends

## Introduction

It sounds strange and contradictory to say it but death *is* a fact of life. When death happens close to or even within our own community we are often thrown back on our inner faith or caused to reflect on those values which we hold most dear.

The following contrasting poems help us to think about death and what it means to friends who have come to terms with the passing of someone they know and love.

# Reading

## *Stop all the clocks*

Stop all the clocks, cut off the telephone,
Prevent the dog from barking with a juicy bone,
Silence the pianos and with muffled drum
Bring out the coffin, let the mourners come.

Let aeroplanes circle moaning overhead
Scribbling on the sky the message He Is Dead,
Put crêpe bows round the white necks of the public doves,
Let the traffic policemen wear black cotton gloves.

He was my North, my South, my East and West,
My working week and my Sunday rest,
My noon, my midnight, my talk, my song;
I thought that love would last for ever: I was wrong.

The stars are not wanted now: put out every one;
Pack up the moon and dismantle the sun;
Pour away the ocean and sweep up the wood;
For nothing now can ever come to any good.

*W. H. Auden*

## *For Andrew Wood*

What would the dead want from us
Watching from their cave?
Would they have us forever howling?
Would they have us rave
Or disfigure ourselves, or be strangled
Like some ancient emperor's slave?

None of my dead friends were emperors
With such exorbitant tastes
And none of them were so vengeful
As to have all their friends waste
Waste quite away in sorrow
Disfigured and defaced.

I think the dead would want us
To weep for what *they* have lost.
I think that our luck in continuing
Is what would affect them most.

But time would find them generous
And less self-engrossed.

And time would find them generous
As they used to be
And what else would they want from us
But an honoured place in our memory,
A favourite room, a hallowed chair,
Privilege and celebrity?

And so the dead might cease to grieve
And we might make amends
And there might be a pact between
Dead friends and living friends.
What our dead friends would want from us
Would be such living friends.

*James Fenton*

## Reflections

\*    The first poem captures the extreme sense of loss we feel when a loved one dies. All purpose in life seems lost. The tone is sombre and bleak. It reflects an utterly natural set of reactions:

'For nothing now can ever come to any good.'

But in the second poem James Fenton leaves us with two lines echoing:

'What our dear friends would want from us
Would be such living friends.'

The friends of Andrew Wood insist that though death has taken away someone they have loved, vibrant memories will live on. The poem seems to be suggesting that if we experience the death of someone close to us, we owe it to them to go on living our own lives generously and to the full:

'I think that our luck in continuing
Is what would affect them most.'

We need to have faith in the future, even though the tragic immediacy of a friend's death can make us feel frozen, empty and desolate in the way W. H. Auden describes: 'Stop all the clocks.'

# 8 A different way to say goodbye

## Introduction

To mark key rites of passage in our lives – birth, coming of age, marriage, death – we usually turn to our religious background and its related rituals and customs.

Churches, synagogues, temples, mosques – these buildings continue to play a vital role in human beings' significant personal steps. But how do you mark the end of a precious life if you do not hold religious beliefs?

The following bereaved families and friends chose alternative funerals. What are your reactions?

# Reading

## *Sailing into the stars, like Wynken, Blynken and Nod*

*Donna Kantaris, 32, gave birth to Christopher, a stillborn baby. The year before, she lost her first child, Ashley, because of an ectopic pregnancy.*

There is no meaning to the death of our two children. It just happened. I wanted a commemoration for both children that was free of cant and hypocrisy and so-called meaning. But I did want to be left with a bit of hope.

It was so frustrating. We'd lost the opportunity to look after our children for a lifetime. We'd lost all those years during which we could have loved and cared for our babies. I wanted to show that I cared about my children. I wanted to say a personal good-bye – not a good-bye which followed a universal script.

The words used by Vivienne, our officiant from the British Humanist Society, were quite hard to take. She said that these things happen – people die. She didn't try to explain the deaths of our babies. But she did say that it is also in the nature of things that life gets better. It was very comforting because one cannot deny the truth of both statements.

The funeral was called a farewell ceremony, which I thought was lovely. Vivienne didn't just stick to our script – she ad libbed. At one point a robin turned up and hung around: the earth had been turned over and the bird was attracted to the worms. She brought him into the service. 'Look,' she said. 'Life carries on.' She showed such empathy. She even cried. I found her understanding so comforting.

I read a poem at the farewell ceremony, a Victorian poem called 'Wynken, Blynken and Nod'. It is a lullaby about sailing into a sea of stars and catching the stars in a net. Even though I am not religious, my children do exist in my head. When I think of my babies I think of them as being safe and warm and asleep.

I asked people not to wear black at the funeral. We wanted the ceremony to be a celebration of life. The hearse was covered with bunches of brightly coloured ribbons, there were ribbons on the white coffin, too. I made Christopher a swaddling cloth of bright colours. He was too small to wear clothes.

I wrote my children a letter which I put in the coffin. And I drew them a picture of the most perfect place – a cottage and trees and flowers and birds. I hope that if they are anywhere, they would be there. We also put the top tier of our wedding cake on the lid of the coffin – my husband and I had saved it to celebrate the birth of our first baby. Other people may have found the gesture depressing, even morbid. But to us it just felt right.

Baby graves in cemeteries often look so forlorn it breaks my heart to look. I wanted to take pleasure in the place where my children were buried so that I could bring future babies to visit. I made the grave into a tiny garden covered with flowers. It has a bird table. I want the birds to come back.

The plaque is made of clay; the glaze is vivid. It just has their names on it –

Christopher and Ashley and the words 'pleasant dreams'. It doesn't have the words 'die' or 'stillborn' on it. It is a celebration of life. They lived. And they are still alive in me.

*Donna Kantaris*

## A bottle of whisky beside the coffin

*Edward Marshall, 23, was killed in a motorbike accident. Andrew Gillmore was one of Ed's closest friends.*

The night before Ed's funeral, I drove up to the family's house in Auchenairn on the Scottish borders, with a group of mutual college friends. The house was already brimming with people. A tombstone was being carved in the basement; people were pinning trinkets and photographs of Ed on to a board; paper chains were being linked together – each with a story about Ed written on it.

We'd all been asked by the family to bring a present for Ed. The idea was that we could take it into the room containing his coffin and take it in turns to say good-bye. When I went in I found he'd been dressed in his favourite clothes. Beside his coffin was a bottle of whisky and some candles. I'd never seen a corpse. I kept expecting him to get up and say: 'Just kidding!' But he didn't. I felt deeply upset.

I talked to him a bit. I couldn't think of much to say. I touched his hand – I wanted to believe he was dead. His skin had a cold, strange texture. That finalised it. Ed had definitely gone.

The next day we got up early. Ed's coffin had to be carried to the graveyard. When we tried to lift the coffin we found that it was purely decorative. If we were to carry the coffin by the handles the bottom would drop out! In the end we had to support the bottom using straps and sticks and webbing. It was quite funny at the time but also annoying.

It took about an hour to carry the body across the fields to the church. It was quiet apart from the noise of us walking through the grass and the sound of someone playing the flute. After a bit we came to a place which was too muddy to cross. We changed direction and all these cows started coming towards us. I had visions of having to drop the coffin and run, because they looked like bullocks. But someone got some branches and shooed them away.

The coffin lid was pulled back before Ed was lowered into the grave. We wanted to know that it was Ed we were burying. His mother came and talked about him and kissed him and said good-bye. Then he father talked about him. I didn't say anything. I felt it had all been said. Then we all took turns to fill the hole. For a bit we could still see his face as we threw earth on it. Again it forced the point: Ed had died.

*Andrew Gillmore*

# Reflections

* What is evident in these 'alternative funerals' is the wish of family and friends to mark death in a way which the dead person would have approved of, or in a way which meant something of value to the friends and family themselves.

We may find their actions unusual but we should respect their views. Faith and belief are deeply personal issues. It is important to recognise the right of others to interpret ceremonies in the way they feel best fits the particular circumstances. As Donna Kantaris observes about placing the wedding cake on the coffin-lid:

'Other people may have found the gesture depressing, even morbid. But to us it just felt right.'

# 9  In search of the self

## Introduction

One of the central ideas in religion and philosophy is concerned with the quite difficult question: 'What is the self?' Many writers and thinkers have argued that we cannot live full and rewarding lives until we know our inner selves. As we grow up we begin to shape our own value-system and to reflect on ourselves as human beings. From time to time we might even ask the difficult questions: 'How do other people see me?' 'What is their opinion of me?'

The following passage is taken from a celebrated novel called *Siddhartha*. It tells of an Indian's search for, if you like, the meaning of life and his own self. The Brahmins mentioned are the Hindu priests and Atman is the God within us.

## Reading

*In search of the self*

Siddhartha himself was not happy. Wandering along the rosy paths of the fig garden, sitting in contemplation in the bluish shade of the grove, washing his limbs in the daily bath of atonement, offering sacrifices in the depths of the shady mango wood with complete grace of manner, beloved by all, a joy to all, there was yet no joy in his own heart. Dreams and restless thoughts came flowing to him from the river, from the twinkling stars at night, from the sun's melting rays. Dreams and a restlessness of the soul came to him, arising from the smoke of the sacrifices, emanating from the verses of the Rig-Veda, trickling through from the teachings of the old Brahmins.

Siddhartha had begun to feel the seeds of discontent within him. He had begun to feel that the love of his father and mother, and also the love of his friend Govinda, would not always make him happy, give him peace, satisfy and suffice him. He had begun to suspect that his worthy father and his other teachers, the wise Brahmins, had already passed on to him the bulk and best of their wisdom, that they had already poured the sum total of their knowledge into his waiting vessel; and the vessel was not full, his intellect was not satisfied, his soul was not at peace, his heart was not still. The ablutions were good, but they were water; they did not wash sins away, they did not relieve the distressed heart. The sacrifices and the supplication of the gods were excellent – but were they everything? Did the sacrifices give happiness? And what about the gods? Was it really

Prajapati who had created the world? Was it not Atman, He alone, who had created it? Were not the gods forms created like me and you, mortal, transient? Was it therefore good and right, was it a sensible and worthy act to offer sacrifices to the gods? To whom else should one offer sacrifices, to whom else should one pay honour, but to Him, Atman, the Only One? And where was Atman to be found, where did He dwell, where did His eternal heart beat, if not within the Self, in the innermost, in the eternal which each person carried within him? But where was this Self, this innermost? It was not flesh and bone, it was not thought or consciousness. That was what the wise men taught. Where, then, was it? To press towards the Self, towards Atman – was there another way that was worth seeking? Nobody showed the way, nobody knew it – neither his father, nor the teachers and wise men, nor the holy songs. The Brahmins and their holy books knew everything, everything: they had gone into everything – the creation of the world, the origin of speech, food, inhalation, exhalation, the arrangement of the senses, the acts of the gods. They knew a tremendous number of things – but was it worthwhile knowing all these things if they did not know the one important thing, the only important thing?

Many verses of the holy books, above all the Upanishads of Samaveda, spoke of this innermost thing. It is written: 'Your soul is the whole world.' It says that when a man is asleep, he penetrates his innermost and dwells in Atman. There was wonderful wisdom in these verses; all the knowledge of the sages was told here in enchanting language, pure as honey collected by the bees. No, this tremendous amount of knowledge, collected and preserved by successive generations of wise Brahmins, could not be easily overlooked. But where were the Brahmins, the priests, the wise men, who were successful not only in having this most profound knowledge, but in experiencing it? Where were the initiated who, attaining Atman in sleep, could retain it in consciousness, in life, everywhere, in speech and in action? Siddhartha knew many worthy Brahmins, above all his father – holy, learned, of highest esteem. His father was worthy of admiration; his manner was quiet and noble. He lived a good life, his words were wise; fine and noble thoughts dwelt in his head – but even he who knew so much, did he live in bliss, was he at peace? Was he not also a seeker, insatiable? Did he not go continually to the holy springs with an insatiable thirst, to the sacrifices, to books, to the Brahmins' discourses? Why must he, the blameless one, wash away his sins and endeavour to cleanse himself anew each day? Was Atman then not within him? Was not then the source within his own heart? One must find the source within one's own Self, one must possess it. Everything else was seeking – a detour, error.

*Hermann Hesse*

# Reflections

* The rest of the novel goes on the explore Siddhartha's quest to conquer suffering and fear. His tortuous road leads him through all kinds of temptations and towards the fulfilment of his destiny: self-knowledge.

  It is of course an allegory of all human life – our growth as a human being leads us to find out things about ourselves that we don't necessarily like but which we must learn to live with or try and change. As Siddhartha concludes here, on the way to finding and clarifying our values and beliefs we all make detours and errors. Learning to grow through those detours and errors is important; and those around us in our homes and friendship groups help us everyday – even though we might not always recognise it, or thank them, at the time.

Siddhartha's quest is everyone's quest; his experience is our experience, albeit in a different culture and country.

# 10 The nation's soul

## Introduction

From time to time in our society we see around us particularly troubling events. And because of the power of TV these events and their aftermath are often beamed into our houses within minutes of their happening. It may be a riot on a housing estate; the discovery of a child's battered body; a family taken hostage by a father desperate for attention; the brutal mugging of an elderly couple.

What is our reaction to such events? Do we just shrug our shoulders and say – 'that's life today?' In the following passage Cardinal Hume, the Archbishop of Westminster, speaks about how he sees society today, from his standpoint as a religious leader. Do you agree with his views? Think especially about his thoughts on the family.

## Reading

*The nation's soul*

A society that has suddenly caught its image in the mirror and dislikes what it sees can either shrug its shoulders and walk away, or pause and ask why.

Any genuine moral reflection has to start with self. We need to search our own hearts before we probe the hearts of others, and face the fact that the potential for evil, pride, greed, lust and envy is within us. We all have a tendency to do or tolerate wrong. Conversely, each person has an innate capacity for good. The recognition of failure and of evil, whether by an individual or a nation, is surely a sign of that goodness.

Morality is very much concerned with how we treat other people. We are normally individually responsible for our own actions. We are, none the less, all powerfully influenced by the culture we inhabit; the social and economic conditions of life. In seeking to understand human behaviour it is wrong to exclude either individual responsibility or social conditions.

In recent years morality, like so much else, has often been reduced to individual choice, a matter of opinion, and is seen as purely private. There are, in fact, basic moral values such as personal integrity, self-discipline, generosity, compassion, fidelity in relationships and respect for human life that we should be able to share. These are founded on the fundamental dignity of being human and are not a matter of arbitrary selection. They are essential to society's survival. Without such shared values, society loses its way and starts to disintegrate. This is happening now and the process must be reversed.

Without indulging in a false nostalgia, we must discover a new sense of community. Membership of a community makes demands and confers benefits. We have to recognise that living in a civilised society imposes on each of us duties and responsibilities; it also means that all citizens have legitimate claims on the society to which they belong. It is ominous that many people now feel they do not belong; that they have no stake in society, that they do not feel wanted, needed or valued. This is why, for example, endemic unemployment, especially among young people, is such a corroding social sore.

But where do we first experience belonging and learn its benefits and demands? In a family. The family is the basic community. It is the place where the deepest experiences of love, trust, self-acceptance and growth in intimacy can take place. Parents are the first and principal educators of their children, and it is in the family that moral values are inculcated and practised, where right and wrong are learnt and where respect for life and love become instilled. The influence of a parent for good or ill is incalculable. To be a parent is perhaps the greatest responsibility a person can undertake.

That, I realise, is the ideal. In reality, and with devastating results, too many families in our society fail to become sources of love and stability. And as an institution the family has been severely undermined in recent decades. A healthy family is fundamentally at odds with our culture because it is radically anti-individualist. Taking family responsibilities seriously leads people away from seeing themselves as the centre of their world, to acknowledge the claims made by partner, children and parents. This process is bound to be painful as well as rewarding.

There is a kind of suffering love, struggle and sacrifice that every family will experience if it is to survive and grow strong. Is it not so that such an experience lies at the heart of true love? Difficulties in relationships, where they are not mutually destructive, are often the growing pains of a mature and lasting love. But in today's society, struggle and self-sacrifice are not generally seen as positive and creative. Our culture presents pain and suffering, in whatever context, as unmitigated disasters always to be avoided. people are urged to limit any commitment, to avoid total involvement; to hold on to what they have, rather than to give themselves away. The lifelong commitment promised at marriage enables a stable family to provide the best environment for children. It is wrong if such a lifelong commitment is seen as impossible or undesirable.

The breakdown in family life is not, of course, the sole cause of our moral malaise. There are many complex factors involved, and family breakdown is as much a symptom of what is wrong, as a cause. But if families are the building blocks of society, what happens if they are crumbling? Without judging or in any way penalising those who, through no fault of their own, find themselves lacking a traditional or stable family, we have to restore family life. Furthermore, I do not forget that there are those who, by circumstance, have the vocation to be single persons. But it is essential for the regeneration of our society to discover the integrity of family life and to find new ways of supporting and protecting it.

In making a claim for the rediscovery of shared moral values, I am speaking from my religious standpoint. My belief in God leads me to ground moral values in Him and to see them as reflecting His plan for the wellbeing of people in society. Furthermore, it is my conviction that a sense of God and the demands He makes upon us are an essential basis for the proper conduct of human affairs. Of course, I recognise there are many who, while advocating the same basic moral values, do not subscribe to any religious belief. It is also true that some professedly religious people behave in immoral ways.

We need to examine candidly the fruits of recent decades of experience which, as much as anything, indicate where we have gone wrong. It would be a hopeful sign and an encouragement to many if our society grasped the opportunity to begin a change for the better.

*Cardinal Basil Hume*

# Reflections

* As a man of the Christian church Cardinal Basil Hume at once reminds us that human beings have the capacity for good or evil. He further reminds us that the healthy community is one in which basic moral values such as self-discipline and compassion should be able to be shared. He doesn't pretend that people with sound religious beliefs have the answers, but he does strongly suggest that without certain core values society cannot flourish.
The family for him is crucially important. He hopes society in the coming years can support and protect good family life for the sake of the children growing up within them.

* We all need to reflect upon our own contribution to our families. What do we take? What do we give? How tolerant are we? What are we learning now from our parents and guardians that we would want to pass on to our own children in time?

'To be a parent is perhaps the greatest responsibility a person can undertake.'

# The Twenty-First Century

*The future is not what it was.*

*I have the audacity to believe that peoples everywhere can have three meals a day for their bodies, education and culture for their minds, and dignity, equality and freedom for their spirits. I believe that what self-centred men have torn down, other-centred men can build up.*

Martin Luther King

# 1 Areas of darkness

## Introduction

Predicting the future is a notoriously difficult business. Some trends in society which we feel will happen suddenly don't. Other things arrive from nowhere to dominate our lives. The following passage comes from a writer whose book titled *The World in 2020* suggests some racing certainties for our future world, but admits there are quite a few areas of darkness.

## Reading

### Areas of darkness

Start with demography. We know that the 5.5 billion or so people on earth now will have increased to about 8.5 billion by 2020. We know that almost the entire rise will take place in the developing world. And we know that the age structure of developed countries will change so that there will be a much higher proportion of elderly people than there are today. The rich world will be old; the poor world will be young.

Can we feed another 3 billion people? Probably, but the food will tend to be in the wrong place. The farmers of North America and Europe can crank out a lot more food – at the moment they are being paid *not* to produce it – but the population growth will be mainly in Africa, the Indian sub-continent and China. Land and, more important, water for irrigation are already quite tight, so even assuming a continued rise in crop yields, it will be difficult for these regions to feed themselves. They will have to develop products to export to help to pay for imports of food, and we will have to buy them.

Will there be sufficient other resources, for example energy? Here we *can* be reasonably confident, for the supply of most natural resources appears adequate for at least one more generation. There will only just be enough oil, but as the price rises substitutes will be developed. Rising energy demand will, however, lead to greater use of fossil fuels which will in turn increase global warming. While we are likely to see only the very early consequences of that by 2020, it will have become a greater concern to the world.

We can predict the technologies that *might* be in everyday use in a generation because they exist in some form now. It takes the best part of a generation from discovery to popular use: the integrated circuit, which brought both the fax and the computer down to a price and size suitable for home use, was invented as far back as 1958. What is much harder to judge is which technologies will be commercially successful and so enter all our lives. The Boeing 747 and Concorde were developed at the same time: one has revolutionised inter-continental travel; the other is a quirky example of what technology can – and cannot – achieve if enough resources are put into it.

We can already see, to take one extreme example, that housing technology will hardly change. A generation from now we will be living in similar homes to those of today, though they will be equipped with even more electronic gadgetry. Homes are home are homes, and the nicest ones seem to have been built at least 100 years ago.

To move up one stage, electro-mechanical technology will continue its incremental advance – but change will only be gradual, for the basic laws of physics apply. So we will be driving in cars that are much the same as today's though safer and more efficient. We will be riding around in trains that look very much like the ones we will travel in to Paris later this year and go a little faster. And we will travel in aircraft that are merely a development of what we have already.

The revolution will come in communications and electronics, where the technologies of fibre optics and data compression will combine to race ahead. This will have a string of economic and social effects. For example, it will make communications very cheap indeed. We do not need to make heroic guesses about technology to say that in 25 years' time it will cost less than 10p in today's money to phone Australia ... on a video phone. The technology exists now.

Cheap communications will change the world in much the same way as cheap air travel has done. Anyone whose work is largely screen-based can choose where they live. Countries with educated and numerate workers will be able to get into the new export market of 'white-collar' services. The *Financial Times* has much of its software written in India; workers in Ireland process US companies' insurance claims.

The hardest part is seeing the social implications of technological change and predicting what will become socially and politically acceptable. To what extent, for instance, will technology be used to cut crime? Few people would quarrel with video cameras monitoring shopping malls, or even city centres, but we might feel uncomfortable if this became the norm for suburban streets. Should there be a national DNA register for all criminals? Should it be extended to cover parking offenders? Or everyone?

It is the interaction between economic, technical and social change that presents the greatest puzzles. If electronic technology enables a significant minority of the population of the developed world to choose their location, the relationship between governments and people is bound to change. Governments will be rated on their performance not just by the people who elect them, but by would-be migrants. Countries will find themselves competing against each other in much the same way that US states do today.

At least in social questions it is possible to see the issues reasonably clearly, whatever judgement we make about the ways in which governments (and, more important, electorates) respond. When we move one stage further in the argument – to the political shape of the world a generation from now – however, even the issues seem unclear. And the better guide to what is to come may not be economics, but history.

Take the relationship between China and Japan, the most important political issue in East Asia. In overall economic terms, China will inevitably outstrip Japan, but Japan will remain far richer per head and have access to more sophisticated technology – technology China will need. It ought to be an ideal economic relationship. But you look back into the tangled history of these ancient cultures and ask how close an economic union these countries actually want.

Closer to home, look at the relationship between Britain and the European Union. It is extraordinary how ancient distrusts repeatedly threaten closer economic co-operation in petty ways: how uncomfortable we felt about BMW taking control of Rover; how the French sought to exclude UK airlines from Orly; how Germany is banning imports of British beef.

But history does provide a guide of sorts. Europe has a common culture which is quite different from that of North America, and that culture is the product of centuries during which the European peoples have lived together, quite often in harmony. It preceded the nation state – indeed several European nations are quite recent inventions. If Europe is seen as a collection of peoples, some long organised into nations, others not, it is possible to hazard a guess at how the political union of Europe might proceed. It surely *feels* more like a common cultural and economic entity than a common political one.

And the United Kingdom? Well, it is worth observing that these islands may make more sense split into the separate nations they once were than pretending that the present UK is the only appropriate constitutional model. But there we really do leave the worlds of economics and technological development far behind.

*Hamish McRae*

## Reflections

\*    From what you've heard, which of the predictions seem more or less likely? Are there some which you look forward to and some you fear?

Hamish McRae's thought-provoking predictions remind us that the global village grows smaller and smaller in terms of advancing communications and technologies. He also makes us aware how, increasingly, people around the world will be economically and socially dependent on one another. Our own local community will need to be less insular as the 21st century advances if it is to flourish.

And might England, Wales, Scotland, Northern Ireland not only have their own football teams but actually be separate countries before the 21st century is out?

# 2 Will robots rule?

## Introduction

Science fiction novels and films have been predicting that robots will run our lives for several decades now. Will it ever happen? Can you imagine a time when your visit to the doctor is replaced by plugging yourself into a computer?

The following passage hints at where technology might be taking us – and at some possible social implications.

# Reading

## Will robots rule?

It is 2025 in suburban Middle England and the intelligent home of the future has arrived. Outside, a robot lawnmower gently grazes on the grass like a good-natured sheep, weeding, feeding and mending the bare patches as it goes. The central house computer is conducting a digital conversation with the nanoprocessors in the car and transmits an electronic update to the garage, ready for the next service.

Inside the house, all is well. Through the intelligent doors, which can recognise family members by their faces and fingerprints, and the weather-sensitive windows, which clean themselves without ever being asked, the domestic robots are going about their chores with a silent solemnity. An anti-static vacuum device dusts, the laundry system sorts, cleans and folds away clothes, and the kitchen's fat controller prepares the day's calorie-counted meals. Meanwhile, the all-sensing house computer checks the weather forecast and re-sets its energy-saving programmes.

Beyond the virtual realism of suburbia lies the nightmare of the information underclass. Here there is no home shopping, telenetworking and videoconferencing. The information revolution has left the underclass behind, fenced into their urban ghettos by squalor, ignorance and data deprivation. Their only contact with the digitised society of the future is when the facial-recognition cameras operated by the data police spot them in a crowd in the wrong part of town.

Nightmare or dream, we all face futures dominated by computers and information technology. And technology pundits are convinced that developments in these fields will be as rapid in the next three decades as they have in the past three. In the Sixties, computers occupied entire office floors and were little more than giant calculators. Now they are faster, more versatile and sit on desk-tops. By the end of this decade it will be possible to put 10 Bibles on a single computer chip. By 2005, a chip will be able to hold all 32 volumes of the *Encyclopaedia Britannica*, pictures as well as text. In 25 years' time computers will be a million times faster than they are today, working in a way that mimics the human brain. Already scientists are talking of the possibility of fitting chips inside the brain to improve memory and so have a portable library literally inside our heads.

These are not wild guesses, but realistic predictions based on what is already known to be feasible, says Ian Pearson, a futurologist at BT Laboratories at Martlesham in Suffolk. The credibility of the company's own technology calendar up to 2025 relies heavily on the accelerating improvements in the speed and memory of the computer chip.

With the information superhighway running past the front door of every future home, the ability to transform a living-room into a virtual office, art gallery, library, museum or whatever else takes your fancy will be almost limitless. Flat video screens that hang on the wall are already being developed that offer high definition, three-dimensional images. This will mean that a whole wall can be turned into, for example, your mother's front parlour, with her as a life-sized image sharing the same virtual space. Forget talking. 'It's good to interact,' may be the BT slogan of the early 21st century.

Is all this inevitable? Not necessarily. David Gann, a technology analyst at the

Science Policy Research Unit at Sussex University, says that there have been ample examples in the past of inventions that nobody wanted to buy. 'Either we had no need for them, or they were too expensive, or too difficult or cumbersome to use.' Room lights operated by a sophisticated programmable controller never took off, he points out. 'It was easier to turn a switch on.'

Dr Gann has recently returned from Japan, where technology is revered like a religion. One of the great goals there is to diagnose illness in the home using telemedicine. An 'intelligent toilet' has been designed which analyses urine, while connected devices monitor pulse and blood pressure at the same time; the data obtained in this way can be sent direct to the local hospital computer. It is a technology directed as much towards saving money on needlessly sending out doctors and ambulances as it is towards helping the patient, Dr Gann says. The only drawback, with this as with all other technological advances, is the question of whether machines can ever really be trusted to work when they are needed most.

But the worst fear that most people have about the future is not that the technology won't work, but that people will not be able to work with it. Are we all in danger of being left behind? Will those who cannot programme a computer, or find their way around the information highways of the future, become unemployable – or find themselves at the mercy of an élite of techno-initiates? It depends who you are. For most people, technology will become more accessible, not less Physically, computers and related products will become easier to use, responding to voices or simple movements of the hand or even eye, rather than cumbersome keyboards and 'mice'. Meanwhile, software will become more user-friendly through constant refinement. As long as you are in the right situation in the first place – that is, educated, working, in touch with technology-users and with access to a certain amount of equipment – you have no more to fear from not being a computer whizz that you currently have to fear from not being an electrician or plumber. You may be dependent on the effective functioning of technology that you don't understand – but then you probably are already.

The problems will come for those who are largely outside the system in the first place: not working, not educated, without access to a computer. As society increasingly goes about its business in 'cyberspace', those who cannot find their way into and around that brave new virtual world will, inevitably, be in danger of exclusion.

The nightmare scenario, according to BT's Ian Pearson, is that society will become riven in two, with the employed information literate having as little as possible to do with the unemployable illiterates in the underclass. 'I sincerely hope this does not happen, but it's a distinct possibility,' he says.

Ultimately, it will be other factors in society and the economy that will dictate which people can afford to live and work in the increasingly technological future. The dominance of technology will grow, but how fast remains to be seen. It is unlikely, for example, that the written word, or even the printed page, will ever be superseded. Ian Pearson says that the watershed will come when computers can design other computers. Then, he says, computers may actually begin to replace skilled people who were once thought to be immune from digital progress. 'People don't really know what people will do in 30 years' time, when computers can do their jobs better,' he says. But he does know one thing: 'We are moving towards an information economy.'

*Steve Connor*

# Reflections

\* Hearing how our world might change challenges us to manage that change in a way that is beneficial to everyone in society. Warnings that there may be an illiterate underclass shut out from the technology revolution need to be taken seriously – especially by schools.

The pace of change in the various fields of technology is extremely fast. The actual impact it has on our everyday lives varies; as the passage suggests, some new inventions never capture the public imagination, while others suddenly become not just luxuries but necessities.

The challenge for us all is to manage this introduction of new technologies in a way that is socially just and does not exaggerate the divides that do exist between those who have and those who have not.

\* Some advice on how to survive technological change:

1 Don't fear technology, or become a slave to it. It's more important to learn what it can do for you than to understand how it is done.

2 Develop your career in a direction where technology could be a valuable asset. Information services, for instance, are likely to continue to be a growth area of the economy. Be prepared to be an independent worker.

3 Remember that knowledge – of all kinds – is power. Even in a world of computers, information of all sorts will be invaluable, and books will remain the primary reference and information source for some time to come.

4 Machines will never replace people totally, so don't forget to be nice to others.

5 Faced with more than one button to press at any given time, remember the oldest technology maxim of all: don't panic!

# 3 A perfect baby

## Introduction

One area of our lives which has been significantly affected by extraordinary advances in technology has been the area of human reproduction. 'Test-tube babies' was the newspaper headline twenty years ago. But now scientists are moving quickly down a path of genetically made families which may have unpredictable consequences.

What's your verdict on this vision of the future? It's titled *A Perfect Baby*. It is 2095 and time Sharon's Mum told her the facts of life. The story is worth following quite carefully.

## Reading

*A perfect baby*

For Trevor and Tracy, it was the moment every parent finds difficult. Sharon, their eldest, had started asking The Question: where did I come from, Mummy?

As she patted her daughter's blond hair (catalogue number: HC 205) and looked into her perfect cornflower blue eyes (EC 317), Tracy decided that, in 2095, there was nothing to be squeamish about.

Sharon had heard disturbing rumours about how in the old days, when a man and a woman wanted to have a baby, they went to bed with each other and left the outcome to passion and chance. Well, this was not the way her father and mother had set about bringing their daughter into the world, Tracy assured her.

It was virtually inconceivable that any responsible parent could permit a child to be born whose genes had been left to the chance shuffling of natural processes, although there were rumours of underground groups that still practised 'chance childbirth' as it was called. No, that was quite obscene. No parent would allow a foetus to go through nine months of development without knowing the colour of its eyes, or whether it had straight hair or wavy. Good grief, no one would ever conceive a child without specifying the genes for its intelligence quotient, which would help determine its chances in education and subsequent employment.

No, Sharon had to understand that Trevor and Tracy had been thorough. They had gone to the Ideal Baby exhibition at Olympia and they had combed through months of back issues of *Genes and Babies* magazine. They had window-shopped hopefully at the Harrods' Baby Counter (but the prices were prohibitive) and had leafed carefully through the glossy pages of a Swedish genetic superstore's *DNA Catalogue* for novel ideas. They would have liked to go to one of the specialist gene designers, who trawled the world's gene banks, for the most exotic mixtures and the latest models. In the end, though, Trevor was only a relatively humble virtual manager and they could afford only to go along to their local mass-retailer, the Genes 'R' Us supermarket to choose Sharon's genes.

All children these days were put together according to their parents' specifications. And, of course, Trevor and Tracy would have sent back any baby which did not conform to their wishes. The right of return with full refund had been written into the recent Consumer Protection (Human DNA) Act. The Act was passed after a long debate following a couple of controversial High Court cases in which the judges had ruled that any human baby merited the law's protection whether it met the parents' specification or not. Their rulings had met with a howl of protest from parents insisting that the gene-retailers and baby farmers should be forced to keep to their contracts.

As Colchester's Anglican vicar, Tracy felt she had a moral duty to explain to her daughter the facts of life.

Tracy explained that the 'blueprint' for all living things, plants and animals alike, is contained in a substance called DNA. The set of instructions which tells a fertilised egg that it is to develop into a human being and not a chimpanzee is written out in chemical letters along the DNA. Family resemblances arise, Tracy explained, because children inherit their DNA from their parents, transmitted in the egg and sperm. Or at least that was how matters had been before technology and civilisation had allowed parents to choose their child's genetic inheritance at will. That was why Sharon had fair hair, blue eyes and creamy-pink skin whereas her mother and father both had brown eyes, dark skin and hair.

But the Church paid its priests poorly and there had been a recession at the genetically engineered food factory where Trevor worked, so, Tracy reflected, it might be better not to mention the fact that they had not been able to afford the most expensive high intelligence genetic profile for Sharon. Over the previous two decades, high intelligence genes had been hoarded by a giant Chinese corporation, which traded under the name GeneSoft. Prices had been driven beyond the reach of ordinary consumers like Trevor and Tracy.

They had settled for a cheaper model (catalogue number: IQ 200). Sharon would therefore always be less intelligent than her school-friend Charlotte, whose grandparents had taken out a second mortgage to help purchase for her the genes guaranteeing ultra-high intelligence (catalogue number IQ 300).

Tracy decided to tell Sharon about the history of human reproduction and genetics. She settled Sharon down in front of their Netscreen module and told it to call up the history service, which then through holographic clips, graphics and 3D-images began to explain how society had put scientific knowledge to use to arrive at the genetic superstores of 2095.

The first step on the road away from superstition and towards the decency of the 21st century came in the 1960s, when The Pill first became available. For the first time in history, women were freed from the burden of biology and could choose when to have a baby.

Technology moved on very quickly, the Netscreen virtual environment explained, using dated television news clips from 1978 to tell the story of Louise Brown, the world's first test-tube baby. The technique, 'in vitro fertilisation' offered another way for people to take control of their biology. IVF meant a woman could carry in her womb a child to which she bore no genetic relationship.

In 1985, Britain's first commercial surrogate mother, Kim Cotton, was paid £6,500 to have an American couple's baby. By 1993 Italian doctors had implanted a fertilised egg, donated by a white woman, into the womb of a black woman, thus altering one of the most firmly established of all inherited traits: that a child should resemble its parents. Now prospective parents could choose the skin colour and racial grouping of their offspring.

Yet something far more profound was going on elsewhere. At a cost of more than $3bn, scientists in the major developed countries were sifting through the human genome: the compendium of all the genes in humanity's inherited blueprint. When this international Human Genome Project was complete, scientists had read the set of instructions written in DNA: they began to rewrite it as well.

On 14 September 1990, doctors at the US National Institutes of Health near Washington DC conducted the first successful attempt to treat disease by transplanting human genes into a four-year-old girl who suffered from an inborn defect of her immune system that had left her defenceless against infection. Within weeks of her gene therapy, the girl was going dancing and taking skating lessons without fear of infection.

At that point Trevor returned from work. As she saw him Tracy felt, as always, joy that he was still alive. In an unpleasant incident at work involving the plutonium and the cobalt-60 source of gamma-rays, Trevor's spleen, liver and kidneys had been destroyed. But the two of them were fortunate that they had taken out extra health insurance to cover genetic engineering of a pig, which was bred to provide organs suitable for transplant and which were virtually guaranteed not to be rejected by Trevor's immune system.

Trevor and Tracy had made sure that, when Sharon was born, they had invested in breeding a line of customised pigs containing copies of Sharon's genes in case she needed organ transplants later.

Yet science was not the only force at work. Commerce became increasingly powerful. Commerce was at the forefront of the Human Genome Project. Many genetics researchers in the USA and several in Britain were directors of private biotechnology companies, while receiving research grants from public funds or from charities. It was the greatest privatisation programme of the 21st century: the privatisation of DNA.

The scientific power of the new genetics, to fabricate what was previously seen as natural, was harnessed not by the public sector but by the market and giant corporations. Genetic engineering research had led to prototypes, which had led to production for general consumption. Soon the genetics industry was following the same path of software, information technology and semi-conductors in the 20th century. The huge R&D costs had to be covered by worldwide sales. Those were the commercial and scientific roots of the genetics superstores of 2095.

'All very interesting', said Sharon, wriggling on he sofa, 'but *Neighbours* will be on in a minute, can't you just tell me where I came from?' Tracy wondered why they hadn't spent a bit more money to get one of the higher-powered patience genes that had just come on the market. So she told her daughter the story.

By the middle of the 21st century advances in science had produced female gorillas with a virtually human reproductive system. So a human egg fertilised in vitro could be implanted in the uterus of such a gorilla. That was how Sharon had been born. After Tracy and Trevor had chosen her genes, they had come back to Genes 'R' Us nine months later to pick up their new child which had been nurtured in the surrogate womb of a genetically engineered female gorilla. Tracy, happily, was spared the bother and inconvenience of having to be pregnant or the difficulties and pain of birth.

*Tom Wilkie*

## Reflections

* What is clever about this piece of writing is that it moves step-by-step from where biological science has been and is now to what it might just become. We are perhaps both intrigued and horrified at the thought of choosing babies from Genes 'R' Us catalogues.

  There will unquestionably continue to be great advances in the 21st century in the fields of human reproduction and genetics. It will be for us to help persuade our law makers that certain social and human values are held onto in the face of galloping technological change.

  And – maybe – there are some scientific advances which we may want to say 'no' to – enough is enough. But that is not in the nature of human endeavour and the constant cry for progress!

# 4 Eating sushi

## Introduction

There is the old saying 'you are what you eat.' And if you are interested in living a long life, then copy the female Japanese diet – Japanese women live longer on average than any other people on earth!

Food is something we all take for granted in this country. But with the world's population growing, might we have to change our own diet to ensure there is enough food globally to go round? The writer in this passage puts forward some of the arguments.

Sushi is a Japanese dish consisting of cold rice and raw fish!

# Reading

## Eating sushi

If we in the rich industrial nations do not eat less meat, the world will starve.

This stark message came from the Worldwatch Institute in Washington.

It deserves to be taken seriously, not just because of Worldwatch's reputation as a sensible, non-alarmist environmental organisation, but because since the mid-Eighties the world's population/food equation has deteriorated sharply.

If there are more people and less food per head, the only way of averting starvation is to cut down on the amount of basic food which is recycled through animals, for they are an inefficient way of converting one form of food (usually grain) into another (meat).

On one side of the equation is the steady rise in global population, now at 5.5 billion, by 93 million a year. Given the youthful age structure of the world, it is hard to see a population of less than 8 billion by 2020. At some stage during the next century world population growth will almost certainly level off, but demographers are much less hopeful than they were 10 years ago that this levelling-off will happen in the first part of the century.

The other side of the equation is equally disturbing. Until the second half of the Eighties the world's food supply was keeping ahead of population growth by a decent margin. More land was being irrigated, more fertiliser was being used, new strains of rice were being developed and grain production was climbing steadily. The world was eating more meat per head, particularly pork and poultry, and the fish catch was increasing. Pessimists who had warned of global food shortages seemed to be wrong.

Now the outlook is more complicated. Irrigation, unless done very carefully, leads to salination (the cause of the decline of the ancient civilisations of Mesopotamia). Excessive fertiliser use leads to other environmental problems, such as the poisoning of water supplies. New strains of grain have proved less disease-resistant and less fertiliser-efficient than older ones. And the world's fish catch has been falling since 1989, probably because of over-fishing.

Since 1984, then, grain production per head has been falling. As a result, it is beginning to look as though the world needs another step-change in food production technology. It may come: advances in biotechnology may achieve in the next two decades what new strains of grain and greater use of fertiliser achieved in the last. If not, we eat less meat.

People in North America, Australia, New Zealand and France eat between 2,500 and 3,000 calories of food a day, unless they are on some expensive diet and have to cope on 800 until they reach their 'target weight'. But actually they are consuming about 15,000 calories of 'food equivalent' a day.

That 15,000 calories is the amount of plant food they eat – the bread, vegetables, cornflakes and so on – plus the seed to grow that plant food; plus, most dramatically, the animal feed for the meat, fish and dairy products they eat.

People in most other industrial countries, including Britain, eat a bit less (12,000–14,000 calories), because they eat less meat. The average diet in the world is about 6,000 calories, and in the Indian sub-continent 3,000 calories. Remember that this figure is a food equivalent: it can translate into less than 2,000 calories of food actually consumed, which may well be short of minerals and protein.

At that level it is difficult to lead an active working life. It would, however, seem pretty boring to most Westerners to live even on 6,000 calories of food equivalent. Yet the Japanese diet is very interesting: it is extremely healthy (Japanese women live longer on average than any other people on Earth) but, because it has a relatively small amount of meat or dairy products, it is only about 9,000 calories. Thus it is perfectly possible to have an interesting, varied diet on two-thirds of the food resources that we use here in Britain.

Worldwatch argues that we have reached some sort of global turning point and really have to change our ways if the world is not to face grave difficulties in the next century. Yet the plain fact remains that whatever happens to the world food balance, physical shortages of food will not become obvious in the supermarkets of the West.

The link between a tightening of the world's food supply and our own eating habits is not a straightforward economic one. It is bound up with social attitudes, too. Western dietary habits, which are already changing, will probably continue to do so, but more for reasons of taste than necessity.

Look at the changes in diet that have already taken place over the last generation: the decline of the cooked breakfast; the trend towards 'lighter' food in general; the emphasis on health in many prepared foods; more detailed labelling so that people can count their E-numbers for themselves; the advance of the designer lettuce across the supermarket shelves; smaller portions being served in posh restaurants.

No one would claim that the growth of either fast-food or prepared meals necessarily leads to healthier eating. But, thanks to those industries' clever marketing people, it does mean that changes in eating habits can spread much more quickly. And of course our own ability to eat more healthy, varied diets has also been transformed by the range of fresh produce which is now available in the local supermarket.

I suspect that if the world's food supply tightens and many people face misery or worse, we in the rich West will try to moderate our eating habits in a such a way that we eat less animal protein. We will try to eat better, rather than eat more. We will not be required to eat the classic Japanese breakfast of miso soup, pickles, seaweed and rice. But maybe we will have sushi more often for lunch.

*Hamish McRae*

# Reflections

* There is certainly an increasing awareness amongst young people about the environmental implications of different food production techniques. And we are all more aware nowadays of how animals are reared and slaughtered, of

the labels on packets we buy, of the critical importance of a healthy diet.

Given the rise in the world's population are we in the wealthy countries of the world prepared to change our eating habits? Or will we have those habits changed by force of circumstance, whether we like it or not?

What we all need to remember is that we do live in an increasingly inter-dependent world. What we do in the UK has an inpact on the lives of people on the other side of the globe. There is an international social responsibility to review food production and consumption. And, selfishly, eating sushi might just lead to a healthier life …

# 5 University challenge, AD 2020

## Introduction

Higher Education over recent years has undergone considerable change in this country. But for some critics of the system change hasn't gone far enough. For those about to embark on applying for or entering a university, college, or institute of Higher Education the following makes for fascinating listening.

## Reading

### University challenge, AD 2020

The antiquated structures of faculties and departments leave today's universities as the academic equivalents of Henry Ford's early cars, when the customer could have 'any colour, so long as it's black'. Ours are mass-production universities. Yet the ideas and technology already exist to ensure that no two students need follow exactly the same educational path. What is lacking is the insight and the will among academics and bureaucrats to make this happen.

To provide 21st-century education as soon as we can, live lectures and tutorials must be backed up not merely by books but also by films, television programmes and videotapes by the world's leading academics and presenters, and by interactive computers. An educational adviser will help each student to use these, together with personal contacts with academics and others, to pursue his or her 'own' education as effectively as possible. The boundaries we impose between subjects – even between 'arts' and 'sciences' – will, and should, then go.

Disputes over whether it would be feasible to run conversion courses to prepare art students who may otherwise be denied university places for entry into science faculties show how benighted most of us are. It would be better to begin at once to create less-specialised degree courses for the new millennium. For another issue that bedevils the arts-versus-science dispute is specialisation.

The two biggest problems with scientists are these: first, they believe too strongly in specialisation; and second, most scientists have acquired a specialism too narrow to make them good at educating the young and almost always too narrow to allow them to become good businessmen or administrators.

Sir John Mason, former director of the Meteorological Office, frequently insists that 'anyone can become a world expert in anything in two years'. Without going so far, the fact remains that scientific and intellectual fields are easier to enter and understand than most experts within them contend.

The looming competitive threat to Britain now comes from the Pacific – from South-east Asia as much as Japan. To compete with an area where pay is low and economic growth as rapid as at any time in human history, we need to be highly innovative. To help us to succeed, 21st-century universities will also have to be innovators: in what they do, in how they do it, and in the skills they pass to those they educate and train.

The assumption that has been allowed to justify the whole of university expansion since the Sixties is that more people educated to 'acceptable levels' would make the country more productive and civilised. Too few of us were far-sighted enough to challenge at least the first part of that assumption and to do so early enough.

On the all-too-rare occasions when the structure of degrees is questioned, it is by academics seeking to produce others like themselves. Even if this gives us more civilised people, it will produce more productive people by accident, if at all. To do that, we need to grasp and apply more generally the second implication of the fact that scientific fields are easier to enter than experts would have us think. This is that there is no need for *any* undergraduate courses to be as specialised as they are.

For those who will spend their lives mainly in business and administration, the prime requirements are an ability to learn, to think and to communicate. Good mathematical and literary skills should be required of all undergraduates. They should also appreciate the implications of the intellectual movements of their day, including the significance of scientific developments.

As if this were not itself a sufficiently dramatic challenge, there are others. Professor Howard Gardner, of the Harvard Graduate School of Education, a respected American writer, insists that well-educated people need rather more than mathematical, logical and linguistic skills.

It may well be that providing interpersonal, physical (e.g. sport), spatial (e.g. art and architecture) and work skills is not the role of the university. But everyone needs at least some of these. All the more reason to make the most radical change of all and abandon the notion that the lifetime skills an individual needs in our rapidly changing world can be acquired in three years, and normally between the ages of 18 and 24. Far-sighted institutions have for years been offering sandwich courses that mix spells of academic learning with work experience. Perhaps all universities should begin to provide lifelong sandwich courses.

This would lead to the most necessary change of all. Universities would at last become open, with more older people attending them, who would insist that standards of presentation, relevance and individual guidance were dramatically improved. They would insist that teaching was no longer the handmaiden of research. And, with the links this would create with the community, well-qualified outsiders would become available as speakers and tutors.

For the fact is that graduates in jobs outside universities are increasingly working in similar fields to academics, using similar talents. They do so more innovatively and with more vigour because they are not burdened with academic traditions and preconceptions. They will, in the end, force abandonment of the pretence that only a university faculty can run a university. The republic of the intellect will have arrived.

*Douglas Hague*

# Reflections

* Douglas Hague makes some important points for us to reflect on:

  - the need for change in styles of learning; have schools also begun to antici-pate these?

  - the need to close the divide between 'arts' and 'sciences'; has the curricu-lum between 16 and 19 yet started to do this?

  - the over-specialisation of much of our system, particularly in the sciences; how can schools assist?

  - the need for universities and the business world to work more closely together, as in the USA.

  - the need to recognise that all life's learning cannot be packaged into three short years at college; people should have the opportunity to study throughout their working lives.

  His ideas clearly throw down the gauntlet to our current system. And change *is* coming. It will be for present and future generations of school leavers to shape how universities and colleges respond to the challenges of that change.

* How far would you agree with the quotation from Sir John Mason – 'anyone can become a world expert in anything in two years'?!
  And what does the final line mean here: 'The republic of the intellect will have arrived'?


# 6 In place of schools

## Introduction

If you were crystal-ball gazing, would you say that two or three decades into the 21st century students would still be attending schools as we know them today? Will society need schools if technological change makes it possible to learn in the home? What would be the social implications?

Listen to the following vision of what might happen to formal education.

## Reading

### In place of schools

It is Friday, 28th December in the year 2029. The hour is 0808 EST (European Standard Time). Susan Smith checks this on her personal computer screen together with the local weather and traffic news, and her day's appointments.

Susan, born in the first hour of the first day of the first year of the 21st century, is a professional personal tutor to nineteen children aged from eight to ten years.

She tutors the children with their parents, or in small groups, in their homes, in her home, in community resource centres, in field stations, in museums and art galleries, in concert halls and theatres, in libraries and sports centres, and in other places where, in her professional opinion, advantage to her clients will accrue.

Susan is not a teacher in the 19th- or 20th-century sense of the word. She does not teach in a school. There are no teachers and there are no schools. There are simply personal tutors, pupils, parents, and extensive support facilities.

Susan possesses, for each of the children in her tutorial group, a personal study programme. She devised each programme with the help of the child, his parents, and colleagues' notes on the child's earlier achievements. She did this before the child first came to her from his previous tutor at the age of eight. The programme outlines the child's studies for the next two years and Susan reviews it each month – again with the help and concurrence of the child's family. She calls on help from colleagues and such other support agencies as she feels are needed. She then sets a detailed study programme for the child for the days immediately ahead.

Susan takes responsibility for the appropriateness of each ongoing programme. This is her professional task: sound educational 'prescriptions' for her clients and the acceptance of full responsibility for the efficacy of what she prescribes.

Susan Smith is happy in her work. She can think of no other career she would rather have. She is benefiting, as are her fellow tutors, her pupils, their parents and the whole of society, from quite desperate decisions made about education in the dying months of the last century. Those decisions were made reluctantly and implemented spasmodically. They came as a result of two factors combining to force a decision: the realisation that after 130 years the school-based system of teaching had run its course, and that rapidly-evolving technology, combined with personal tuition, presented a viable and possibly far superior alternative.

What the school could offer, with individual teachers working largely alone in classrooms, was meagre compared with the vast choice of material emanating from the electronic media. Satellite transmissions from all over the world, fibre optic cable, multi-channelled television and radio, and sophisticated facsimile machines, had made possible the despatch and reception of an immense range of programmes, lessons, experiences and responses to almost any place at any time. All could be supported by supplementary material and background notes for adult and child at any level of comprehension. This had been barely imaginable only a generation earlier. Some could not digest the implications, while others chose not to. But changing social circumstances in the nation forced all to examine what lay ahead.

At the turn of the millennium three groups had worked together in haste. These were politicians, amalgamations of worried teachers acting – amazingly – in unison, and parents, anxious to participate in any scheme likely to aid them in the difficult task of bringing up their children. They had all decided that the great potential of the rapidly-developing media should be used to the benefit of society. Particularly it should be utilised in the education of young children. What was needed, they agreed, was a means whereby the skills of the teacher in relating to children could be fully utilised, with the teacher released from the time and energy-consuming tasks of preparing, quite uneconomically, teaching materials. Such a scheme was devised almost fortuitously, and when its implementation began it was seen also that far more had been done for the professional enhancement of teachers than had ever been foreseen or even intended. Everyone had gained.

A huge central library of transmittable material had been created, approved and stored ready for instant retrieval and direct delivery to the homes of tutors, their pupils and their parents and any other citizens who chose to receive it. So vast had the store become and so wide, varied and appealing its range, that within five years it was possible for a knowledgeable tutor to devise a personalised curriculum capable of meeting the individual academic and social needs of each child in her care. A tutor, such as Susan Smith with her eight- and nine-year-olds, could then amend or fine-tune each curriculum as the child's requirements were seen to develop, or the wishes of the parents change.

The media – largely the electronic media – had become the provider of lessons – the 'teacher' of the old school-based system. Part of the personal tutor's work had become the prescription of 'lessons' to be taken and the study that would arise from each. But, as had been laid down by a far-seeing member of the parliamentary select committee which had devised the new system, the reading of literature, selected and aided by a tutor who now had the time and skills necessary for the work, would be an intrinsic element in any curriculum and have priority over anything else that was included.

Thus, from the moment such media potential was understood and the means of utilising it within a viable personal-tutoring system was devised, the days of the traditional school and classroom were numbered. Social problems, which in some schools had grown acute by late 1999, precipitated the movement. Then, seen in terms of educational change, the end was remarkably swift. By 2020 all but a very few of the old-fashioned schools had gone and the institution's 150 year life had drawn to a close. There had been few mourners at the graveside. Many a teacher, near to the end of her tether, had been glad to see it buried. The memorial headstone, paid for many times over by generous public subscription, had read simply:

**The School, 1870–2020.**
**It lived beyond its years.**

*John Adcock*

# Reflections

\*   What would your verdict be: 'It lived beyond its years'?
This extract comes from a book titled *In place of schools*. Its view of the future is premised on five key developments into the 21st century:

1  An expansion of the electronic media into every home,

2  A rise in the amount of non-working time available to most adults,

3  The willingness of the country to think about alternatives to schools as we know them,

4  The wish to see children remaining largely within the family for their early education,

5  The supply of professional tutors for all families.

You may or may not think these might come about. If they did, what might society lose? This is a question that makes us think afresh, not only about the academic learning that takes place in classrooms but also about the important social learning that goes on in every school. What do we really value as a school community?

* How old will you be in 2020? Watch this space!

# 7 Learning to live with the city

## Introduction

Though we do not always recognise it, *where* we live has quite an impact on *how* we live. We all recognise how very hot or very cold weather affects our lifestyle at different times of the year. But have we reflected on the importance of our environment in shaping how we think, feel and act?

Increasing numbers of the world's population live in cities. Many writers about the future think that how human kind develops cities will decide whether we survive or not on this planet. The brilliant architect Richard Rogers believes passionately that we must find ways to make cities more humane places in which to live.

## Reading

*Learning to live with the city*

It is a shocking revelation – especially to me as an architect – that the world's environmental crisis is being driven by our cities. For the first time in history, half the world's population lives in cities. In 1900 it was only one-tenth. In 30 years, it may be as much as three-quarters. The urban population of the world is increasing at a rate of a quarter of a million people per day – think of it as a new London every month.

The scale, and the rate of increase, of our consumption of resources, and the pollution it inflicts, is catastrophic.

Yet cities, which are now failing to provide the most basic needs of society, can provide a healthy and civilising environment for our citizens. I passionately believe that the art of city building has never been so crucial to our future.

My cause for optimism in the face of grim evidence comes from the growing acceptance of ecological thought worldwide. Scientists, philosophers, economists, architects, and artists, often working with local communities, are now using a global perspective to explore strategies to sustain our future.

The classic statement of this approach is the United Nations report 'Our Common Future', which laid down the concept of sustainable development as the backbone of a global economic policy. The core of this approach is a new notion of wealth, incorporating environmental elements previously considered limitless and free – clean air, fresh water, fertile land and sea. The ultimate aim of sustainable economic development is to leave to future generations a stock of environmental wealth that equals or exceeds our own inheritance.

I believe environmental 'sustainability' needs to become the guiding law of modern urban design – an innovation that would have an impact on the 21st-century city as radical as that of the industrial revolution on its 19th-century counterpart.

As it stands, cities and buildings are the most important destroyers of the ecosystem. In London, for example, massive traffic congestion causes more air pollution today than there was before the Clean Air Act banned the burning of coal in 1956. Foul air is blamed for the fact that one in seven city children in Britain now suffers from asthma.

In Japan, Tokyo alone dumps an estimated 20 million tonnes of waste every year. The city has already saturated its bay with waste, and is now running out of sites on land.

But although cities are breeding environmental disaster, there is nothing in the nature of city living that makes this inevitable. On the contrary, I believe that cities can be transformed into the most environmentally balanced form of modern settlement.

The social aspects of city life are vital to a city's sustainability. It is only if our cities offer a vibrant, healthy and secure urban life that we can dissuade people from fleeing to the suburbs, with all the problems – environmental and social – that this exodus continues to create.

Cities have grown and changed so much that it is hard to remember they exist first and foremost for people. They are the cradle of civilisation, a place for societies to come together and exchange ideas. They concentrate physical, intellectual and creative energy.

I am passionate about the choice and diversity of city life. I love the combination of ages, races, cultures, and activities, the mix of community with the unknown, familiarity and surprise – even the sense of dangerous excitement they can generate. I enjoy the animation that pavement cafés bring to the street, the informal liveliness of the public square, the mixture of shops, offices and homes, that makes a living neighbourhood.

One of the exhilarating moments of my career was when the Parisian authorities agreed to give half the site they had set aside for the Pompidou Centre to a public piazza. Today, to my great delight, the Place Beaubourg and the Pompidou Centre teem with life, and this has led to a wholesale renewal of the areas around it.

I have been talking about the importance of a vibrant urban life – to my mind, the essential ingredient of a good city. And yet today this quality is increasingly missing.

Just ask anybody what they think of city life now. He or she will more likely talk about congestion, pollution and fear of crime, than community, animation, or beauty.

*Richard Rogers*

# Reflections

* What are your thoughts? Do those who live in cities or visit them think of them as places of congestion, pollution and fear of crime? Or do they talk of community, animation and beauty?

Certainly how we shape our cities of the future is a vital social challenge – for all of us, wherever we live.

Richard Rogers believes we must become more active as citizens by influencing our built environment. We shouldn't just accept that pollution and crime in urban settings have to be as they are. We must pass on to future generations cities of great animation which are a pleasure to be in.

He has written further:

'Educating our children is a necessary first step towards the participation of communities in decision-making. It is on this that we must focus our National Curriculum. Teaching children about biology and history, but not about their actual environment – the built one – leaves them ill-equipped to participate in the process of respecting and improving the city that so critically affects their lives.'

(See also **Midtown Manhattan**, p. 162)

# 8 A sound of thunder

## Introduction

Do we fear the future? Are we afraid of what it might bring by way of change? Or do we look forward to meeting new people, new challenges, visiting new places – and then perhaps finding our life changes as a result? It is true to say that society today continues to change rapidly, so rapidly that we sometimes feel we are not in control of events; rather, events control us.

One way of looking at our future is to dig into our past. The following extract from a short story by science fiction author Ray Bradbury offers a fascinating perspective on the past – and possible futures.

## Reading

*A sound of thunder*

The sign on the wall seemed to quaver under a film of sliding warm water. Eckels felt his eyelids blink over his stare, and the sign burned in his momentary darkness:

TIME SAFARI, INC.
SAFARIS TO ANY YEAR IN THE PAST.
YOU NAME THE ANIMAL.
WE TAKE YOU THERE.
YOU SHOOT IT.

A warm phlegm gathered in Eckel's throat, he swallowed and pushed it down. The muscles around his mouth formed a smile as he put his hand slowly out upon the air, and in that hand waved a cheque for ten thousand dollars to the man behind the desk.

'Does this safari guarantee I come back alive?'

'We guarantee nothing,' said the official, 'except the dinosaurs.' He turned. 'This is Mr. Travis, your Safari Guide in the Past. He'll tell you what and where to shoot. If he says no shooting, no shooting. If you disobey instructions, there's a stiff penalty of another ten thousand dollars, plus possible government action on your return.'

Eckels glanced across the vast office at a mass and tangle, a snaking and humming of wires and steel boxes, at an aurora that flickered now orange, now silver, now blue. There was a sound like a gigantic bonfire burning all of Time, all the years and all the parchment calendars, all the hours piled high and set aflame.

A touch of the hand and this burning would, on the instant, beautifully reverse itself. Eckels remembered the wording in the advertisements to the letter. Out of chars and ashes, out of dust and coals, like golden salamanders, the old years, the green years, might leap; roses sweeten the air, white hair turn Irish-black, wrinkles vanish; all, everything fly back to seed, flee death, rush down to their beginnings, suns rise in western skies and set in glorious easts, moons eat themselves opposite to the custom, all and everything cupping one in another like Chinese boxes, rabbits into hats, all and everything returning to the fresh death, the seed death, the green death, to the time before the beginning. A touch of a hand might do it, the merest touch of a hand.

'Lord, Lord,' Eckels breathed, the light of the Machine on his thin face. "A real Time Machine.' He shook his head. 'Makes you think. If the election had gone badly yesterday, I might be here now running away from the results. Thank God Keith won. He'll make a fine President of the United States.'

'Yes,' said the man behind the desk. 'We're lucky. If Deutscher had gotten in, we'd have the worst kind of dictatorship. There's an anti-everything man for you, a militarist, anti-Christ, anti-human, anti-intellectual. People called us up, you know, joking but not joking. Said if Deutscher became President they wanted to go live in 1492. Of course, it's not our business to conduct Escapes, but to form Safaris. Anyway, Keith's President now. All you got to worry about is –'

'Shooting my dinosaur,' Eckels finished it for him.

'A *Tyrannosaurus rex*. The Thunder Lizard, the damnedest monster in history. Sign this please. Anything happens to you, we're not responsible. Those dinosaurs are hungry.'

Eckels flushed angrily. 'Trying to scare me!'

'Frankly, yes. We don't want anyone going who'll panic at the first shot. Six Safari leaders were killed last year, and a dozen hunters. We're here to give you the greatest thrill a *real* hunter ever asked for. Travelling you back sixty million years to bag the biggest game in all Time. Your personal cheque's still there. Tear it up.

Mr. Eckels looked at the cheque for a long time. His fingers twitched.

'Good luck,' said the man behind the desk. 'Mr. Travis, he's all yours.'

They moved silently across the room, taking their guns with them, towards the Machine, towards the silver metal and the roaring light.

First a day and then a night and then a day and then a night, then it was day – night – day – night – day. A week, a month, a year, a decade! A.D. 2055. A.D. 2019. 1999! 1957! Gone! The Machine roared.

They put on their oxygen helmets and tested the intercoms.

Eckels swayed on the padded seat, his face pale, his jaw stiff. He felt the trembling in his arms and he looked down and found his hands tight on the new rifle. There were four other men in the Machine. Travis, the Safari Leader, his assistant, Lesperance, and two other hunters, Billings and Kramer. They sat looking at each other, and the years blazed around them.

'Can these guns get a dinosaur cold?' Eckels felt his mouth saying.

'If you hit them right,' said Travis on the helmet radio. 'Some dinosaurs have two brains, one in the head, another far down the spinal column. We stay away from those. That's stretching luck. Put your first two shots into the eyes, if you can, blind them, and go back into the brain.'

The Machine howled. Time was a film run backward. Suns fled and ten million moons fled after them. 'Good God,' said Eckels. 'Every hunter that ever lived would envy us today. This makes Africa seem like Illinois.'

The Machine slowed; its scream fell to a murmur. The Machine stopped.

The sun stopped in the sky.

The fog that had enveloped the Machine blew away and they were in an old time, a very old time indeed, three hunters and two Safari Heads with their blue metal guns across their knees.

'Christ isn't born yet,' said Travis. 'Moses has not gone to the mountain to talk with God. The Pyramids are still in the earth, waiting to be cut out and put up. *Remember* that. Alexander, Caesar, Napoleon, Hitler – none of them exists.'

The men nodded.

'That' – Mr. Travis pointed – 'is the jungle of sixty million two thousand and fifty-five years before President Keith.'

He indicated a metal path that struck off into green wilderness, over steaming swamp, among giant ferns and palms.

'And that,' he said, 'is the Path, laid by Time Safari for your use. It floats six inches above the earth. Doesn't touch so much as one grass blade, flower, or tree. It's an anti-gravity metal. It's purpose is to keep you from touching this world of the past in any way. Stay on the Path. Don't go off it. I repeat. *Don't go off.* For *any* reason! If you fall off, there's a penalty. And don't shoot any animal we don't okay.'

'Why?' asked Eckels.

They sat in the ancient wilderness. Far birds' cries blew on a wind, and the smell of tar and an old salt sea, moist grasses, and flowers the colour of blood.

'We don't want to change the Future. We don't belong here in the Past. The government doesn't *like* us here. We have to pay big graft to keep our franchise. A Time Machine is damn finicky business. Not knowing it, we might kill an important animal, a small bird, a roach, a flower even, thus destroying an important link in a growing species.'

'That's not clear,' said Eckels.

'All right,' Travis continued, 'say we accidentally kill one mouse here. That means all the future families of this one particular mouse are destroyed, right?'

'Right.'

'And all the families of the families of the families of that one mouse! With a stamp of your foot, you annihilate first one, then a dozen, then a thousand, a million a *billion* possible mice!'

'So they're dead,' said Eckels. 'So what?'

'So what?' Travis snorted quietly. 'Well, what about the foxes that'll need those mice to survive? For want of ten mice, a fox dies. For want of ten foxes, a lion starves. For want of a lion, all manner of insects, vultures, infinite billions of life forms are thrown into chaos and destruction. Eventually it all boils down to this: fifty-nine million years later, a cave man, one of a dozen on the *entire world*, goes hunting wild boar or sabre-tooth tiger for food. But you, friend, have *stepped* on all the tigers in that region. By stepping on *one* single mouse. So the cave man starves. And the cave man, please note, is not just *any* expendable man, no! He is an *entire future nation*. From his loins would have sprung ten sons. From *their* loins one hundred sons, and thus onward to a civilization. Destroy this one man, and you destroy a race, a people, an entire history of life. It is comparable to slaying some of Adam's grandchildren. The stomp of your foot, on one mouse, could start an earthquake, the effects of which could shake our earth and destinies down through Time, to their very foundations. With the death of that one cave man, a billion others yet unborn are throttled in the womb. Perhaps Rome never rises on its seven hills. Perhaps Europe is forever a dark forest, and only Asia waxes healthy and teeming. Step on a mouse and you crush the Pyramids. Step on a mouse and you leave your print, like a Grand Canyon, across Eternity. Queen Elizabeth might never be born, Washington might not cross the Delaware, there might never be a United States at all. So be careful. Stay on the Path. *Never step off!'*

'I see,' said Eckels. 'Then it wouldn't pay for us even to touch the *grass?'*

'Correct. Crushing certain plants could add up infinitesimally. A little error here would multiply in sixty million years, all out of proportion. Of course maybe our theory is wrong. Maybe Time *can't* be changed by us. Or maybe it can be changed only in little subtle ways. A dead mouse here makes an insect imbalance there, a population disproportion later, a bad harvest further on, a depression, mass starvation, and, finally, a change in *social* temperament in far-flung countries. Something much more subtle, like that. Perhaps only a soft breath, a whisper, a hair, pollen on the air, such a slight, slight change that unless you looked close you wouldn't see it. Who knows? Who really can say he knows? We don't know. We're guessing. But until we do know for certain whether our messing around in Time *can* make a big roar or a little rustle in history, we're being damned careful. This Machine, this Path, your clothing and bodies, were sterilized, as you know, before the journey. We wear these oxygen helmets so we can't introduce our bacteria into an ancient atmosphere.'

*Ray Bradbury*

# Reflections

\*   You will need to read the rest of this intriguing tale to find out what happens; a clue – when they return to the present President Keith is not the US President!

   What Ray Bradbury's story does is highlight that what *each* of us does – no matter how small our contribution – affects how society is shaped for the future. Actions we take today, for example, in the natural environment – lakes, rivers, seas, forests, ice-caps, deserts – will have long-term effects.

   The pace of change may sometimes appear to overwhelm us. Nonetheless, we should never underestimate our individual power and influence. The future can be what we want it to be.

*    Futurist Alvin Toffler once wrote in flowery terms:

'Accustomed to coping with lower diversity and slow change, individuals and institutions suddenly find themselves trying to cope with high diversity and high-speed change. The cross-pressures threaten to overload their decisional competence.'

Fellow futurist Tom Peters encourages all of us these days to thrive *on* chaos!

# 9 A silicon chip in your head

## Introduction

Scientists have been saying since the advent of computerised systems and robotic devices that the human brain itself would never be replaced by machines. But is that last frontier about to be partly crossed? What *would* be the social and moral implications of the human brain being enhanced, if not replaced, by the silicon chip?

## Reading

### A silicon chip in your head

The human brain may be connected directly to computers within the next 50 years, according to a far reaching study by one of Britain's leading technology 'futurologists'.

The study by Professor Peter Cochrane, the head of BT's high-tech laboratories at Martlesham Heath, Suffolk, predicts that by 2020 scientists will start to develop ways to link powerful silicon chips directly to the brain, possibly by growing nerve cells on the chip.

Such a link would allow someone to carry around the entire *Encyclopedia Brittanica* on a chip inserted into their head. The link would create a physical connection between the carbon-based memory of the human brain to the silicon memory of the computer chip.

The link would hugely augment the power of a brain because by that stage silicon chips will match the brain's ability to store and retrieve information. Professor Cochrane's research suggests that should be possible by 2015.

The amount of digital information transmitted by optical fibres is doubling every year and the size of memory chips is increasing almost as fast.

This will create an ever-accelerating improvement in computer power, Professor Cochrane said.

'At 2015 the computer will be equal to you and I in terms of storing the stuff you and I can store,' he said.

Computer memories are growing so much 'very soon we will be able to put all 24 million volumes in the library of the US Congress in the living room', he said.

The direct link between computer chips and the brain is the most startling conclusion of Professor Cochrane's study on technology trends. It also includes these predictions:

- Daily health checks by computers over the phone by the year 2000.

- Automatic dialling by talking to a phone that can recognise individual voices by 2006.

- Artificial noses that can detect the entire array of odours identifiable to humans by 2008.

- Medical devices that can roam inside human blood vessels under their own power by 2011.

- Portable machines that can translate a simple conversation in two or more languages by 2011.

Professor Cochrane said that past attempts to predict the future course of technology have suffered from being too conservative. 'My wristwatch wields more power than some 1970s mainframe computers. Ordinary cars today have more intelligence than the original lunar lander.'

The computers of 2015 that will match human brain power will be large supercomputers. Five years after that they will be desktop computers.

These computers will talk and listen to their owners, with apparent feeling.

*Steve Connor*

## Reflections

\* What are your reactions to such developments? On the one hand we probably wonder at the skill of the scientists; on the other hand we want to say to them that they need to be careful they don't produce a Frankenstein!

Can we imagine the front door that opens when we ask it to; the bath that turns on its taps automatically at our pre-arranged bath-time; the cooker that responds to our voice control; or wearing virtual reality glasses to go shopping?

These are set to feature in some homes within a few years. We might ask ourselves: where does convenience end and dependence begin? As always, how we manage, use and come to terms with new technology will decide who is master/mistress over whom. Or should that be: what is master/mistress over what?!

# 10 Grand Tour: 2484

## Introduction

Despite all the talk about the great pace of change our globe is currently experiencing, it's probably safe to say that human beings are quite a conservative lot. We feel familiar with what we have, rooted as it often is, in the past. George Orwell once memorably wrote in his own futuristic novel *1984*: 'Who controls the past controls the future: who controls the present controls the past.'

The following imaginative essay written in 1984 is set five hundred years hence. It suggests humans are fond of and significantly shaped by their past. The 'Canaveral' mentioned in the passage is the base from which the Americans first launched their moon missions in the 1960s.

# Reading

## *Grand Tour 2484*

On some morning in the year 2484, five hundred incredible years from now, a family named Peregrine, a good name for far-traveling folks, will bound out of bed on the Moon or Mars, or farther out on some colonial pod circling Alpha Centauri, and ask themselves what to do On Vacation.

Home might be the answer. Home meaning, of course, Earth, where we all started from. The Seedbed Vacation, it might well be called.

Let's go back, someone suggests, to see what's left of it. See what we did wrong and then did right.

No, let's not, half the family argues. There's nobody left there, only a few genetic retards, so why go back? There are other planets we can visit first. On each one we'll find something like Earth. Let's see the other worlds first. After that – maybe – Earth.

So the Peregrines board their Leapfrogs. Leapfrogs? Yes, that is what they might call their fast-as-the-speed-of-light spaceships. Once aboard, they would blast off on not a short vacation at all. It would be a long haul spanning many years, making landfall at impossible places with incredible climates.

But – with *familiar* architectures! ...

So on their long day's journey through night, our vacationers will indeed find the familiar architectural faces of Rome here, Venice there and Waukegan, Illinois, just beyond. So the journey will be a journey not only through space but through time and all the ways we had of living and seeing ourselves in shapes and sizes, in colors and textures, most of them brand new, on Mars or wherever we could make a lean-to and turn it into a Southern Manse or Northern Castle.

All of this, of course, because in the far traveling we will accomplish, we will be forced by time and distance and memory, which hurts, to resurrect the dead in order to go on living. The towns we loved as Earth children will be the towns, sometimes larger, sometimes smaller, that we will facade across any halfway-habitable satellite or world. We will carry along stained-glass windows and build entire houses around them. We will tote a brick from the Via Veneto and, halfway to Andromeda, which is too far by several billion years; we will put up an awning and two chairs, and wink at passing Beasts.

In sum, we will travel in 2484 much as we have done in our time, to revisit the Past that strengthens our Present before we turn back to the sometimes uncertain Futures awaiting us.

And as we travel back down through the universe, we will revisit the entire history of mankind. We will cross paths with the vast firework calligraphies we left behind with our rocket exhausts on our way to seeding star worlds with our harvest children.

And depending on which national or ethnic group settled this world or that, we will find the whims and fancies and late-night nostalgias of Arabs who built mosques, or Swiss who cobbled up fake Alps on planets as pancake-flat as Kansas, or Japanese who left a Shinto shrine and a robot factory behind as they said farewell.

And arriving back on Earth for what might well be our last visit, we will tour Canaveral, where the gantries, still standing, tossed our flags to the Moon. Then, we'll go see New York, rebuilt in 1999 and again in 2050, the year they blew up every other block of ugly buildings and planted gardens in their place. The neatest real-estate trick of the age! And then on to Chicago, which finished its rebuilding in 2020 and at last was beautiful. And Los Angeles, which went on growing into the twenty-second century and still had no center.

And then on to Moscow, which finally accepted the true revolution of the twenty-first century: technology.

A trifle of politics but a huge serving of the automobile, the train, the jet, the Xerox and the Fax, the radio, the TV, the videocassette and the telephone instead of the dull hammer and the blunted sickle. Moscow with architectures, by some miracle at last, somewhat lovely.

But why go on? Obviously, Moscow by A.D. 2233, wasn't a bad place to visit. You wouldn't want to go there summers because there are too many American tourists, but …

There you have the grand tour, 2484 style. Back down in time, to a mostly empty Earth, because everyone couldn't resist heading out and up – or to the New West, as it was called. And the empty cities began to be taken by grass and dust, as the inhabitants of New Earths in separate star systems came back for reunions here in Nantucket or Bombay. Home but no longer home. Mother but no longer mother.

And we turn around and blast back off, up past the Moon and its abandoned colonies, and Mars and its Martians (all with strangely familiar Cherokee faces), we will fix a last stare at the bloodshot eye of Jupiter, ricochet through Saturn's rings, then head for our home away from home.

What a time and tour it will be, far beyond 1984, which turned out to be a bore and not Big Brother after all.

We, the hyper-ventilating generation, bursting with star-seed, can hardly wait to explode up out-away, so we can come back on a lightship trek for a strange visitation, a peculiar vacation.

And if not I, or you, or our children – who?

*Ray Bradbury*

# Reflections

* There are some arresting lines here from science fiction writer Ray Bradbury. What does he mean by them?

    – 'Let's go back, someone suggests, to see what's left of it. See what we did wrong and then did right.'

    – 'We will be forced by time and distance and memory to resurrect the dead in order to go on living.'

    – 'We will travel to revisit the Past that strengthens our Present.'

The future is, almost by definition, uncertain. *Grand Tour 2484* perhaps hints that it may not be so very different from how we live today. There are certain familiar truths and landmarks we keep coming back to – whether we shall live on Earth, Mars or on one of Saturn's rings.

# Success and Failure

*A celebrated French general was once tactlessly asked, after a famous victory, if it hadn't* really *been won by the second-in-command.*

*The general thought for some time before answering: 'Maybe so. But one thing is certain. If the battle had been lost I would have lost it!'*

*To lose the argument is as enlightening as to win it. To be defeated by the truth is to experience the one defeat which is also victory.*

Rabbi Jonathan Sachs

# 1 Heroic failures

## Introduction

It is a fact that when we are successful at something everyone is happy to congratulate us; on the other hand failure can attract some pretty sharp looks and comments. G. K. Chesterton once wrote: 'If a thing is worth doing, it is worth doing badly.' But that's not how the world normally sees things.

That said, it is a rare person who is successful and has never experienced failure. Maybe incompetence *is* what we're good at, even though we spend a lot of time talking about success!

Listen to the following extracts from *The Book of Heroic Failures*. They may put some of our own grand failures in perspective.

## Reading

*Heroic failures*

### 1 The least successful newspaper

Described on billboards as 'Britain's most fearless newspaper', the *Commonwealth Sentinel* opened on 6th February, 1965 and closed on the 7th. Designed to cater for all Commonwealth citizens, the paper was founded by Mr Lionel Burleigh in London. He spent a hectic week collecting the advertisements, writing the stories and seeing the first issue through the press. Then Mr Burleigh received a phone call from the police.

'Are you anything to do with the *Commonwealth Sentinel*?' asked a constable, encouraged by an hysterical hotel porter. 'Because there are 50,000 of them outside the entrance to Brown's Hotel and they're blocking Albemarle Street.'

'We had forgotten to arrange any distribution,' Mr Burleigh said later, 'and they were just dumped outside the hotel where I was staying. To my knowledge we only sold one copy. I still have the shilling in my drawer'. It was sold by Mr Burleigh's daughter to a passer-by. This caused so much excitement that a photograph was taken of the transaction.

### 2 The vet who surprised a cow

In the course of his duties in August 1977, a Dutch veterinary surgeon was required to treat an ailing cow. To investigate its internal gases he inserted a tube into that end of the animal not capable of facial expression and struck a match. The jet of flame set fire first to some bales of hay and then to the whole farm causing damage estimated at £45,000. The vet was later fined £140 for starting a fire in a manner surprising to the magistrates. The cow escaped with shock.

### 3 The least convenient post box

In March 1979 workmen at Ballymacra, County Antrim, replaced a telegraph pole upon which a pillar box was fixed.

The workmen did not have the official keys needed to release the clips that fastened the box to the pole. So they raised it over the top of the old one and then slipped it down the new one. The new pole turned out to be thicker than the old one and the post box came to rest nine feet above the ground.

It remained in this position for three weeks during which time some post still managed to get through. 'I am told', said Mr Ernie McDermott, the postmaster, 'that someone provided a step ladder. The mind boggles.'

### 4  The worst bus service

Can any bus service rival the fine Hanley to Bagnall route in Staffordshire? In 1976 it was reported that the buses no longer stopped for passengers.

This came to light when one of them, Mr Bill Hancock, complained that buses on the outward journey regularly sailed past queues of up to thirty people.

Councillor Arthur Cholerton then made transport history by stating that if these buses stopped to pick up passengers they would disrupt the time-table.

### 5  The soldiers who fought the Second World War for longest

Lieutenant Hiroo Onoda of the Japanese army fought the Second World War until 3 p.m. on 10 March 1974, despite the continued absence of armed opposition in the later years. He used to come out of the jungle on his remote island in the Philippines and fire the odd bullet on behalf of Emperor Hirohito. In 1945 'come home' letters were dropped from the air but he ignored them believing it was just a Yankee trick to make him surrender. After he was found in 1974 it took six months to finally convince him that the war really was over.

But even after this surrender the Second World War still continued on the Island of Morotai where Private Teruo Nakamura maintained unbending resistance to the Allied Forces. This Indonesian island was finally liberated nine months later in December 1974.

### 6  The least successful firework

The most unsuccessful firework so far ignited was the 'Fat Man' Roman candle perfected in 1975 by Mr George Plimpton of New York. It weighed 720 pounds, was forty inches long and was developed to break the record for the most spectacular firework ever. It succeeded admirably.

Lighting it, Mr Plimpton confidently predicted that it would reach an altitude in excess of 3,000 feet. Instead of this, however, it hissed, whistled and blew a ten-foot crater in the earth.

*Stephen Pile*

# Reflections

*   The collector of all these stories decided to set up The Not Terribly Good Club of Great Britain, of which he is President. The stories are all about failure but they are also about people – in the main – trying hard to make something work. Success and failure do lie either side of the same coin.

    The serious point for a school community is to recognise when someone has done their very best to succeed, even though that success has finally escaped them. Heroic failures like the firework we can properly laugh at; but that should never extend to making fun of failure if that means putting down someone's sincere efforts.

# 2 Grapes of wrath

## Introduction

Coming to terms with failure is often very difficult for many of us. When our failure also involves others – perhaps our family – our sense of pain and frustration can be particularly acute. But it is how we then live with and learn from failure that is important.

The following passage comes from John Steinbeck's powerful novel *Grapes of Wrath*, in which he tells the story of the farming families who moved westwards across America during the 1930s in search of work. This passage comes from the closing chapters and describes the increasing desperation of the men and their families as they fail to find jobs and have nothing to live on. They have only their old cars and tents to shelter in.

## Reading

*Grapes of Wrath*

When the first rain started, the migrant people huddled in their tents, saying, It'll soon be over, and asking, How long's it likely to go on?

And when the puddles formed, the men went out in the rain with shovels and built little dikes around the tents. The beating rain worked at the canvas until it penetrated and sent streams down. And then the little dikes washed out and the water came inside, and the streams wet the beds and the blankets. The people sat in wet clothes. They set up boxes and put planks on the boxes. Then, day and night, they sat on the planks.

Beside the tents the old cars stood, and water fouled the ignition wires and water fouled the carburettors. The little gray tents stood in lakes. And at last the people had to move. Then the cars wouldn't start because the wires were shorted; and if the engines would run, deep mud engulfed the wheels. And the people waded away, carrying their wet blankets in their arms. They splashed along, carrying the children, carrying the very old, in their arms. And if a barn stood on high ground, it was filled with people, shivering and hopeless.

Then some went to the relief offices, and they came sadly back to their own people.

They's rules – you got to be here a year before you can git relief. They say the gov'ment is gonna help. They don't know when.

And gradually the greatest terror of all came along.

They ain't gonna be no kinda work for three months.

In the barns, the people sat huddled together; and the terror came over them, and their faces were gray with terror. The children cried with hunger, and there was no food.

Then the sickness came, pneumonia, and measles that went to the eyes and to the mastoids.

And the rain fell steadily, and the water flowed over the highways, for the culverts could not carry the water.

Then from the tents, from the crowded barns, groups of sodden men went out, their clothes slopping rags, their shoes muddy pulp. They splashed out through the water, to the towns, to the country stores, to the relief offices, to beg for food, to cringe and beg for food, to beg for relief, to try to steal, to lie. And under the begging, and under the cringing, a hopeless anger began to smoulder. And in the little towns pity for the sodden men changed to anger, and anger at the hungry people changed to fear of them. Then sheriffs swore in deputies in droves, and orders were rushed for rifles, for tear gas, for ammunition. Then the hungry men crowded the alleys behind the stores to beg for bread, to beg for rotting vegetables, to steal when they could.

Frantic men pounded on the doors of the doctors; and the doctors were busy. And sad men left word at country stores for the coroner to send a car. The coroners were not too busy. The coroners' wagons backed up through the mud and took out the dead.

And the rain pattered relentlessly down, and the streams broke their banks and spread out over the country.

Huddled under sheds, lying in wet hay, the hunger and the fear bred anger. Then boys went out, not to beg, but to steal; and men went out weakly, to try to steal.

The sheriffs swore in new deputies and ordered new rifles; and the comfortable people in tight houses felt pity at first, and then distaste, and finally hatred for the migrant people.

In the wet hay of leaking barns babies were born to women who panted with pneumonia. And old people curled up in corners and died that way, so that the coroners could not straighten them. At night the frantic men walked boldly to hen roosts and carried off the squawking chickens. If they were shot at, they did not run, but splashed sullenly away; and if they were hit, they sank tiredly in the mud.

The rain stopped. On the fields the water stood, reflecting the gray sky, and the land whispered with moving water. And the men came out of the barns, out of the sheds. They squatted on their hams and looked out over the flooded land. And they were silent. And sometimes they talked very quietly.

No work till spring. No work.

And if no work – no money, no food.

Fella had a team of horses, had to use 'em to plow an' cultivate an' mow, wouldn' think a turnin' 'em out to starve when they wasn't workin'.

Them's horses – we're men.

The women watched the men, watched to see whether the break had come a last. The women stood silently and watched. And where a number of men gathered together, the fear went from their faces, and anger took its place. And the women sighed with relief, for they knew it was all right – the break had not come; and the break would never come as long as fear could turn to wrath.

Tiny points of grass came through the earth, and in a few days the hills were pale green with the beginning year.

*John Steinbeck*

## Reflections

* The migrant families – driven westwards in search of a new life – find themselves destitute. The men, in particular, feel extreme failure because they have brought their families thousands of miles across America to California for nothing, or worse than nothing. But what John Steinbeck is interested in exploring is how they do not let their anger at the way they are being treated become destructive:

'the break would never come as long as fear could turn to wrath.'

He portrays the men as angry at failure, yes, but equally resolute to survive and find a way forward. The conclusion to the novel is not an optimistic one, but his characters remind us of the importance of self-dignity at times of failure. Even under the most desperate conditions the human spirit has the will to triumph.

# 3  The four-minute mile

## Introduction

There are certain moments in sport which go down in a special way in the record books. One such moment was the first time a human being ran the mile in under four minutes. As with so many sporting achievements, one person's name went into the record books but the record could not have been set without a team effort.

This is Roger Bannister's account of how he came to run that magic mile back in 1954 in Oxford. Brasher and Chataway were his friends and fellow runners who had planned this attempt on the mile record.

## Reading

### The Four-Minute Mile

Failure is as exciting to watch as success, provided the effort is absolutely genuine and complete. But the spectators fail to understand – and how can they know – the mental agony through which an athlete must pass before he can give his maximum effort. And how rarely, if he is built as I am, he can give it.

No one tried to persuade me. The decision was mine alone, and the moment was getting closer. As we lined up for the start I glanced at the flag again. It fluttered more gently now, and the scene from Shaw's *Saint Joan* flashed through my mind, how she, at her desperate moment, waited for the wind to change. Yes, the wind was dropping sightly. This was the moment when I made my decision. The attempt was on.

There was complete silence on the ground ... a false start ... I felt angry that precious moments during the lull in the wind might be slipping by. The gun fired a second time ... Brasher went into the lead and I slipped in effortlessly behind him, feeling tremendously full of running. My legs seemed to meet no resistance at all, as if propelled by some unknown force.

We seemed to be going so slowly! Impatiently I shouted 'Faster!' But Brasher kept his head and did not change the pace. I went on worrying until I heard the first lap time, 57.5 seconds. In the excitement my knowledge of pace had deserted me. Brasher could have run the first quarter in 55 seconds without my realizing it, because I felt so full of running, but I should have had to pay for it later. Instead, he had made success possible.

At one and a half laps I was still worrying about the pace. A voice shouting 'Relax' penetrated to me above the noise of the crowd. Unconsciously I obeyed. If the speed was wrong it was too late to do anything about it, so why worry? I was relaxing so much that my mind seemed almost detached from my body. There was no strain.

I barely noticed the half-mile, passed in 1 minute 58 seconds, nor when, round the next bend, Chataway went into the lead. At three-quarters of a mile the effort was still barely perceptible; the time was 3 minutes 0.7 second, and by now the crowd was roaring. Somehow I had to run that last lap in 59 seconds. Chataway led round the next bend and then I pounced past him at the beginning of the back straight, three hundred yards from the finish.

I had a moment of mixed joy and anguish, when my mind took over. It raced well ahead of my body and drew my body compellingly forward. I felt that the moment of a lifetime had come. There was no pain, only a great unity of move-ment and aim. The world seemed to stand still, or did not exist. The only reality was the next two hundred yards of track under my feet. The tape meant finality – extinction perhaps.

I felt at that moment that it was my chance to do one thing supremely well. I drove on, impelled by a combination of fear and pride. The air I breathed filled me with the spirit of the track where I had run my first race. The noise in my ears was that of the faithful Oxford crowd. Their hope and encouragement gave me greater strength. I had now turned the last bend and there were only fifty yards more.

My body had long since exhausted all its energy, but it went on running just the same. The physical overdraft came only from greater willpower. This was the crucial moment when my legs were strong enough to carry me over the last few yards as they could never have done in previous years. With five yards to go the tape seemed almost to recede. Would I ever reach it?

Those last few seconds seemed never-ending. The faint line of the finishing tape stood ahead as a haven of peace, after the struggle. The arms of the world were waiting to receive me if only I reached the tape without slackening my speed. If I faltered, there would be no arms to hold me and the world would be a cold, forbidding place, because I had been so close. I leapt at the tape like a man taking his last spring to save himself from the chasm that threatens to engulf him.

My effort was over and I collapsed almost unconscious, with an arm on either side of me. It was only then that real pain overtook me. I felt like an exploded flashlight with no will to live; I just went on existing in the most passive physical state without being quite conscious. Blood surged from my muscles and seemed to fell me. It was as if all my limbs were caught in an ever-tightening vise. I knew that I had done it before I even heard the time. I was too close to have failed, unless my legs had played strange tricks at the finish by slowing me down and not telling my tiring brain that they had done so.

The stop-watches held the answer. The announcement came – 'Result of one mile … time, three minutes' – the rest lost in the roar of excitement. I grabbed Brasher and Chataway, and together we scampered round the track in a burst of spontaneous joy. We had done it – the three of us!

We shared a place where no man had yet ventured – secured for all time, however fast men might run miles in future. We had done it where we wanted, when we wanted, how we wanted, in our first attempt of the year. In the wonderful joy my pain was forgotten and I wanted to prolong those precious moments of realization.

I felt suddenly and gloriously free of the burden of athletic ambition that I had been carrying for years. No words could be invented for such supreme happiness, eclipsing all other feelings. I thought at that moment I could never again reach such a climax of single-mindedness. I felt bewildered and overpowered. I knew it would be some time before I caught up with myself.

*Roger Bannister*

## Reflections

* The record was set before a modest crowd and, of course back in the 1950s, by a group of amateur athletes – a far cry from the razzmatazz of today's professional televised events with their endless slow-motion replays. It is their very amateurism which makes their achievement all the more exciting, an excitement and intensity which Bannister's words capture. And putting into words such a physical and emotional experience is not easy.

He also has some interesting things to say about his achievement:

- 'Failure is as exciting to watch as success, provided the effort is absolutely genuine and complete.'

- 'I drove on, impelled by a combination of fear and pride.'

- 'I felt suddenly and gloriously free of the burden of athletic ambition that I had been carrying for years.'

- 'I felt bewildered and overpowered.'

In success and failure there often is an intensity of mixed emotions. Bannister reminds us, that it is better to have competed and lost, than never to have competed at all! And that applies to sport but equally to so many other aspects of our lives.

# 4 The angel of the candy counter

## Introduction

Have you ever found yourself in a situation where something went wrong? Things didn't turn out as you would have wished; you felt a sense of failure; but *later* you imagined that things had turned out rather differently – successfully and to your advantage.

In the following extract – set in the southern states of America in the 1940s – a young black girl, Maya, goes with her mother to the dentist. The dentist bluntly refuses to treat black people even though he owes the mother a favour. The young girl *then* imagines a scene in which her Momma turned the tables on Dentist Lincoln.

# Reading

## *The angel of the candy counter*

Momma knocked on the back door and a young white girl opened it to show surprise at seeing us there. Momma said she wanted to see Dentist Lincoln and to tell him Annie was there. The girl closed the door firmly. Now the humiliation of hearing Momma describe herself as if she had no last name to the young white girl was equal to the physical pain. It seemed terribly unfair to have a toothache and a headache and have to bear at the same time the heavy burden of Blackness.

It was always possible that the teeth would quiet down and maybe drop out of their own accord. Momma said we would wait. We leaned in the harsh sunlight on the shaky railings of the dentist's back porch for over an hour.

He opened the door and looked at Momma. 'Well, Annie, what can I do for you?'

He didn't see the towel around my jaw or notice my swollen face.

Momma said, 'Dentist Lincoln. It's my grandbaby here. She got two rotten teeth that's giving her a fit.'

She waited for him to acknowledge the truth of her statement. He made no comment, orally or facially.

'She had this toothache purt' near four days now, and today I said, "Young lady, you going to the Dentist."'

'Annie?'

'Yes, sir, Dentist Lincoln.'

He was choosing words the way people hunt for shells. 'Annie, you know I don't treat nigra, colored people.'

'I know, Dentist Lincoln. But this here is just my little grandbaby, and she ain't gone be no trouble to you … '

'Annie, everybody has a policy. In this world you have to have a policy. Now, my policy is I don't treat colored people.'

The sun had baked the oil out of Momma's skin and melted the Vaseline in her hair. She shone greasily as she leaned out of the dentist's shadow.

'Seem like to me, Dentist Lincoln, you might look after her, she ain't nothing but a little mite. And seems like maybe you owe me a favor or two.'

He reddened slightly. 'Favour or no favour. The money has all been repaid to you and that's the end of it. Sorry, Annie.' He had his hand on the doorknob. 'Sorry.' His voice was a bit kinder on the second 'Sorry,' as if he really was.

Momma said, 'I wouldn't press on you like this for myself but I can't take No. Not for my grandbaby. When you come to borrow my money you didn't have to beg. You asked me, and I lent it. Now, it wasn't my policy. I ain't no money-lender, but you stood to lose this building and I tried to help you out.'

'It's been paid, and raising your voice won't make me change my mind. My policy … ' He let go of the door and stepped nearer Momma. The three of us were crowded on the small landing. 'Annie, my policy is I'd rather stick my hand in a dogs mouth than in a nigger's.'

He had never once looked at me. He turned his back and went through the door into the cool beyond. Momma backed up inside herself for a few minutes. I forgot everything except her face which was almost a new one to me. She leaned over and took the doorknob, and in her everyday soft voice she said, 'Sister, go on downstairs. Wait for me. I'll be there directly.'

Under the most common of circumstances I knew it did no good to argue with Momma. So I walked down the steep stairs, afraid to look back and afraid not to do so. I turned as the door slammed, and she was gone.

[And now comes the scene imagined by Maya]

*Momma walked in that room as if she owned it. She shoved that silly nurse aside with one hand and strode into the dentist's office. He was sitting in his chair, sharpening his mean instruments and putting extra sting into his medicines. Her eyes were blazing like live coals and her arms had doubled themselves in length. He looked up at her just before she caught him by the collar of his white jacket.*

*'Stand up when you see a lady, you contemptuous scoundrel.' Her tongue had thinned and the words rolled off well enunciated. Enunciated and sharp like little claps of thunder.*

*The dentist had no choice but to stand at R.O.T.C. attention. His head dropped after a minute and his voice was humble. 'Yes, ma'am, Mrs. Henderson.'*

*'You knave, do you think you acted like a gentleman, speaking to me like that in front of my granddaughter?' She didn't shake him, although she had the power. She simply held him upright.*

*'No, ma'am, Mrs. Henderson.'*

*'No, ma'am, Mrs. Henderson, what?' Then she did give him the tiniest of shakes, but because of her strength the action set his head and arms to shaking loose on the ends of his body. He stuttered much worse than Uncle Willie. 'No, ma'am, Mrs. Henderson, I'm sorry.'*

*With just an edge of her disgust showing, Momma slung him back in his dentist's chair. 'Sorry is as sorry does, and you're about the sorriest dentist I ever laid my eyes on.' (She could afford to slip into the vernacular because she had such eloquent command of English.)*

*'I didn't ask you to apologize in front of Marguerite, because I don't want her to know my power, but I order you, now and herewith. Leave Stamps by sundown.'*

*'Mrs. Henderson, I can't get my equipment ... ' He was shaking terribly now.*

*'Now, that brings me to my second order. You will never again practice dentistry. Never! When you get settled in your next place, you will be a vegetarian caring for dogs with the mange, cats with the cholera and cows with the epizootic. Is that clear?'*

*The saliva ran down his chin and his eyes filled with tears. 'Yes, ma'am. Thank you for not killing me. Thank you, Mrs. Henderson.'*

*Momma pulled herself back from being ten feet tall with eight-foot arms and said, 'You're welcome for nothing, you varlet, I wouldn't waste a killing on the likes of you.'*

*On her way out she waved her handkerchief at the nurse and turned her into a crocus sack of chicken feed.*

*Maya Angelou*

# Reflections

* A lovely parting gesture! What actually happens is that, having been turned away by Dentist Lincoln, they have to travel further afield to find a dentist who will treat the black family. What Maya *imagines* is of course her way as a young child of coming to terms with the rejection by the dentist. She wants to believe that her Momma cannot be treated in this rude and prejudiced way.

The extract comes from the novel by Maya Angelou titled *I Know Why The Caged Bird Sings*. It is essentially her autobiography and has many powerful scenes describing the racial tensions of the time. The scene we have heard is both a powerful condemnation of prejudice and a witty account of how we can turn failure into success in our own minds, as a way of coming to terms with rejection.

Rewriting our own personal history – often with the wisdom of hindsight – is something human beings regularly do. It helps us manage difficult moments!

(See also **Stereotypes**, p. 201)

# 5 It was a very bad year ... (1)

## Introduction

Life can often deal out some extraordinary slaps in the face. When it happens to us we can feel very indignant, depressed or got at, especially if someone is unkind enough to say 'serves you right.' Of course, when the tables are turned we sometimes find it difficult to stop laughing at other people's misfortunes.

Here are a series of true stories, recorded month by month, from one year's news. They're meant to cheer us up! And put our own troubles in perspective ...

## Reading

*It was a very bad year ... (1)*

January

*Police*, the journal of the boys in blue, reported that a suspicious-looking cardboard box has been found outside a Territorial Army centre in Bristol. The TA called the police, who called an Army bomb disposal unit, which blew the box up – to discover it was full of leaflets on how to deal with suspicious-looking packages.

\* \* \*

Because a hunt saboteurs' demonstration was anticipated, Police Constable John Dawson was briefed to attend the Buccleuch Hunt in the Scottish Borders. He set off on his mission, drove round a bend near Hawick, saw the huntsmen in full flight, and ran over the fox.

## February

On the weekend of 13–14 February, a man, unnamed in press reports, was heading for Toulouse on a TGV high-speed train. The train's lavatory had a voracious drainage system which swallowed the man's wallet with a triumphant snap as he was bending to adjust his clothing. As the man tried to retrieve his wallet, the loo's jaws clamped savagely round his wrist. Somehow, he managed to pull the alarm and the train screeched to a half near Tours. Firemen had to destroy the vicious appliance with metal cutters. France's television viewers saw the unfortunate traveller being carried away on a stretcher, his wallet in one hand and the lavatory bowl still wrapped around his wrist.

## March

After his house in Tabot Woods, Bournemouth, had been burgled three times, David Dower was determined to be a model of crime prevention. So, before attending the England–Scotland rugby match at Twickenham, he fitted an alarm and left a dummy reclining on his sofa. On his return, he was confronted by both a broken front door and the police. His alarm had gone off accidentally and the police, thinking the dummy was a corpse, had smashed their way in.

## April

On 22 April, neighbours ignored a blaze at the Bermondsey studios where the television series *London's Burning* is filmed – they thought the conflagration was part of the show. When fire crews arrived at the four-storey building to tackle the outbreak, the same residents complained about the noise.

## May

At the beginning of May, Darryl Hayes, the manager of a furniture store, was too late to pay the day's £3,000 takings into the bank, so he stashed the money in a leather wallet which he put at the back of his microwave oven at home in Torbay, Devon, to keep it safe from thieves. That evening Darryl's fiancée, Jane Butlin, forgot about the money, put some sprouts in the oven to cook and switched it on. The metal strips in the notes turned red hot, ignited the paper and reduced the cash to ash. The sprouts were fine.

\* \* \*

Two weeks later, detectives called to a disturbance outside a pub in Southampton found a severed ear, which they packed in ice and popped into the police station fridge. When the ear's 23-year-old owner rang them the next day, he was told that it was too late: the ear had 'gone off'. Detective Inspector Ray Burt said: 'Unfortunately, it had been there too long. It was next to an egg roll and that had gone off as well, so there was nothing we could do.'

## September

In Bolivia, 150 football-mad villagers let off fireworks to celebrate their country's

3–1 win over Uruguay. Unfortunately, the bangers landed on the thatched roofs of their houses and burned down 40 buildings.

\* \* \*

In Dublin, Father Sean O'Leary jumped up and down as he urged his choir to put more effort into singing the hymn 'I Wonder Where I'm Bound'. An iron grid collapsed under his weight and he disappeared into a heating duct.

### October

On 12 October, a woman driver had her handbag snatched from her car as she was waiting at traffic lights in Birmingham. Apoplectic with rage, she revved up her Mercedes and gave chase to the thieves. The thieves dropped the bag, and she got out of the car to retrieve it. As she picked the bag up, they leapt into her car and drove away in it, leaving her stranded.

### November

Lelli Ellul decided to smuggle four baby moustache parrots, worth £8,000, from Thailand to Australia. On arriving at Adelaide airport, he switched the birds from his suitcase to his underpants. When customs officers heard chirping noises emanating from Ellul's trouser fly, they searched him. He was fined £10,000.

### December

Residents gathered in their apartment block in Rome to protest against their landlord's refusal to conduct repairs – and were injured when the floor gave way beneath them.

\* \* \*

Kurt Kubler was hired, at a wage of £700 a week, as an efficiency expert by council officials in Mannheim. His first suggestion was by way of a joke: 'Sack me,' he said. They did.

## Reflections

\*   Do we feel better?!
    How might we have reacted in these situations?!
    Do the victims get our sympathy?!

# 6  It was a very bad year ... (2)

## Introduction

Another selection of true stories, recorded month by month, from one year's news. Fate's fickle finger not only visited misfortune on some, it made them look utterly ridiculous.

# Reading

*It was a very bad year ... (2)*

### January

The hospital attached to the Weifang Medical Institute in the Chinese city of Shangdong invited a television crew to film its first attempt at open-heart surgery. Unfortunately, nurses mixed up the medical records of two young boys. Liu Dalong and Xu Tong; so the one who had been admitted for a tonsillectomy had open-heart surgery while the critically ill boy had his tonsils removed by a trainee surgeon.

* * *

Ornithologists were excited by the arrival in Gosport, Hampshire, of a hoopoe, a foot-long bird which normally leaves its Mediterranean quarters to winter in Africa. Several twitchers actually managed to see the bird, but hundreds more had their hopes dashed when the rare visitor was killed by a local tomcat.

* * *

Four hundred and fifty top seismologists were attending a conference on earthquakes in Wellington, New Zealand, when a quake measuring 4.4 on the Richter scale took place. About half of them failed to notice: 'Apparently, one or two delegates thought it was just the cleaners,' commented an organiser.

### February

Bill Kale of Hibbing, Minnesota, was wandering home after having downed four cans of medium-strength lager when he started to feel 'pretty snoozy'. He broke into the nearest available house, climbed the stairs and leapt on to a bed. This turned out to be a folding bed which immediately snapped shut, trapping Mr Kale within. 'The thing was like a shark.' he said later. 'I couldn't move. I tried to cry out, but my face was wedged into the mattress so nobody could hear.' Five days later, the householders returned from a holiday to discover Mr Kale, trapped, dehydrated and delirious.

### March

Six masked raiders ambushed an armoured security van carrying a million pounds a Crawley near Winchester, forced it off the road and burned a two-foot hole in its side with blow torches. Alas for them, thousands of banknotes were burnt to ashes while further bundles were left unusable, damaged by the smoke and heat. The robbers fled empty-handed.

### April

A man suffering from amnesia walked into a police station in Hanau, Germany, and asked officers to find out who he was. Minutes later he was behind bars after detectives identified him as Manfred Bissiner, wanted on fraud charges.

* * *

Paul Rose, 16, from Romsey, Hampshire, who had been given crutches after spraining his ankle in a football match, was reaching for the doorhandle in the door's surgery when another patient opened the door and sent him flying, breaking his ankle. He had to spend six weeks in plaster.

## May

Chinese acrobat Ke Wang walked 27 miles on his hands in a romantic bid to propose to his girlfriend. The latter was reportedly 'impressed' when she heard about the walk, but got tired of waiting and married a local suitor instead. 'It took me 37 days. I guess that was too long,' mused Ke Wang. The girl's parents were said to be delighted with her decision, as they belied Ke Wang to be 'too unstable'.

* * *

A Brazilian artist tried a similar ruse. He tried to win back his girlfriend by walking nine miles on his knees, cushioning his kneecaps with pieces of car tyre. After 14 hours, Marcio da Silva, 21, arrived at the home of his beloved, Katia de Nascimento, 19. She had left the house to avoid seeing him.

## June

After 226 days underground, a 73-yer-old miner emerged from a pit in Colorado, thinking that he had achieved a new best for the *Guinness Book of Records*, only to be told that the record was, in fact, 463 days.

## July

The Disastrous Wedding of the Year award goes to Kirk Wilson and Sara Manners. During Sara's hen night, her mother's camera developed a fault and none of the pictures came out. On the morning of the wedding in Bundall, Norfolk, Jonathan Manners, the bride's brother and chief usher, fainted in the heat and had to be supported throughout the ceremony by his mother. At the reception, the icing on the wedding cake melted and the top tier collapsed, falling upside down on the floor. When the bride arrived at the honeymoon suite of their Norwich hotel, the roses in her bouquet triggered an asthma attack an she discovered she had not packed her inhaler. At 3 am she was rushed to hospital with her husband holding an oxygen bottle, but she was able to return to the hotel for breakfast. Later that morning, the groom's brother, James Wilson, drove the newlyweds to Stansted airport for their flight to the Canary Islands. His car caught fire as he pulled into the airport car park and they had to douse the engine with cans of cold drink. Meanwhile, the wedding video, still inside the camcorder, had been stolen in a burglary at a friend's house in Blofield. They are, however, still married.

* * *

An undertaker had driven his hearse 560 miles on his journey from the western German town of Bottrop to a funeral in Zagreb, Croatia, when a colleague telephoned him at the Austro–German border and pointed out that he had forgotten the body.

### September

David Johnson escaped from a low-security jail in September. At first, things went well and he managed to get a lift in a police petrol car; it was during the second ride he picked up that his world fell apart. 'I hope you don't mind, but I'm an escaped prisoner,' he told the driver, one Steve Wynder. 'Not if you don't mind that I'm a prison officer,' replied Mr Wynder. Mr Johnson was soon back behind bars.

### October

Three hundred tons of sand put down to make a new bathing beach at Burnham-on-Crouch, Essex, disappeared when the tide went out.

### November

John Cook returned home to Nelson, New Zealand, from a holiday in America to find that his wooden five-bedroom house had been stolen; not a trace of it anywhere.

* * *

A disabled woman was stranded in a car for four days in California's San Fernando Valley when her husband forgot where he had left it.

### December

Raiders stole 200 training shoes from a sports shop in Alfreton, Derbyshire. They may be hard pressed to find a ready market: the shoes were all left-footed.

## Reflections

* Are we cheered up?!
  Do you feel sorry for any of these people?!
  Wait – what might be just around the corner for any one of us?!

# 7 Humility

## Introduction

We've probably all come across someone who thinks they know-it-all. Or the arrogant person who boasts of their successes and won't admit to failure. Perhaps when we meet such a person we wish something would happen to teach them a little humility.

Listen to the following story of revenge.

# Reading

## *The Conjurer's Revenge*

'Now, ladies and gentlemen,' said the conjurer, 'having shown you that the cloth is absolutely empty, I will proceed to take from it a bowl of goldfish. Presto!'

All around the hall people were saying, 'Oh, how wonderful! How does he do it?'

But the Quick Man on the front seat said in a big whisper to the people near him, He – had – it – up – his – sleeve.'

Then the people nodded brightly at the Quick Man and said, 'Oh, of course', and everybody whispered round the hall, 'He – had – it – up – his – sleeve.'

'My next trick,' said the conjurer, 'is the famous Hindustani rings. You will notice that the rings are apparently separate; at a blow they all join (clang, clang, clang) – Presto!'

There was a general buzz of stupefaction till the Quick Man was heard to whisper, 'He – must – have – had – another – lot – up – his – sleeve.'

Again everybody nodded and whispered, 'The – rings – were – up – his – sleeve.'

The brow of the conjurer was clouded with a gathering frown.

'I will now,' he continued, 'show you a most amusing trick by which I am enabled to take any number of eggs from a hat. Will some gentleman kindly lend me his hat? Ah, thank you – Presto!'

He extracted seventeen eggs, and for thirty-five seconds the audience began to think that he was wonderful. Then the Quick Man whispered along the front bench, 'He – has – a – hen – up – his – sleeve,' and all the people whispered it on. 'He – has – a – lot – of – hens – up – his – sleeve.'

The egg trick was ruined.

It went on like that all through. It transpired from the whispers of the Quick Man that the conjurer must have concealed up his sleeve, in addition to the rings hens, and fish, several packs of cards, a loaf of bread, a doll's cradle, a live guinea-pig, a fifty-cent piece, and a rocking-chair.

The reputation of the conjurer was rapidly sinking below zero. At the close of the evening he rallied for a final effort.

'Ladies and gentlemen,' he said, 'I will present to you, in conclusion, the famous Japanese trick recently invented by the natives of Tipperary. Will you, sir,' he continued, turning toward the Quick Man, 'will you kindly hand me your gold watch?'

It was passed to him.

'Have I your permission to put it into this mortar and pound it to pieces?' he asked savagely.

The Quick Man nodded and smiled.

The conjurer threw the watch into the mortar and grasped a sledge hammer from the table. There was a sound of violent smashing, 'He's – slipped – it – up – his – sleeve,' whispered the Quick Man.

'Now, sir,' continued the conjurer, 'will you allow me to take your handkerchief and punch holes in it? Thank you. You see, ladies and gentlemen, there is no deception; the holes are visible to the eye.'

The face of the Quick Man beamed. This time the real mystery of the thing fascinated him.

'And now, sir, will you kindly pass me your silk hat and allow me to dance on it? Thank you.'

The conjurer made a few rapid passes with his feet and exhibited the hat crushed beyond recognition.

'And will you now, sir, take off your celluloid collar and permit me to burn it in the candle? Thank you, sir. And will you allow me to smash your spectacles for you with my hammer? Thank you.'

By this time the features of the Quick Man were assuming a puzzled expression. 'This thing beats me,' he whispered. 'I don't see through it a bit.'

There was a great hush upon the audience. Then the conjurer drew himself up to his full height and, with a withering look at the Quick Man, he concluded:

'Ladies and gentlemen, you will observe that I have, with this gentleman's permission, broken his watch, burnt his collar, smashed his spectacles, and danced on his hat. If he will give me the further permission to paint green stripes on his overcoat, or to tie his suspenders in a knot, I shall be delighted to entertain you. If not, the performance is at an end.'

And amid a glorious burst of music from the orchestra the curtain fell, and the audience dispersed, convinced that there are some tricks, at any rate, that are not done up the conjurer's sleeve.

## Reflections

* At what point in the story did you guess how the revenge might come? Clearly a story in which we are – like the conjurer's audience – satisfied that the Quick Man has got his come-uppance. Here is an occasion when the practical joke has its place; sometimes it just doesn't.

* And this is also a tale which does give us pause for thought on the subject of humility. Some people in any community are naturally good at many things and enjoy great success. Some will be arrogant with that success while others will be a little more sensitive about things. It is right to celebrate achievement and success, but not if that celebration becomes a way of putting down others. A touch of humility is usually quietly admired, while we tire of the Quick Men and Women.

# 8  Capturing animals

## Introduction

Artists of all kinds strive hard to capture – as well as they can – ideas and images from the world around them. It might be said they are constantly in search of truth. In the following passage, poet Ted Hughes describes a time when, for him, he really succeeded as a writer.

# Reading

## *Capturing Animals*

An animal I never succeeded in keeping alive is the fox. I was always frustrated: twice by a farmer, who killed cubs I had caught before I could get to them, and once by a poultry keeper who freed my cub while his dog waited. Years after those events I was sitting up late one snowy night in dreary lodgings in London. I had written nothing for a year or so but that night I got the idea I might write something and I wrote in a few minutes the following poem: the first 'animal' poem I ever wrote. Here it is – *The Thought-Fox*.


I imagine this midnight moment's forest:
Something else is alive
Beside the clock's loneliness
And this blank page where my fingers move,

Through the window I see no star:
Something more near
Though deeper within darkness
Is entering the loneliness:

Cold, delicately as the dark snow,
A fox's nose touches twig, leaf;
Two eyes serve a movement, that now
And again now, and now, and now

Sets neat prints into the snow
Between trees, and warily a lame
Shadow lags by stump and in hollow
Of a body that is bold to come

Across clearings, an eye,
A widening deepening greenness,
Brilliantly, concentratedly,
Coming about its own business

Till, with a sudden sharp hot stink of fox
It enters the dark hole of the head.
The window is starless still; the clock ticks,
The page is printed.

This poem does not have anything you could easily call a meaning. It is about a fox, obviously enough, but a fox that is both a fox and not a fox. What sort of a fox is it that can step right into my head where presumably it still sits ... smiling to itself when the dogs bark. It is both a fox and a spirit. It is a real fox; as I read the poem I see it move, I see it setting its prints, I see its shadow going over the irregular surface of the snow. The words show me all this, bringing it nearer and nearer. It is very real to me. The words have made a body for it and given it somewhere to walk.

If, at the time of writing this poem, I had found livelier words, words that could give me much more vividly its movements, the twitch and craning of its ears the slight tremor of its hanging tongue and its breath making little clouds, its teeth bared in the cold, the snow-crumbs dropping from its pads as it lifts each one in turn, if I could have got the words for all this, the fox would probably be even more real and alive to me now, than it is as I read the poem. Still, it is there as it is. If I had not caught the real fox there in the words I would never have saved the poem. I would have thrown it into the wastepaper basket as I have thrown so many other hunts that did not get what I was after. As it is, every time I read the poem the fox comes up again out of the darkness and steps into my head. And I suppose that long after I am gone, as long as a copy of the poem exists, every time anyone reads it the fox will get up somewhere out in the darkness and come walking towards them.

So, you see, in some ways my fox is better than an ordinary fox. It will live for ever, it will never suffer from hunger or hounds. I have it with me wherever I go. And I made it. And all through imagining it clearly enough and finding the living words.

*Ted Hughes*

# Reflections

\*    'Till, with a sudden sharp hot stink of fox
      It enters the dark hole of the head.'

With these lines from the poem Ted Hughes skilfully describes how a writer's imagination suddenly grasps something which he has been wrestling with for some time. He reminds us that the painter, the sculptor, the musician, the poet – all encounter these magic, rare moments when they are trying hard to create something which others will then enjoy and appreciate.

\*    The following poem – often read by Ted Hughes at poetry readings – draws a neat parallel between the work of a writer and the work of a cat as they both go about their respective tasks. Think carefully about the words here.

## Pangur Bán

*Written by a student of the monastery of Carinthia on a copy of St Paul's Epistles, in the eighth century*

I and Pangur Bán, my cat,
'Tis a like task we are at;
Hunting mice is his delight,
Hunting words I sit all night.

Better far than praise of men
'Tis to sit with book and pen;
Pangur bears me no ill-will,
He too plies his simple skill.

'Tis a merry thing to see
At our tasks how glad are we,
When at home we sit and find
Entertainment to our mind.

Oftentimes a mouse will stray
In the hero Pangur's way;
Oftentimes my keen thought set
Takes a meaning in its net.

'Gainst the wall he sets his eye
Full and fierce and sharp and sly;
'Gainst the wall of knowledge I
All my little wisdom try.

When a mouse darts from its den,
O how glad is Pangur then!
O what gladness do I prove
When I solve the doubts I love!

So in peace our tasks we ply,
Pangur Bán, my cat, and I;
In our arts we find our bliss,
I have mine and he has his.

Practice every day has made
Pangur perfect in his trade;
I get wisdom day and night
Turning darkness into light.

*Anon (from the Gaelic; trans. Robin Flower)*

\*   Success, the poem hints, comes in various shapes and forms:

'In our arts we find our bliss,
I have mine and he has his.'

# 9 The road not taken

## Introduction

Throughout our lives we face choices and decisions which take us in one direction rather than another. Some choices we make lead to success, others to failure. From time to time we look back on particular decisions and wonder whether they were the right ones. Would things have been different if …?

These two poems develop these ideas.

## Reading

*The Road Not Taken*

Two roads diverged in a yellow wood,
And sorry I could not travel both

And be one traveler, long I stood
And looked down one as far as I could
To where it bent in the undergrowth;

Then took the other, as just as fair,
And having perhaps the better claim,
Because it was grassy and wanted wear:
Though as for that the passing there
Had worn them really about the same,

And both that morning equally lay
In leaves no step had trodden black.
Oh, I kept the first for another day!
Yet knowing how way leads on to way,
I doubted if I should ever come back.

I shall be telling this with a sigh
Somewhere ages and ages hence:
Two roads diverged in a wood, and I –
I took the one less traveled by,
And that has made all the difference.

*Robert Frost*

## The Choosing

We were first equal Mary and I
with the same coloured ribbons in mouse-coloured hair,
and with equal shyness
we curtsied to the lady councillor
for copies of Collins Children's Classics.
First equal, equally proud.

Best friends too Mary and I
a common bond in being cleverest (equal)
in our small school's small class,
I remember
the competition for top desk
or to read aloud the lesson
at school service.
And my terrible fear
of her superiority at sums.

I remember the housing scheme
Where we both stayed.
The same house, different homes,
where the choices were made.

I don't know exactly why they moved,
but anyway they went.
Something about a three-apartment
and a cheaper rent.
But from the top deck of the high-school bus

I'd glimpse among the others on the corner
Mary's father, mufflered, contrasting strangely
with the elegant greyhounds by his side.

He didn't believe in high-school education,
especially for girls,
or in forking out for uniforms.

Ten years later on a Saturday –
I am coming home from the library –
sitting near me on the bus,
Mary
with a husband who is tall,
curly haired, has eyes
for no one else but Mary.
Her arms are round the full-shaped vase
that is her body.
Oh, you can see where the attraction lies
in Mary's life –
not that I envy her, really.

And I am coming from the library
with my arms full of books.
I think of the prizes that were ours for the taking
and wonder when the choices got made
we don't remember making.

*Liz Lochhead*

## Reflections

* What do you think prompted these two poems? What might have happened
  to the poets in their own lives to lead them to write as they have?
  Robert Frost, while travelling alone, stood at a fork in the road, undecided
  which path to take. He indicates that the road he chose is in fact the only road
  he could have taken – and that has shaped his life.
  In *The Choosing* two friends grew up together but somewhere along the way
  made particular choices that have led them towards rather different adult lives.
  Do we detect a note of regret, envy, missed opportunity in either poem?
  A key part of our growth as human beings is learning to live with the decisions we make, whether they prove to lead on to successful or less successful
  outcomes.

# 10 If ...

## Introduction

It is often said that the Devil has the best tunes – in other words, living a morally
good, blameless life is beyond the reach of most of us. To err is to be human.

Temptation to break with what we know is right is all around us every day of our lives. The purpose of formal education, it is argued, is as much about helping young people develop a moral code of conduct as it is about passing academic examinations.

The following celebrated poem by Rudyard Kipling was written about a century ago, and still rings very true today. It repeats the word *If* and moves towards a conclusion that suggests *if* we can face up to certain challenges through life, we'll be successful and fulfilled human beings. He was addressing the poem to a boy – and, by implication, *all* young people.

# Reading

*If ...*

If you can keep your head when all about you
Are losing theirs and blaming it on you,
If you can trust yourself when all men doubt you,
But make allowance for their doubting too;
If you can wait and not be tired by waiting,
Or being lied about, don't deal in lies,
Or being hated, don't give way to hating,
And yet don't look too good, nor talk too wise:

If you can dream – and not make dreams your master;
If you can think – and not make thoughts your aim;
If you can meet with Triumph and Disaster
And treat those two imposters just the same;
If you can bear to hear the truth you've spoken
Twisted by knaves to make a trap for fools,
Or watch the things you gave your life to, broken,
And stoop and build 'em up with worn-out tools:

If you can make one heap of all your winnings
And risk it on one turn of pith-and-toss,
And lose, and start again at your beginnings
And never breathe a word about your loss;
If you can force your heart and nerve and sinew
To serve your turn long after they are gone,
And so hold on when there is nothing in you
Except the Will which says to them: 'Hold on!'

If you can talk with crowds and keep your virtue,
Or walk with Kings – nor lose the common touch,
If neither foes nor loving friends can hurt you,
If all men count with you, but none too much;
If you can fill the unforgiving minute
With sixty seconds' worth of distance run,
Yours is the Earth and everything that's in it,
And – which is more – you'll be a Man, my son!

*Rudyard Kipling*

# Reflections

* Do you agree with the qualities he admires? What others might you add? Are there any thoughts you don't particularly agree with?
Probably the most often quoted lines of the poem are:

'If you can meet with Triumph and Disaster
And treat those two impostors just the same'

They are two lines worth learning to say to yourself, whether on the sports field or at the end of an argument with parents!

* Here is a more contemporary working of Kipling's ideas; again, reflect carefully on the words and see if you agree with them.

## *Children Learn What They Live*

If children live with criticism
   they learn to condemn
If children live with hostility
   they learn to fight
If children live with ridicule
   they learn to be shy
If children live with shame
   they learn to feel guilty
If children live with tolerance
   they learn to be patient
If children live with encouragement
   they learn confidence
If children live with praise
   they learn to appreciate
If children live with fairness
   they learn justice
If children live with security
   they learn to have faith
If children live with approval
   they learn to like themselves
If children live with acceptance and friendship
   they learn to find love in the world.

# International Scenes

*The old law of an eye for an eye leaves everybody blind.*

*Things fall apart; the centre cannot hold;*
*Mere anarchy is loosed upon the world,*
*The blood-dimmed tide is loosed and everywhere*
*The ceremony of innocence is drowned.*

W. B. Yeats

# 1 Poverty as pornography

## Introduction

For information about other parts of the world we tend to rely on what we see on television or film. Travel abroad of course gives us an opportunity to see and feel first-hand how other cultures work and flourish.

But have you thought about the kinds of images that TV tends to promote about certain countries or continents? What comes into your mind when the following are mentioned – Australia? Japan? Jamaica? Bangladesh? Ethiopia?

The following passage comes from a newspaper column previewing a television programme. It is critical of how the media generally present the Developing (Third) World.

## Reading

*Poverty as pornography*

Oxfam will be filling the *Open Space* slot on BBC 2 with a programme that challenges the media's use of images of starvation. In 'Framing the Famine', it asks whether the desperate, negative images of starving children and poverty-stricken people that are coming out of Africa do not, in fact degrade their subjects – victims first of famine and then of the camera lens – thereby doing more harm than good.

Commentators such as Jon Snow, Lenny Henry and Michael Buerk will question the value, even under the guise of information, of programmes that suggest millions of Africans have no place or power in the world, except as bearers of a begging bowl proffered towards the West. Such programmes may extract a few hundred thousand pounds, just as charity concerts and telethons extract a few million, but this is small help beside the vastness of the need. It serves to salve the conscience of the givers, but does nothing to stimulate long-term economic change.

Can concerts or images – especially beautiful, harrowing images – ever *change* anything? And if you reply, that is not the job of the media ... it is up to the politicians/aid agencies/charities/climate to change, I would answer: in that case, why show such programmes at all?

Even if we accept the need for news reports about Third World catastrophes, many documentaries move swiftly beyond information to an indulgent exploitation of those they purport to pity. In much the same vein, a new and worrying sort of programme is becoming more frequent. A recent film about street violence in Brazil was one particularly horrific example among many. Blurbed as 'a disturbing documentary journey though poverty, crime and violence', it had little commentary, offered no hope and no conclusion and seemed merely to cater to the 'there but for the grace of God go I' mentality.

Viewers comfortably ensconced on their sofas at home were regaled with photogenic details of the brutality of the lives of Brazil's urban poor. Behold – cue for close-up – this 12-year-old's amputated leg. See this emaciated dog in its death throes. Observe the moment of decapitation, as a bullock is sacrificed. Shudder at the faeces-filled streams that run through the shanty town, displayed in a lingering, arty camera shot.

These programmes do not appeal for my help, either in purse or person. They offer no solutions, and indeed, it is impossible to think of any. The lives depicted are usually the inescapable result of over-crowded cities, over-fertile families living in slums without access to family planning; low or non-existent incomes leading to high crime rates; poor educational facilities leading to a thriving drug culture; drugs and crime both producing a gun-toting underworld; the whole producing police brutality. At what point can this vicious circle be interrupted, least of all by me? Will they be seen by the police or politicians of these tortured communities? You bet your life they won't.

What, then, is the purpose of these beautifully filmed programmes about street crime in Buenos Aires or Rio de Janeiro; prostitution in Bangkok or the Philippines; beggars in Bombay? Can it be that viewers revel in the smugness of knowing they belong to the fortunate quarter of the globe?

In my case, the only consequence is guilt: for having watched, and more importantly, for being helpless. I cannot affect these lives, not unless I abandon mine and travel to countries whose languages I do not speak and whose customs I do not know. I cannot even affect, by more than a handful of small change, the lives of *London's* street poor. Am I any the better for knowing that a child dies violently – was it every 90 seconds or every 90 minutes? – on the streets of Rio?

This guilt merely blankets me in impotent despair. I can support Amnesty or Oxford or the Red Cross; I can educate an orphan child or two: but these programmes do not solicit such actions. They are nothing but the pornography of poverty. I resolve not to watch any more.

*Angela Lambert*

# Reflections

* The journalist – feeling 'guilt' and 'despair' – has some strong words at the end:

'They are nothing but the pornography of poverty.'

She is clearly expressing a view that much of our television tends to indulge in highlighting scenes of poverty, to the exclusion of presenting other more positive images of Developing countries.

There is also the deeply-held viewpoint – which most of us probably share when we see child poverty – that we are pretty helpless to do anything about it. And we become rather careless about such statistics as to whether in the streets of Rio de Janeiro a child dies violently every 90 seconds or 90 minutes.

The journalist Angela Lambert resolves not to watch any more. What is our response? How can we make ourselves better informed about some of these global scenes? How can we avoid creating in our minds certain stereotypical images of people living in different countries of our world?

# 2 Blood and belonging

## Introduction

Turning on our television for the 6, 7 or 10 o'clock news each evening we might be forgiven for thinking that much of the world is at war. Not a day goes by without our seeing on our screens a reporter, clad in battle-dress, speaking against the backcloth of tanks and gunfire.

Have you asked yourself the question why nations continue to fight other nations, or why groups within a country seem to find it impossible to live peacefully alongside one another?

Here is how one writer about international affairs concludes his book on this subject. The book has an interesting title – *Blood and Belonging* – and recounts the writer's travels around the world to try and find out why nations go to war. He visited the former Yugoslavia, Germany, Quebec, Kurdistan, Ukraine and Belfast.

## Reading

### Blood and belonging

Throughout my travels, I kept remembering the scene in *Romeo and Juliet* when Juliet is whispering to herself on the balcony in her nightgown, unaware that Romeo is in the shadows listening. She is struggling to understand what it means for her, a Capulet, to fall in love with a Montague. Suddenly she exclaims,

'Tis but thy name, that is my enemy;
Thou art thyself though not a Montague.
What's a Montague? it is not hand, nor foot
Nor arm, nor face, nor any other part
Belonging to a man. O! be some other name:
What's in a name?

In the front lines of Bosnia, in the estates of Loyalist and Republican Belfast, in all the places where the tribal gangsters – the Montagues and Capulets of our day – are enforcing the laws of ethnic loyalty, there are Juliets and Romeos who still cry out 'Oh, let me not be a Croatian, Serbian, Bosnian, Catholic or Protestant. Let me only be myself.'

Being only yourself is what ethnic nationalism will not allow. When people come, by terror or exaltation, to think of themselves as patriots first, individuals second, they have embarked on a path of ethical abdication.

Yet everywhere, in Belfast, in Belgrade and Zagreb, in Lvov, in Quebec and Kurdistan, I encountered men and women, often proud patriots, who have stubbornly resisted embarking on that path. Their first loyalty has remained to themselves. Their first cause is not the nation, but the defence of their right to choose their own frontiers for their belonging.

But such people are an embattled minority. The world is not run by sceptics and ironists, but by gunmen and true believers and the new world they are bequeathing to the next century already seems a more violent and desperate place than I could ever have imagined. If I had supposed, as the Cold War came to an end, that the new world might be ruled by philosophers and poets, it was because I believed, foolishly, that the precarious civility and order of the states in which I live must be what all people rationally desire. Now I am not so sure. I began the journey as a liberal, and I end as one, but I cannot help thinking that liberal civilization – the rule of laws not men, of argument in place of force, of compromise in place of violence – runs deeply against the human grain and is only achieved and sustained by the most unremitting struggle against human nature. The liberal virtues – tolerance, compromise, reason – remain as valuable as ever, but they cannot be preached to those who are mad with fear or mad with vengeance. In any case, preaching always rings hollow. We must be prepared to defend them by force, and the failure of the sated, cosmopolitan nations to do so has left the hungry nations sick with contempt for us.

Between the hungry and the sated nations, there is an impassable barrier of incomprehension. I've lived all my life in sated nation states, in places which have no outstanding border disputes, are no longer ruled by foreigners or oppressors, are masters in their own house. Sated people can afford to be cosmopolitan; sated people can afford the luxury of condescending to the passions of the hungry. But among the Crimean Tartars, the Kurds and the Crees, I met the hungry ones, peoples whose very survival will remain at risk until they achieve self-determination, whether in their own nation state or in someone else's.

What's wrong with the world is not nationalism itself. Every people must have a home, every such hunger must be assuaged. What's wrong is the kind of nation, the kind of home that nationalists want to create and the means they use to seek their ends. A struggle is going on wherever I went between those who still believe that a nation should be a home to all, and that race, colour, religion and creed should be no bar to belonging, and those who want their nation to be home only to their own. It's the battle between the civic and the ethnic nation. I know which side I'm on. I also know which side, right now, happens to be winning.

*Michael Ignatieff*

# Reflections

\* Michael Ignatieff reminds us that thriving countries – wherever they are on our planet – need to celebrate the liberal virtues of tolerance, compromise, reason. In our own local communities we must remember that these are equally important watchwords.

He feels it is important that people live where they can feel secure about their identity, and that race, colour, religion, creed should not be obstacles. Yet the reality is that, all around the world, he encountered in his travels groups who wanted their nation to be, as he puts it, 'home only to their own'.

Michael Ignatieff is not optimistic in his conclusion. But it is vital that in our own school community we should – remembering *Romeo and Juliet* – encourage the Capulets and the Montagues to live side by side. Even if some international scenes constantly present us with conflict, there are many others where people of all different backgrounds flourish in one community. Future gener-

ations need to strive hard to ensure that the virtues of compromise and tolerance win over intolerance and violence.

# 3 Zlata's Diary

## Introduction

Many young people around the world have their childhood almost taken away
from them by war. They grow old before their time. At the same time young eyes
see scenes of war with great sharpness and, throughout history, have written
powerfully about their experiences. *The Diary of Anne Frank* from the Second
World War (1939–45) is one celebrated example.

The following extracts are from *Zlata's Diary*, the writings of an 11-year-old girl
caught up in the war in former Yugoslavia. She lived at this time in the city of
Sarajevo and the name she gives to her diary is 'Mimmy'.

## Reading

*Zlata's Diary*

*Monday, 20 April 1992*

Dear Mimmy,

War is no joke, it seems. It destroys, kills, burns, separates, brings unhappiness.
Terrible shells fell today on Baščaršija, the old town centre. Terrible explosions.
We went down into the cellar, the cold, dark, revolting cellar. And ours isn't even
all that safe. Mummy, Daddy and I just stood there, holding on to each other in a
corner which looked safe. Standing there in the dark, in the warmth of my parents' arms, I thought about leaving Sarajevo. Everybody is thinking about it, and
so am I. I couldn't bear to go alone, to leave behind Mummy and Daddy,
Grandma and Grandad. And going with just Mummy isn't any good either. The
best would be for all three of us to go. But Daddy can't? So I've decided we
should stay here together. Tomorrow I'll tell Keka that you have to be brave and
stay with those you love and those who love you. I can't leave my parents, and I
don't like the other idea of leaving my father behind alone either.

Yours Zlata

*Thursday, 7 May 1992*

Dear Mimmy,

I was almost positive the war would stop, but today … Today a shell fell on the
park in front of my house, the park where I used to play with my girlfriends. A lot
of people were hurt. From what I hear Jaca, Jaca's mother, Selma, Nina, our neighbour Dado and who knows how many other people who happened to be there
were wounded. Dada, Jaca and her mother have come home from hospital, Selma

lost a kidney but I don't know how she is, because she's still in hospital. AND NINA IS DEAD. A piece of shrapnel lodged in her brain and she died. She was such a sweet, nice little girl. We went to kindergarten together, and we used to play together in the park. It is possible I'll never see Nina again? Nina, an innocent eleven-year-old little girl – the victim of a stupid war. I feel sad. I cry and wonder why? She didn't do anything. A disgusting war has destroyed a young child's life. Nina, I'll always remember you as a wonderful little girl.

Love, Mimmy,

Zlata

*Wednesday, 13 May 1992*

Dear Mimmy,

Life goes on. The past is cruel, and that's exactly why we should forget it.

The present is cruel too and I can't forget it. There's no joking with war. My present reality is the cellar, fear, shells, fire.

Terrible shooting broke out the night before last. We were afraid that we might be hit by shrapnel or a bullet, so we ran over to the Bobars'. We spent all of that night, the next day and the next night in the cellar and in Nedo's flat. (Nedo is a refugee from Grbavica. He left his parents and came here to his sister's empty flat.) We saw terrible scenes on TV. The town in ruins, burning, people and children being killed. It's unbelievable.

The phones aren't working, we haven't been able to find out anything about Grandma and Grandad, Melica, how people in other parts of town are doing. On TV we saw the place where Mummy works, Vodoprivreda, all in flames. It's on the aggressor's side of town (Grbavica). Mummy cried. She's depressed. All her years of work and effort – up in flames. It's really horrible. All around Vodoprivreda there were cars burning, people dying, and nobody could help them. God, why is this happening?

I'M SO MAD I WANT TO SCREAM AND BREAK EVERYTHING!

Your Zlata

*Sunday, 17 May 1992*

Dear Mimmy,

It's now definite: there's no more school. The war has interrupted our lessons, closed down the schools, sent children to cellars instead of classrooms. They'll give us the grades we got at the end of last term. So I'll get a report card saying I've finished fifth grade.

Ciao!

Zlata

*Wednesday, 27 May 1992*

Dear Mimmy,

SLAUGHTER! MASSACRE! HORROR! CRIME! BLOOD! SCREAMS! TEARS! DESPAIR!

That's what Vaso Miskin Street looks like today. Two shells exploded in the street and one in the market. Mummy was near by at the time. She ran to Grandma's and Grandad's. Daddy and I were beside ourselves because she hadn't come home. I saw some of it on TV but I still can't believe what I actually saw. It's unbelievable. I've got a lump in my throat and a knot in my tummy. HORRIBLE. They're taking the wounded to the hospital. It's a madhouse. We kept going to the window hoping to see Mummy, but she wasn't back. They released a list of the dead and wounded. Daddy and I were tearing our hair out. We didn't know what had happened to her. Was she alive? At 16.00, Daddy decided to go and check the hospital. He got dressed, and I got ready to go to the Bobars', so as not to stay at home alone. I looked out the window one more time and ... I SAW MUMMY RUNNING ACROSS THE BRIDGE. As she came into the house she started shaking and crying. Through her tears she told us how she had seen dismembered bodies. All the neighbours came because they had been afraid for her. Thank God, Mummy is with us. Thank God.

A HORRIBLE DAY, UNFORGETTABLE.

HORRIBLE! HORRIBLE!

Your Zlata

*Zlata Filipovic*

## Reflections

\*    The simplicity and clarity of Zlata's writing brings home the true horrors and immediacy of civil war – more than reading a journalist's account. Imagine our own local streets turned into the kind of battle-zone Zlata witnessed in Sarajevo – a city in fact only about 800 miles from us.

The fact that so many of the world's children have their everyday lives completely taken over by war must make us value afresh those things around us which we take for granted. Having school abruptly shut down may seem appealing – but the death of a friend and wondering whether your family can cross the street without being shot is quite another thought.

\*    Zlata cannot help pondering the futility of it all – 'I cry and wonder why ... There's no joking with war'.

Our thoughts should be with all children caught up in war, wherever they may be in the world.

# 4 Refugees

## Introduction

A recent international report presented a staggering statistic. It estimated that about 25 million of the world's people could be described as refugees – having been displaced within their own country or moved across frontiers into other countries. The dictionary defines a refugee as a person who has fled from some danger or problem, especially political persecution. It is a striking feature of our contemporary world that the numbers of refugees continue to increase.

Here is an extract from a play about Mirad, a 13-year-old boy who is a refugee living in Holland. He has fled from a place called Foça, in Bosnia. At this point in the play his Aunt Fazila and Uncle Djuka (also refugees in Holland) are reading something Mirad has written about his father.

# Reading

## *Mirad, a boy from Bosnia*

*Fazila.*    Nunspeet, 29th September 1992.
Dear Sir,
I am Mirad Balic from Foca.
You asked me to write down what happened
to my father.
That's what I am going to do for you now.
Please excuse my handwriting
because I tremble a bit sometimes.
That is because of the war.
In school in Foca I didn't tremble at all.
The last time I saw my father
was on the 6th July.
After that nobody saw him
because he didn't exist any more.
That day we were taken out of the prison
that we had been put in some days before.
When the Serbs took Foca,
we didn't get anything to eat,
only some water
and we were beaten up many times.
I knew one of the guards,
he used to be our neighbour.
The second night
some of the men were taken outside
and beaten terribly with sticks,
gunbutts and chains.
My father was one of them
and he told me
that our neighbour had beaten him with an iron
stick on the soles of his feet.
The man used to be friendly and polite.
My father couldn't understand,
nor could I.

*Djuka.*    That day about fifty men and boys
were taken for a 'technical expedition',
they said.
We walked out of the city
and reached a field full of clover.
We had to stand next to each other
and join hands.

Then the Serbs told us to walk slowly
into the clover-field.
Suddenly one of the prisoners,
Mister Poljac,
the father of my friend Ante,
cried out: 'Don't do it, don't go,
the field is heavily mined.'
As he cried out he was shot.
Nobody was allowed to pick him up.
Not even Ante.
Then we walked into the mined field.
Never before had I been so afraid,
not all my life,
because every step could be your last.
But I was most afraid for my father,
that he would step on a mine.
My father didn't walk beside me,
that was forbidden,
he was at a distance at the end of the line.
The line was a bit curved
so that I could see him.
I was glad about that.
And then it happened.
I looked at the ground
for I saw something small sticking out
and I was afraid it was a mine.
Then I heard a loud explosion.
Somebody had stepped on a mine.
I looked to my father
but all I saw
was a cloud of mud and blood.
I shouted 'Daddy'
and I ran without thinking
right over the field
to the spot where my father had walked.
Then, one right after another
there were more explosions.
Everybody wanted to run away in panic
but the Serbs were still behind us
and started to shoot with machine guns.
All over the field were dead bodies and wounded
people.
Some men were crying horribly
because their arms or legs had been blown off by a mine.
So the Serbs left the engine of their tank running,
very loudly,
so that nobody could hear the
shooting and crying any more.
They kept shooting until nobody walked

over the clover-field any more.
Then they left.
I was lying very still all the time,
as if I was shot at the first firing.
But also because I'd found the hand of my father,
the hand with the little finger
without a nail.
So I knew he was dead.
I felt dead too.
All the shooting and crying didn't bother me any
more.
I don't know how long I lay in the clover-field
holding my father's hand in my hand.
When it grew dark I stood up.
I buried my father's hand
and started walking.
Away from Foca.
Later I thought I could go to Sarajevo,
to Uncle Djuka and Aunt Fazila.

*Ad de Bont*

# Reflections

\* The horror of civil war – where neighbour turns upon neighbour – is brought home to us in this very moving account. Later in the play Mirad leaves Holland to return to Bosnia to search for his mother. In many ways it is the classic tale of a refugee, driven from his or her homeland by war, later returning to see whether any of their family has survived.

At another point in the play Uncle Djuka, finding himself feeling very alone in a strange new country, says:

'But I am no refugee
for I did not flee.
I have been blown away
like a leaf from a tree …

Refugees are never welcome.
Nowhere.
Everybody knows that.
History has proven it so often.
Why should you flee then?

Why a slow death in a strange country
if you can die on the threshold
of your own home?
Refugees don't exist.
Only blown away people exist,
people blown by the wind
all over the world.'

# 5 Russia's railway children

## Introduction

Homelessness is a blight in so many societies, even and especially in those countries of the world which are rich in resources – like our own, or France, America, Canada, Australia. It is particularly in evidence in some of the world's capital cities; side by side with expensive hotels and palatial office blocks we can see young and old alike sleeping in doorways and on top of iron-grids through which hot air comes from subway trains.

Listen to the following report from a BBC correspondent based in Moscow.

## Reading

*Russia's railway children*

Suddenly there was a commotion behind me. A woman with a bruised face pushed forward. 'They beat us like dogs,' she sobbed, tugging at my arm. 'They do it every night. I just popped into the pay toilet at Yaroslav station, paid my ten roubles. When I lay down, in they came – the police – and dragged me out by the legs.' Her name was Roza. She was from Moscow, homeless after a spell in prison. The irony was that her only crime had been to be unemployed, which was against the law under the communist regime of the old Soviet Union. By the time she had emerged from prison, the Soviet Union had vanished and her crime with it. But that didn't help Roza: her Moscow flat had also been confiscated. All she could do was to join the down-and-outs at the stations. 'Tell the police not to beat us,' she pleaded, as she finished her tale.

I hadn't come to Kursk station at 11 o'clock at night only to talk to Roza and her unfortunate friends. I also wanted to meet the 'railway children' – the bands of Oliver Twist kids weaving in and out of the crowds of grown-ups, avoiding the gypsy families encamped in corners, and living their own secret station life. For that I needed a guide, 14-year-old Yasha – though he looked no more than ten. After two years' dossing as a vagrant, he had been picked up by Russian charity workers who persuaded him in swap his hideaway under the station stairs for a bed in a children's sanctuary. He was revisiting his old haunt with us by way of an outing. Yasha was small, wiry, with a big grin and quick eyes. The kindly ladies at the charity home warned us to keep an eye on purses and other valuables; Yasha, it seemed, was an experienced pickpocket. As we wandered past the fruit machines, Yasha explained how he had ended up living rough. He had run away from a mother who used to beat him and a father who was always drunk. There were hundreds and hundreds of kids at the stations, he said. They lived by stealing and selling ice-cream.

At that moment, 16-year-old Andrei strolled up. If Yasha looked like Oliver Twist, then sturdy Andrei was the Artful Dodger – surveying the world with a confident swagger in a jacket just a little too big for him. His pockets sagged from the weight of books – a Russian–English phrasebook on one side and a handy volume of science fiction on the other. Andrei proudly listed the merits of station life. He had negotiated a comfortable corner as a permanent bedroom; his education was in hand, since he was learning English and first aid from the charity doctors; and he had several lucrative jobs. 'Excuse me,' he added politely, 'but I must be off, or I'll be late for work.' Work, it turned out, was running a newspaper stall in the bustling, sordid underground passage near the railway tracks. As weary travellers discovered that their trains were late again, there was Andrei – smiling from ear to ear – waiting to proffer a well-thumbed magazine to while away the time.

Around the next corner, we stumbled on Garik, a small, stern boy of about ten. Garik was sitting on his holdall munching sunflower seeds. He had just smuggled his way up from Armenia, a stowaway on a plane. He was 16, he lied boldly, and was looking for a job. 'It's bad back there in Armenia,' he announced in his high-pitched, childish voice. 'They've cut down the trees and there's nothing to eat.' Garik was streetwise. To impress us, he pulled out a jackknife and two guns, letting his sleeve fall open to reveal several electronic watches wound round his arm like silver bangles.

If the Moscow police catch a boy like Garik, they take him to the police detention centre for homeless children; it is hated by the street gangs. I could see why; I had been there the day before: high concrete walls, topped with barbed wire, surround the bleak buildings; the staff are uniformed policemen and women; children with fleas and lice, and, worse, young girls with venereal disease are instantly put into quarantine. A policewoman in a steel-blue uniform unlocked the door in the girls' section to let us in. She locked the door again. Thin, obedient girls shuffled up in a crocodile and chanted, 'Hello.' Half had been deloused – their heads shaven bare like convicts'.

The chief warder pushed forward one tiny, angelic-looking girl with tufty brown hair and a clean, red dress. Ten-year-old Katya perched on a chair, dangled her feet and confessed her sins. 'I'm here for the fourth time,' she whispered. 'I was living at Kursk and Leningrad stations, but the police picked me up. Me and my friend, we were just having a look around. It's nice at the station,' she added wistfully, staring at the floor. 'We sleep in the trains; the police don't find us there. We buy things to eat and have a good time.'

At that, the warder interrupted: 'Go on, Katya, tell the lady what you're really like. Tell her you smoke and thieve and tell lies.' Yes, she did smoke, she admitted; she had started when she was seven. In a loud, disapproving voice, the warder went on: Katya had run away from her children's home so often that no orphanage would take her any more. Her mother was an alcoholic, a degenerate.

'No, she wasn't,' Katya objected.

'And Katya is the worst child in the orphanage,' the warder added.

'There's none worse than this little girl,' a second policewoman joined in. But they admitted that no one knew what to do with her. By law, she could stay locked up for no longer than a month. After that – wherever they sent her – she was sure to steal away to rejoin her station friends.

Back at Kursk station, young Garik from Armenia twisted his knife thoughtfully. 'It's not good here at night,' he volunteered. 'People get beaten up. You wake up in the morning, and you've lost your cap and your knife. They steal everything.'

'Come back with us!' The proposal came from our guide, Yasha 'Come to the children's charity refuge. It's not the police, and they won't lock you up. You can have supper, sleep and leave tomorrow if you want.'

Garik looked doubtful. Then Andrei, the Artful Dodger, appeared. 'You should go, he told the younger boy. 'You'll be all right there.' But he shook his head in amusement at our suggestion that he come, too. He had work to do.

At the station entrance, the Artful Dodger shook our hands and proudly waved goodbye – standing in the doorway in his dirty, baggy jacket like the lord of a stately home. In the car, Garik was having second thoughts. 'I'm not coming if I have to give up my weapons,' he warned. His new friend, Yasha, reassured him that he could stay armed, and begged one of his many watches as a gift. Young Garik began to settle down. Sinking back into the seat, still clutching his bag, he started to sing a clear melody in his high voice. 'One, two, three, four …' he sang in English to please us. Then the words changed to Armenian – a slow, mournful lullaby. And we drove through the black Moscow night to the children's charity refuge.

*Bridget Kendall*

## Reflections

\* The pathetic plight of many of these young people is repeated around the capital cities of the world's wealthy democracies. It is a problem that appears ever on the increase. What seems shameful about it is that these countries have the wealth to provide decent housing for everyone, but somehow it just doesn't happen.

These young women and men in Moscow hold onto a strong spirit to survive – but they are a poor advertisement for the wealth of nations and for democracy in the late twentieth century. Can we think of ways of reducing the problem as we move into the 21st century?

Sadly, some of Britain's politicians seem not to care. One once callously described the homeless as 'the people you step on when coming out of the opera', an ironic reminder of the contrast between the wealthy opera goers and the homeless in London's Covent Garden area. We need to press our politicians and other leaders in our communities to do all in their power to prevent the young, in particular, entering a life on the streets.

(See also **Underclass or just unfortunates**, p. 238)

# 6 'God bless Africa'

## Introduction

History will surely record the name of Nelson Mandela – a leader who would not compromise his ideals, whatever the personal cost – as one of the great statesmen of the twentieth century. Imprisoned for twenty-five years (1964–1989) for his protests against racial oppression and apartheid, he then emerged from prison to be elected President of South Africa in 1994.

'A rainbow nation at peace with itself and the world,' is how he summed up the new-born South Africa. Here is the speech he made as he was sworn in as President.

# Reading

## *God bless Africa*

Today, all of us do, by our presence here, and by our celebrations in other parts of our country and the world, confer glory and hope to newborn liberty.

Out of the experience of an extraordinary human disaster that lasted too long, must be born a society of which all humanity will be proud.

Our daily deeds as ordinary South Africans must produce an actual South African reality that will reinforce humanity's belief in justice, strengthen its confidence in the nobility of the human soul and sustain all our hopes for a glorious life for all.

All this we owe both to ourselves and to the peoples of the world who are so well represented here today.

To my compatriots, I have no hesitation in saying that each one of us is as intimately attached to the soil of this beautiful country as are the famous jacaranda trees of Pretoria and the mimosa trees of the bushveld.

Each time one of us touches the soil of this land, we feel a sense of personal renewal. The national mood changes as the seasons change. We are moved by a sense of joy and exhilaration when the grass turns green and the flowers bloom.

That spiritual and physical oneness we all share with this common homeland explains the depth of the pain we all carried in our hearts as we saw our country tear itself apart in a terrible conflict, and as we saw it spurned, outlawed and isolated by the peoples of the world, precisely because it has become the universal base of the pernicious ideology and practice of racism and racial oppression.

We, the people of South Africa, feel fulfilled that humanity has taken us back into its bosom, that we, who were outlaws not so long ago, have today been given the rare privilege to be host to the nations of the world on our own soil. We thank all our distinguished international guests for having come to take possession with the people of our country of what is, after all, a common victory for justice, for peace, for human dignity.

We trust that you will continue to stand by us as we tackle the challenges of building peace, prosperity, non-sexism, non-racialism and democracy.

We deeply appreciate the role that the masses of our people and their political mass democratic, religious, women, youth, business, traditional and other leaders have played to bring about this conclusion; not least among them is my second Deputy President, the Honourable F. W. de Klerk.

We would also like to pay tribute to our security forces, in all their ranks, for the distinguished role they have played in securing our first democratic elections and the transition to democracy, from blood-thirsty forces which still refuse to see the light.

The time for the healing of the wounds has come.

The moment to bridge the chasms that divide us has come.

The time to build is upon us.

We have, at last, achieved our political emancipation. We pledge ourselves to liberate all our people from the continuing bondage of poverty, deprivation, suffering, gender and other discrimination.

We succeeded to take our last steps to freedom in conditions of relative peace. We commit ourselves to the construction of a complete, just and lasting peace.

We have triumphed in the effort to implant hope in the breasts of the millions of our people. We enter into a covenant that we shall build the society in which all South Africans, both black and white, will be able to walk tall, without any fear in their hearts, assured of their inalienable right to human dignity – a rainbow nation at peace with itself and the world.

As a token of its commitment to the renewal of our country, the new interim government of national unity will, as a matter of urgency, address the issue of amnesty for various categories of our people who are currently serving terms of imprisonment.

We dedicate this day to all the heroes and heroines in this country and the rest of the world who sacrificed in many ways and surrendered their lives so that we could be free. Their dreams have become reality. Freedom is their reward.

We are both humbled and elevated by the honour and privilege that you, the people of South Africa, have bestowed on us, as the first President of a united, democratic, non-racial and non-sexist South Africa, to lead our country out of the valley of darkness.

We understand it still that there is no easy road to freedom.

We know it well that none of us acting alone can achieve success.

We must therefore act together as a united people, for national reconciliation, for nation-building, for the birth of a new world.

Let there be justice for all.

Let there be peace for all.

Let there be work, bread, water and salt for all.

Let each know that for each the body, the mind and the soul have been freed to fulfil themselves.

Never, never and never again shall it be that this beautiful land will again experience the oppression of one by another and suffer the indignity of being the skunk of the world.

Let freedom reign.

The sun shall never set on so glorious a human achievement.

God bless Africa. Thank you.

*Nelson Mandela*

# Reflections

* At a time of great change for a country it is right that the President sets forth a powerful and optimistic manifesto. With its history of racial oppression Nelson Mandela wanted above all else to champion a South African within which everyone could be 'assured of their inalienable right to human dignity.' There are many phrases in the speech worth reflecting on.

* It is also important to remember that South Africa's change came about because of strong and unrelenting pressure from the international community. South Africa's final rejection of apartheid, Nelson Mandela's release from prison and the birth of a stable democracy came about in no small measure because politicians and ordinary people around the world willed it to happen. The interdependence of nations should not be underestimated. Nor should it be forgotten that South Africa's new democracy is still young in heart and deed; it will continue to need international support in the years to come.

# 7 The Terezín ghetto

## Introduction

It remains the most horrific chapter of twentieth century history; a chapter that must never be forgotten: the Holocaust. If you've seen Steven Spielberg's film *Schindler's List*, other films or documentaries on the subject of the Nazi's treatment of millions of Jews in the 1930s, it is a story that is still difficult to believe happened – and yet we *know* it did. The evidence is still all around Europe and the world.

Here is one published account – a translation from the Czech – of one concentration camp, based in the town of Terezín. What made this particular camp so frightening was that to the outside world there seemed at the time (early 1940s) to be an almost normal life going on within it.

## Reading

*The Terezín ghetto*

The imprisoned doctors and nurses cared for the health of the prisoners. During the initial period of the ghetto most primitive instruments were used for treatment and operations. Devoted work of the medical staff resulted in the establishment of a hospital together with other health centres providing the basic medical care. Special wards for the sick were opened together with first aid stations in the big barracks and youth homes. However, there was a permanent shortage of medicaments and sanitary and disinfection materials. There was permanent lack of water, unsuitable sanitation and inadequate hygiene. Exhaustion, hunger and tremendous concentration of people caused diarrhoea, tuberculosis, typhoid fever, skin affections and other diseases often assuming epidemic character. The maximum number of sick persons was in February 1943: over 13,000, i.e. 31 per cent of the total of prisoners. In September 1942, for example, about 127 persons died every day. The old prisoners – weak, often handicapped, chronically ill and deeply shattered by their fate – were among the first who died in great numbers. The Nazis solved the situation in their own way: they sent 9 transports with old people to the east. The promise to stay for the rest of life-time in the ghetto was quickly forgotten. The total number of the dead was shocking: 35,000 persons died in Terezín including prisoners from the evacuation transports at the end of the war.

The dead were first buried in a place outside the fortifications in the lowland of Bohušovice. Nine thousand persons are buried there in individual and common graves. The newly built crematorium was put into operation in September 1942. In November 1944 the Nazis ordered the liquidation of the urns containing the ashes in the columbarium. The ashes were partly taken to Litoměřice and buried near the Richard underground factory and the greater part was thrown into the river Ohře in an effort to obliterate the evidence of the appalling number of the dead.

\* \* \*

Thousands of children came to Terezín both with their parents and from the

Jewish orphanages. At first all children up to 12 years lived in the barracks together with their mothers and boys over 12 with the men. There was a tendency to assemble them in special places and, when the local population moved away, to form in the evacuated houses independent homes for children and teenagers, the so-called heims. Gradually the majority of the youngest prisoners was assembled there. Thus was opened a home for infants and babies, homes for pre-school age children. Older children were separated according to their age and sex. The youth care department with the self-government did everything possible for good management and equipment of those homes to give the young people, at least to a certain extent, protection against the difficult situation in the camp. The adults greatly endeavoured to educate the children in the ghetto in order that, after the end of the war, they may return to normal life without greater problems.

Usually 20–30 children lived in one home. Each 'heim' had its own teachers and attendants who directed the daily activities and, contrary to teachers and attendants who directed the daily activities and, contrary to the Nazi order, secretly taught the basic school subjects. They also provided work for children over 14 years. Reading of books, recitals, discussions, fairy tales and theatre performances were the favourite activities. Sport competitions were also very popular. Older children and teenagers wrote poems, published magazines and diaries. These little literary works contain the thoughts and sorrows of the young prisoners, their homesickness and feelings of injustice but, likewise, the hope for better future. In their drawing lessons, permitted by the Nazi Commandery, the children could also well express their impressions, desires and ideas. The thousands of children drawings which remained hidden in Terezín are often the only evidence of their existence and activities during their internment in Terezín. Because the children were too young to work, they could not be used for labour for the Reich as some of their older fellow prisoners and their deportation from Terezín mostly ended by their death. From 10,000 children dragged by transports to the east only a small percentage survived. The children remaining in Terezín during the whole period of the war were the only ones who could hope for survival.

\* \* \*

There were extraordinary conditions for the development of culture in the Terezín ghetto. At the beginning the Nazi Commandery suppressed all artistic activities. However, since the middle of 1942 and in accordance with the new concept of the camp, considerable freedom was given in that field. The SS-Commandery may have cynically declared 'Let them play!' without any danger of being accused of love towards the Jews because – contrary to the prisoners – they knew their fate after leaving Terezín. It was thus possible to develop arts much more in Terezín than in the whole Protectorate. It was not an expression of benevolence of the SS-men but, rather, their indifference to what was sung, played or performed in the ghetto. Art in Terezín served the Nazis both as alibi and cover of the cruel fate they had prepared a long time ago. The prisoners, however, saw the situation in a different light.

Many outstanding personalities from the spheres of culture, science and political life were assembled in Terezín. They arrived from the Protectorate and from the other occupied countries from which Jews were deported to Terezín. They all decided to live like human beings even under the worst conditions and refused to yield to desperation or fear of the unknown future. Therefore, they organized literary evenings, delivered lectures, gave concerts and staged theatre performances.

The majority of the Terezín artists was sent by transports to the east. Thus were lost or destroyed many paintings, novels, poems or compositions because they refused to part with them to the last moment.

* * *

Practically from its foundation, the Terezín camp was destined to play a significant propaganda role and, therefore, the Nazis made great effort to conceal the actual conditions in the ghetto. Simultaneously with the worsening of Germany's situation in the war theatre, the pressure abroad increased, in particular by the International Red Cross Committee, to obtain permission to visit Terezín in order to verify the Nazi allegations about the ghetto character. At the same time it would assist in the verification of the horrible reports about the extermination of Jews which were gradually seeping out from the concentration camps. Finally, the German authorities decided to grant permission of the visit and use it as a propaganda trick. Terezín underwent a number of improvements already in 1943 and its 're-decoration' culminated in the spring 1944, at the time when the permission was given to the delegate of the International Red Cross to visit the camp. The Nazis were not at all concerned with the improvement of the living conditions of the imprisoned Jews but wanted to disguise the real purpose of the whole place.

*Ludmila Chladkova*

## Reflections

* 'These little literary works contain the thoughts and sorrows of the young prisoners, their homesickness and feelings of injustice but, likewise, the hope for a better future.'

The great power and will of the human spirit to survive and look to the future is a feature of this account of life in Terezín. The fact that few who entered the town survived adds to the sadness and outrage we must feel about this period in European history.

Historians remind us: 'Those who forget the past are condemned to repeat it, but those who anticipate the future are free to shape it.' Each of us – whatever our position in society – must do everything in our power to shape the future, so that the likes of the Terezín ghetto can never again come into being.

# 8 An evil cradling

## Introduction

From time to time we hear on the news that hostages have been taken. It can be in a domestic dispute or a robbery; and on the international stage this may well

involve hijackers or a militant group who want to bring their cause to the attention of the world's media. And by kidnapping others they usually manage to
achieve high profile publicity without much trouble.

But have you thought what it might be like to be a hostage, just not knowing
what was going to happen next? The following passage comes from Brian
Keenan's interesting book titled *An Evil Cradling*. It describes his experiences as a
hostage of a Middle East terrorist group. He spent five years imprisoned,
together with several other British and American men. What you are about to
hear comes from near the end of his book. After years of living in poor and filthy
cells, conditions begin to improve. There is just a hint of release around the corner. But how will Brian react to news of release? John McCarthy and Terry Waite
are the two fellow hostages mentioned.

# Reading

## An evil cradling

We had long recognized that the guards were as much our prisoners as we were
theirs, and they were now more prisoners than ever before. In many respects
they had become our servants. If we asked for anything we were given it immediately. Medicine, a particular kind of food, coffee, hot chocolate – all were given
to us. Only newspapers were refused. In the light of this, we became more confident. To treat us so royally, but yet to refuse magazines or newspapers, suggested strongly that something was happening which they did not want us to
know about. That something, we were sure, was an impending end to our captivity.

Another prisoner was moved into the room beside ours. For some days there
was silence from this other person's room, then inevitably the knocking began. A
man will risk his life or the better part of it to communicate. The knocking told us
who it was, and we were not surprised. We had guessed as much beforehand.
We returned the messages, tapping out our own identity and what news and
information we could pass on. It was a slow, laborious process, but we knew how
hungry Terry Waite must be for news. We had always known that he would be
alone. The fact that he was in this apartment with us now further reinforced our
hopes.

Daily we would be taken to the toilet, returned and exercised. In the afternoon
the guards would come to unchain us, take us one at a time from the room,
across the hall into the kitchen. We would sit on a chair in front of a window. The
window would be opened and in would come the heat and light of the sun, blazing through our blindfolds. A radio was always playing in the kitchen. Often the
guard Bilal, the one who had asked John to teach him to dance, would tune the
radio to some western rock station and we would listen to old and familiar tunes.
Occasionally we caught some quick news flash, half understanding it before the
guards would flick to another station. There was much talk now with the guards,
and jokes were traded.

John sat chained to his wall at one end of the large apartment room and I,
chained to mine, at the other. We would take our socks, stuff them full of paper
or some rag or shirt that we had torn up, wrap the sock around this and make
ourselves a small ball. Chained to the wall we would viciously pass this ball back

and forward, scoring points against each miss. The next morning during exercise we would bring out our secret ball and play soccer or volleyball, choking on the laughter.

'Hope for everything but expect nothing' had long been our motto. But now hope increased expectation, rather than limited it. We spoke little to one another about our possible release. We hoped we would both go together. We expected it would not happen like that. Yet we enjoyed one another's company too much to bear the thought of either of us going before the other.

It comes as all things that change a life must come: without warning. An afternoon visit, suddenly there are many men in the room. A guard kneels down, lifting me by the arm with the command 'Stand, Brian, stand.' I stand, wondering, not really expecting this to be the moment. I am unchained and led from the room and into another. On the floor is a mattress and I am made to sit on it and am chained again. Slowly something is dawning on me. To move me to another room and rechain me is a separation that means something though I cannot allow myself to believe what it might be. Grasping hold of something and then having it instantaneously taken away had hurled many of us in the past into that abyss we all knew too well. But I sit in defiant silence. A man kneels in front of me, his hand gentle on my shoulder. It is the voice of one of the chiefs. Quietly he says, 'Brian, you go home.' I am silent and unstunned 'Home, you mean another place?' I ask, for I have heard these words before.

Again the hand at my shoulder and the voice. 'You go home, family, Dublin.' The sound of the word Dublin suggests that something is imminent. I am still amazingly calm. I ask 'What about my friend?' There is silence, voices mumbled in Arabic. All of them leave the room. Ten minutes later two men return, then ask whether I want anything. That phrase I have heard ten thousand times before. 'I want to speak with my friend John. I want to speak with him now. I will not go without speaking.' My voice is rising in panic, realizing 'My God, it is over.'

They recognize my insistence, the loudness of my voice, the determination in it. A man kneels again in front of me, quietly he asks 'What do you want?' I answer, my voice slow, loud enough so that I hope John will hear. 'I want to speak with John, I will not go from this room until I speak with him.' The figure still squats in silence in front of me. After some minutes he leaves. I am given tea. I sit, the door is left wide open.

I know they have gone into the kitchen and are there talking. After half an hour two men come into the room. 'Brian,' a voice says. I sit silent, 'You douche, take shower.' I sit silent, wondering is this an order or an offer. Again I say to them 'Take me to John, I want to say goodbye.' My voice is more angry now than determined but it's a quiet anger. Again the chief kneels down in front of my blindfolded face. His hand is at my shoulder but not this time in a pat of affection; squeezing and gripping hard again. 'After douche, after some hours you talk with your friend.' I nod, not knowing whether to believe and accept or to face the pointlessness of argument.

I am left for those hours to think. I begin to believe what I have been told and suddenly there is something in me I cannot resolve. I know it is over and within hours or days I will not be wearing a blindfold. I will be unfettered. But I feel it build in me, the weight of my imprisonment. For how much freedom can there be for a man when he leaves one half of himself chained to the wall? I begin to try to order my thinking to see beyond the consequences of any action I can take. I can argue and fight and insist on staying until my friend is released. But if I don't go, how will my family and friends receive it? Perhaps even now they are sitting waiting for the final confirmation. Has their suffering been so little over the past four and a half years that I can refuse this, and thrust them back into their anguish? I think one moment that I am thinking only of myself and then that I am not. I am trying desperately to find a balance in my compassion. I weigh the scales and I move back and forth and I am caught in indecision. My hands stretched out to the man in the room next door and to my family far away. Which has the greater hold and where is the greater pull on me?

*Brian Keenan*

## Reflections

\* It is the indelible bond and friendship that has grown up between those locked together for many years that is the interesting focus of this extract. Brian Keenan finds it difficult to imagine being released and leaving others behind:

'For how much freedom can there be for a man when he leaves one half of himself chained to the wall?'

It is almost impossible for us to imagine the state of mind of the hostages after many years behind bars in a foreign country, never knowing from one day to the next what would be their fate. When we hear of hostages on the news, our thoughts must lie with both the victims and their families. Meanwhile, the international community needs to go on asserting how wrong this kind of terrorism is and seek to prevent it. It corrodes trust between nations.

# 9  Barracuda breakfast

## Introduction

When we think about the origins of many crazy fashions and alternative lifestyles we look no further than the USA. As presented through a thousand films and soap operas, the beaches of California, the streets of New York and the highways of Florida seem to be teeming with the latest in off-beat living.

Listen to the following – the very latest in holiday resorts. Would you fancy an overnight stop?

## Reading

### Barracuda breakfast

Dress codes are usually fairly relaxed in American hotels but at the Emerald Lagoon in Key Largo, 54 miles south of Miami, they won't let you in even if you're not wearing a wetsuit, flippers and a snorkel. It is the world's first and only underwater hotel.

Everything in Florida involves large volumes of water – especially local beers. The southernmost state of the USA is the self-proclaimed water sports capital of the world and now, after all that snorkelling, water skiing, swimming with dolphins, hand-feeding moray eels, plus all those jetties, jacuzzis and glass-bottomed boat rides, you can even sleep the night in water if you want to.

The Jules Verne Lodge, sunk 30 ft. down in the Undersea Park close to the John Pennecamp Coral Reef Park and Key Largo Marine Sanctuary, can accommodate up to six in bunk-style accommodation in two bedrooms. Inside your 11 ft. by 50 ft. undersea sub-Atlantic habitat, formerly a marine research laboratory, you feel odd: as if you had driven along the Interstate One in a large hi-tech caravan, your automatic coaster has suddenly malfunctioned and you have veered off the road through some palms and 'Tackle & Bait' ad hoardings and plunged into the sea only to land right way up on the sandy bottom. The Jules Verne underwater suite is more of a submerged caravan site than a hotel. But it is exclusive. Nobody bothers you for matches or sugar and the only Peeping Toms are barracudas.

Every window, 4 in. thick by 42 in. in diameter, offers a sea view. The Americans are keen to offer you 'limitless opportunities' and 'the ultimate', waking in the morning and drawing the curtain to see a four-foot barracuda staring at you is surely some kind of ultimate. Few Europeans get the chance to observe marine life so close. Likewise the colourful marine life make the most of the limitless opportunities of observing at close-range Europeans in their colourful Marks & Spencer's pyjamas.

When you check-in you need not show your passport, only a diving certificate. If you haven't dived before you can attend a three-hour 'aquatic habitat orientation programme' which involves learning what salt water tastes like and how to put flippers on the right way. The secret of putting flippers on is that there is no secret. There is no right or wrong way to put on flippers. There is no such thing as left or right flipper. If you remember flippers go on your feet you can't go far wrong.

The programme is taken by the world's only full-time professional mermaid, Carla Rush, a 40-year-old from Illinois and former captain of a local dive charter boat.

She has been a 'pro' mermaid for nearly two years and will teach you how to operate your flippers, the rudiments of breathing compressed air, help you in and out of your wetsuit, clean your mask for you with her own spit, bring your meals, wash up, carry your bags and do anything else that needs doing, including pushing you in.

After a short downward swim you emerge up under the hotel into a dive port from where, once Carla has eased you out of your oxygen tank and towelled you down, you are shown to your living chambers. These are equipped with all mod cons. Carla then leaves you to your microwave filet mignon and lobster and returns to terra firma to man the control and wait on every whim. Room service is excellent and if you leave your shoes outside they are clean in the morning.

There isn't much to do underwater. Smoking and drinking are not allowed. But you can watch videos like John Wayne's *Hell Town* and, predictably, *Splash* and *20,000 Leagues Under The Sea*. You can hope that somebody rings you up. Wrong numbers are fun. You can ring anybody in the world. You may attempt to become a member of the Five Fathom Club or merely wonder how much air you have in your 600 square feet of living space.

The brochure boasts 'limitless' air supply as part of your package.

If lucky you might get a sighting of a manatee swimming past your dining room window. A manatee is a curious looking and very rare marine creature which can only be described as weighing 300 lbs, having the head of Bobby Charlton and body of a stout middle-aged woman.

When you check out you decompress. This ensures that you aren't suffering from 'the bends' – something your signature on your Visa and Mastercard can't prove – and receive your treasured Aquanaut certificate which verifies that you have spent the whole night in the sea and enjoyed all the benefits of the experience. These are obvious. Staying underwater in Florida is the best way to avoid sunburn and mosquitos.

*Kevin Pilley*

## Reflections

*   Travel to this hotel would certainly broaden the mind! Indeed, international travel is increasingly an experience many of us have as air travel becomes more accessible to more people. And travelling to glimpse other cultures is important if we are to understand how our global village operates; we come to realise there are other lifestyles which are very different from our own; and we also come to value a little more what we have at home.

# 10  Midtown Manhattan

## Introduction

The major cities of the world continue to be a source of great energy and human activity. In many senses they are the engine-rooms of our international community. But many of them have an increasingly darker side, as the following account of New York's streets reveals.

## Reading

### Midtown Manhattan

The Concise Oxford definition of to mug is to 'thrash; strangle; rob with violence, especially in a public place'. The Webster definition is somewhat less dramatic, but nevertheless insists that a mugging should involve at least some degree of violence. So whatever happened to me in West 44th Street last month was certainly not a mugging.

I was walking at 8.30pm along this somewhat deserted street when a young black man in a leather jacket blocked my path and said in a tense, even frantic, voice: 'I am unemployed. I am desperate. Please give me money.' Before I had decided how to reply, although only a few seconds had passed, he had become angry. 'I'm talking to you,' he said with sudden aggression. 'I'm talking to you.' I reached into my trouser pocket, extracted what turned out to be a $10 bill, and handed it to him. But he was not to be so easily placated. He put his hand inside his jacket and said: 'I know you have money in your wallet. I have a knife. Don't make me use it on you. Take our your wallet. Give me all the money in it – *all* of it – and there will be no problem. You will go your way, and I will go mine.' I did as I was told. I took out my wallet and gave him all the money it contained ($200, unfortunately, it was Friday and I had just stocked up for the weekend).

True to his word, he took the money and went on his way. I also went on mine, feeling perhaps a little shaken, but predominantly grateful that he had not also deprived me of my driving licence and credit cards. I even began to feel that I had struck a rather favourable bargain.

But when I have described this incident to New Yorkers I have been astonished and gratified by their reactions. Almost without exception, they have (1) shown boundless fascination with every detail; (2) insisted, against all the evidence, that I have been well and truly mugged; and (3) congratulated me on my good sense in acceding without argument to the young man's demands. 'But how do I know he had a knife?' I say, hoping that someone at least will suspect me of cowardice. 'Oh, you can never be too careful,' they reply. 'He was probably a crack addict.'

On reflection, I think it highly unlikely he was a crack addict. I even doubt if he had a weapon. I think he may well have been just a spur-of-the-moment beggar who only decided to pose as a mugger when he realised that he might get more money that way. One can hardly blame him, given the conventional wisdom of the New York middle class. This states that you should always hand over all the money you have to anybody who asks for it, if he does so in an even slightly menacing way. Further conventional advice concerns prevention and damage limitation: cross the road if you don't like the look of the person coming towards you, carry only modest amounts of money on you, smile cheerfully if accosted.

There are certainly a lot of weirdos and desperadoes roaming the streets of New York with whom it would be rash to seek a confrontation. But the distinction between a mugger and a beggar is beginning to become rather blurred. There are still beggars who say 'God bless you, sir' if you hand them a quarter. And the advice you are generally given is to treat all of them – good beggars, bad beggars, phoney muggers, real muggers – in much the same manner as you are treated by the bank's cash dispenser when you demand money from it with your plastic card. 'Hello,' the computer says on the little screen. 'How can I help you?' You tap in your request for $200. 'I'm working on it,' the computer replies. Eventually the cash spews out. 'It's always a pleasure to serve you,' the computer concludes.

Far more frightening than the incident on 44th Street, was one that happened to me when I was living in Washington DC. I was walking down a dark and empty street in the middle of the city when I noticed that a large man was approaching from the opposite direction. As he drew nearer, I began to wonder whether I should cross the street, but I felt ashamed at the thought; he had done nothing whatsoever to arouse suspicion. But as I continued walking in his direction, and he in mine, I found that my heart was racing. I told myself there was no reason for fear, and yet my anxiety grew. His footsteps grew louder, my heart beat still faster, until finally we came face to face. Then, with great suddenness, he waved his arms violently in the air, and let out a terrifying roar. I thought my heart would stop, but he did not even pause. He just walked on by, chuckling contentedly.

Feeling not only a nervous wreck but also a complete idiot, I took myself home and poured myself an enormous drink. A long time has passed since then, but that experience remains much more vivid in my memory than my recent financial transaction in midtown Manhattan.

*Alexander Chancellor*

## Reflection

\*    What would you have done? What *would* you do?

It is a sad reflection on our great metropolitan centres that beggars and muggers hunt in this way. To give in to the muggers is to encourage them to become more daring; to resist is to risk injury to the person.

Society needs to look at ways of both dealing with the source of these problems as well as making our city streets safer. But it cannot go down the road, surely, of just shrugging its shoulders and accepting muggers/beggars as inevitable: 'prevention' rather than 'damage limitation' should be our social goal.

The values of right and wrong need to be asserted – we live in a world where criminals can move quickly between different countries. It is important that our streets are not places where, as in this extract, we fear any person walking towards us in an empty street.

# The Human Being and Doing

*The belief that God will do everything for man is as untenable as the belief that man can do everything for himself. It, too, is based on a lack of faith. We must learn that to expect God to do everything while we do nothing is not faith but superstition.*

Martin Luther King

*This is the true joy in life – that being used for a purpose recognized by yourself as a mighty one. That being a force of nature, instead of a feverish, selfish little clod of ailments and grievances complaining that the world will not devote itself to making you happy. I am of the opinion that my life belongs to the whole community and as long as I live it is my privilege to do for it whatever I can. I want to be thoroughly used up when I die. For the harder I work the more I live. I rejoice in life for its own sake. Life is no brief candle to me. It's a sort of splendid torch which I've got to hold up for the moment and I want to make it burn as brightly as possible before handing it on to future generations.*

George Bernard Shaw

# 1 Jailed for life

## Introduction

All communities must have basic rules and codes of conduct if they are to survive and prosper. Anthropologists tell us this has been true since the birth of the human species. So what does any community – a home, a school, a team, a nation – do with those who break the rules?

Listen to the following account (written in 1993) of a man named Harry Roberts. He was jailed for life in 1966 for murdering (with two other men) three policemen. The Home Secretary of the time described him as 'a threat to the whole fabric of society'.

## Reading

*Jailed for life*

The face on the man in the visiting room at Dartmoor Prison is recognisably the same as the one that used to sneer down from the police posters, but now it looks as though it has been doctored by a cartoonist. The flesh on the face has started to sag, the corners of the mouth have dropped and pulled dark lines down through the skin above them. The thick black hair is grey. He has trouble with his back. His hands are stiff. His eyes are going; he says he has glaucoma. He is 56, he looks older and inside himself, as he talks, it begins to seem that the decay runs even deeper.

Harry Roberts is being considered for parole. Police groups say he should never be released. Maybe they are right. Maybe Harry Roberts deserves to rot there for ever – to deter others, to console the bereaved, simply to hurt him for what he did. Maybe this society wants to say that there is no limit to the incarceration of prisoner number 231191. But maybe it is not quite that simple.

It is not just about Harry Roberts. There is a bigger issue which is subtle and difficult and which goes to the heart of criminal justice. If Harry Roberts had committed his offence a year earlier – before the 1965 law which abolished the death penalty for the murder of policemen – he would certainly have hanged. Instead, he was locked up and thus became one of the first examples of a new problem. If hanging is wrong, how much jail is right?

The question is striking not only because it raises the same clash of emotive issues as the death penalty but also because in all the years that have passed since abolition, it has never been answered. While hanging has been debated to the point of exhaustion, the definition of justice for men like Harry Roberts has been decided in private by officials of a section of the Prison Department known as DSP2/LSRS. And they don't talk – not about the rules by which they operate, nor about individual cases, not even to the murderers whose fate they are deciding.

When Harry Roberts starts to talk, he seems at first to be as hard now as he was on the day he shot his victims. 'They keep asking me, "Do you feel remorse,

Harry?" And I say no. We didn't want to murder anyone. That was the last thing we wanted. We shot them because we thought they were going to nick us and we didn't want to go to jail for 15 years. We were professional criminals. We don't react the same way as ordinary people. The police aren't like real people to us. They're strangers, they're the enemy. And you don't feel remorse for killing a stranger. I do feel sorry for what we did to their families. I do. But it's like people I killed in Malaya when I was in the army. You don't feel remorse.'

The hardness has an edge of bravado. Why were they carrying guns that day? 'Because we were gangsters.' How does he feel each time he arrives at a new prison?' I'm going in there, with my shoulders back, saying, 'Right, which one of you lot's done more time than me?' He chuckles like an indulgent father at the football fans who still chant his name to aggravate policemen – 'Harry Roberts, he's our man; he shoots policemen, bang, bang, bang.'

And maybe that's the end of the argument; if he's still so full of himself, he should stay where he is for another 27 years. Maybe that is why he has not been released. Harry Roberts says he does not know. 'They won't tell me. Every time I ask, I get something different. They say, "Look at you Harry. You're too fit to go back on the streets." I say, "I'm old. My friends are old. No one's going to take me on a robbery." Be serious. Who's going to want me along on a job? I'm a liability. They'd get an extra 16 years just for talking to me. I'm past it, aren't I?

'But I can't prove I'm not a risk. I volunteered to go to Grendon Underwood to let the psychiatrists have a look at me. They said I wasn't suitable material. But how can they say that if they haven't looked? Or they say I should go to church. I ask you. I could do it for six months, then I'd have a row with the vicar.

'Once I asked a governor why they wouldn't let me out. He said it was because I was institutionalised. They keep me in here all these years – and then they tell me that!'

Roberts says that for years after he was jailed, he thought of nothing but escape. He forced himself to stay fit so that he was ready to run, and he came up with 22 different escape plans. Most of them simply failed. Once his mother was caught on a visit with a pair of bolt cutters in her bra. Three times he was caught and punished. He never came close to freedom. During all the years, he has never really come close to anything.

He has no radio and no newspapers. For the first 18 years he was a top security Category A prisoner, barred from most opportunities for work or education. When finally he was allowed to mix with other prisoners, he took a couple of O levels in English Language and Literature and passed two engineering exams with distinction. Then they put him to work in the sock shop, sewing up the toes of hundreds of socks, so he stopped messing about with exams. He couldn't see the point. For a while, he painted. He stopped that, too. He says he was no good at it.

Harry Roberts has lost everything. His wife abandoned him soon after his arrest. He had a woman friend, Lillian Perry, but he told her to stop visiting him. 'I got chivalrous. I said, "don't waste your life." Mistake. There you go. She's gone.'

His mother, Dorothy, visited him for years, but she died in 1984. 'We were very close. Then one day they opened the cell door and said, "Your mother died yesterday." Suddenly she's not there any more. I tried to go to the funeral, but they were talking about a security escort and police outriders and I said, "This is a circus – forget it." Someone sent me a couple of photos of the funeral, but they wouldn't let me have 'em. So that's the end of that.'

And as he talks, the truth about the hardness begins to become clear. He remembers a budgie which he kept a few years ago. In the beginning, he only got it because he needed the wire from its cage for an escape plan, but then he started to like the bird. It would sit on his shoulder and he'd stroke its beak and feed it bread crumbs. He told jokes about this bird trying to set up robberies. 'I turned it down. The money he was offering was chickenfeed.' Then the bird died, and that hurt him. 'I could see it was ill. I spent money on a vet. But it died. I nearly cracked up. I'd never have another one. I was really choked and you can't go getting upset in this place.'

He talks about the months after they released him from 18 years in security blocks, when he couldn't focus his eyes on the end of a corridor, when he got lost in the wing because he couldn't cope with the space, when he simply spent hours staring out of his new cell in Gartree watching the fields for the first time in nearly 20 years. It was around then that his mother died. He knew it was all getting to him one night when he was watching athletics on television and he saw Steve Ovett and Sebastian Coe racing for the finishing line, and he started to cry.

Prisoners often say that the system is out to break their spirit and the truth is that Harry Roberts is all but broken. He talks tough, but inside he has been hollowed out. He boasts about being a gangster, because he has nothing else to do. His notoriety is all he has, the nearest thing to self-respect. Maybe that is all they want from him now – not simply to be broken but to admit it. If he does that, maybe they will let him go.

'I'm a criminal. All my life, I've been involved with criminal things. If there's a fiddle in the kitchen in here, if there's a bit of booze, if there's a crooked screw bringing in some gear, I'm going to be there. And of course they all say, "Oh, he's carrying on his criminal life." But it's a game. It's a way of surviving. How can you accept 27 years in jail? A lot of these escapes were a means of surviving. Mentally. I mean, it's a terrible thing they do to people. You know? I want to say to them, "Why are you still punishing me?" I don't know the answer.'

*Nick Davies*

# Reflections

\*   'If hanging is wrong, how much jail is right?'

'Maybe Harry Roberts deserves to rot there for ever – to deter others, to console the bereaved, simply to hurt him for what he did.'

What is your response? How should we deal with major criminals in our society? What should be the purpose of prison?

We need to protect our basic freedoms by excluding from society those individuals who break the laws passed by governments. But we also need to think carefully about the link between crime and punishment. And, crucially, about what happens to that person when they are released to be with other people again.

This passage is about prison. But what are its lessons for society as a whole – and any smaller community like a school, the workplace, the sports club?

What is the most effective way of handling those who seek to break the rules and make life unpleasant for those around them?

# 2 Room 101

## Introduction

Fear is a natural human feeling. And though there are many things we probably all fear in the same way, each of us will have our own particular fears – and it's often difficult to explain to someone else, say, a fear of heights, a fear of water, a fear of spiders!

Philosophers tell us that some fears are rational, others irrational. What is also true is that we each develop our own way of living with and perhaps overcoming a particular fear.

The following reading is taken from George Orwell's powerful novel of the future titled *1984* (written in 1948). In this episode, the central character Winston finds himself in Room 101, being 'interviewed' by the sinister O'Brien.

## Reading

*Room 101*

At each stage of his imprisonment he had known, or seemed to know, where-abouts he was in the windowless building. Possibly there were slight differences in the air pressure. The cells where the guards had beaten him were below ground level. The room where he had been interrogated by O'Brien was high up near the roof. This place was many metres underground, as deep down as it was possible to go.

It was bigger than most of the cells he had been in. But he hardly noticed his surroundings. All he noticed was that there were two small tables straight in front of him, each covered with green baize. One was only a metre or two from him, the other was further away, near the door. He was strapped upright in a chair, so tightly that he could move nothing, not even his head. A sort of pad gripped his head from behind, forcing him to look straight in front of him.

For a moment he was alone, then the door opened and O'Brien came in.

'You asked me once,' said O'Brien, 'what was in Room 101. I told you that you knew the answer already. Everyone knows it. The thing that is in Room 101 is the worst thing in the world.'

The door opened again. A guard came in, carrying something made of wire, a box or basket of some kind. He set it down on the further table. Because of the position in which O'Brien was standing, Winston could not see what the thing was.

'The worst thing in the world,' said O'Brien, 'varies from individual to individual. It may be burial alive, or death by fire, or drowning, or by impalement, or fifty other deaths. There are cases where it is some quite trivial thing, not even fatal.'

He had moved a little to one side, so that Winston had a better view of the thing on the table. It was an oblong wire cage with a handle on top for carrying it by. Fixed to the front of it was something that looked like a fencing mask, with the concave side outwards. Although it was three or four metres away from him, he could see that the cage was divided lengthways into two compartments, and that there was some kind of creature in each. They were rats.

'In your case,' said O'Brien, 'the worst thing in the world happens to be rats.'

A sort of premonitory tremor, a fear of he was not certain what, had passed through Winston as soon as he caught his first glimpse of the cage. But at this moment the meaning of the mask-like attachment in front of it suddenly sank into him. His bowels seemed to turn to water.

'You can't do that!' he cried out in a high cracked voice. 'You couldn't, you couldn't! It's impossible.'

'Do you remember,' said O'Brien, 'the moment of panic that used to occur in your dreams? There was a wall of blackness in front of you, and a roaring sound in your ears. There was something terrible on the other side of the wall. You knew that you knew what it was, but you dared not drag it into the open. It was the rats that were on the other side of the wall.'

'O'Brien!' said Winston, making an effort to control his voice. 'You know this is not necessary. What is it that you want me to do?'

O'Brien made no direct answer. When he spoke it was in the schoolmasterish manner that he sometimes affected. He looked thoughtfully into the distance, as though he were addressing an audience somewhere behind Winston's back.

'By itself,' he said, 'pain is not always enough. There are occasions when a human being will stand out against pain, even to the point of death. But for everyone there is something unendurable – something that cannot be contemplated. Courage and cowardice are not involved. If you are falling from a height it is not cowardly to clutch at a rope. If you have come up from deep water it is not cowardly to fill your lungs with air. It is merely an instinct which cannot be destroyed. It is the same with the rats. For you, they are unendurable. They are a form of pressure that you cannot withstand, even if you wished to. You will do what is required of you.'

'But what is it, what is it? How can I do it if I don't know what it is?'

O'Brien picked up the cage and bought it across to the nearer table. He set it down carefully on the baize cloth. Winston could hear the blood singing in his ears. He had the feeling of sitting in utter loneliness. He was in the middle of a great empty plain, a flat desert drenched with sunlight, across which all sounds came to him out of immense distances. Yet the cage with the rats was not two metres away from him. They were enormous rats. They were at the age when a rat's muzzle grows blunt and fierce and his fur brown instead of grey.

'The rat,' said O'Brien, still addressing his invisible audience, 'although a rodent, is carnivorous. You are aware of that. You will have heard of the things that happen in the poor quarters of this town. In some streets a woman dare not leave her baby alone in the house, even for five minutes. The rats are certain to attack it. Within quite a small time they will strip it to the bones. They also attack sick or dying people. They show astonishing intelligence in knowing when a human being is helpless.'

There was an outburst of squeals from the cage. It seemed to reach Winston from far away. The rats were fighting; they were trying to get at each other through the partition. He heard also a deep groan of despair. That, too, seemed to come from outside himself.

O'Brien picked up the cage, and, as he did so, pressed something in it. There was a sharp click. Winston made a frantic effort to tear himself loose from the chair. It was hopeless; every part of him, even his head, was held immovably. O'Brien moved the cage nearer. It was less than a metre from Winston's face.

'I have pressed the first lever,' said O'Brien. 'You understand the construction of this cage. The mask will fit over your head, leaving no exit. When I press this other lever, the door of the cage will slide up. These starving brutes will shoot out of it like bullets. Have you ever seen a rat leap through the air? They will leap on to your face and bore straight into it. Sometimes they attack the eyes first. Sometimes they burrow through the cheeks and devour the tongue.'

The cage was nearer; it was closing in. Winston heard a succession of shrill cries which appeared to be occurring in the air above his head. But he fought furiously against his panic. To think, to think, even with a split second left – to think was the only hope. Suddenly the foul musty odour of the brutes struck his nostrils. There was a violent convulsion of nausea inside him, and he almost lost consciousness. Everything had gone black. For an instant he was insane, a screaming animal. Yet he came out of the blackness clutching an idea. There was one and only one way to save himself. He must interpose another human being, the *body* of another human being, between himself and the rats.

The circle of the mask was large enough now to shut out the vision of anything else. The wire door was a couple of hand-spans from his face. The rats knew what was coming now. One of them was leaping up and down, the other, an old scaly grandfather of the sewers, stood up, with his pink hands against the bars, and fiercely sniffed the air. Winston could see the whiskers and the yellow teeth. Again the black panic took hold of him. He was blind, helpless, mindless.

'It was a common punishment in Imperial China,' said O'Brien as didactically as ever.

The mask was closing on his face. The wire brushed his cheek. And then – no, it was not relief, only hope, a tiny fragment of hope. Too late, perhaps too late. But he had suddenly understood that in the whole world there was just *one* person to whom he could transfer his punishment – *one* body that he could thrust between himself and the rats. And he was shouting frantically, over and over.

'Do it to Julia! Do it to Julia! Not me! Julia! I don't care what you do to her. Tear her face off, strip her to the bones. Not me! Julia! Not me!'

He was falling backwards, into enormous depths, away from the rats. He was still strapped in the chair, but he had fallen through the floor, through the walls of the building, through the earth, through the oceans, through the atmosphere, into outer space, into the gulfs between the stars – always away, away, away from the rats. He was light-years distant, but O'Brien was still standing at his side. There was still the cold touch of a wire against his cheek. But through the darkness that enveloped him he heard another metallic click, and knew that the cage door had clicked shut and not open.

*George Orwell*

# Reflections

* So Winston escapes his worst fear – rats – by confessing to O'Brien the name of Julia, his partner-in-crime. It is a very powerful passage from a book which

paints the portrait of a future controlled by Big Brother and in which any individual feeling is squashed by those who want to run a particular kind of brutalised society.

Fear is a particularly difficult human emotion. It is one we come to terms with in different, personal ways. Recognising what our fears are is important to us as we develop as human beings. Some we can overcome by sharing our thoughts with other people; some we overcome by actions – for example, conquering a fear of heights by being successful at rock-climbing or abseiling.

As with Winston's fear of rats (linked to a childhood experience in his case) we need to recognise that each of us has fears which may well rest with us much of our lives. Learning to live with them is part of growing up.

# 3  As old as old could be

## Introduction

We often read in news reports of accidents where someone has cheated death – meaning that it was amazing that they escaped or recovered from injury. Scientists for centuries have tackled the task of cheating death in other practical ways, asking whether it's possible to extend life expectancy.

Listen to the following article about one Charlotte Hughes.

## Reading

### As old as old could be

Modern medicine may have done wonders for life expectancy, but it has proved useless at giving us the secrets of immortality. Even with the best possible care and attention, men and women cannot live much beyond the ripe old age of 115, the point at which Charlotte Hughes, the oldest person in Britain, passed away in her sleep. She lived as long as a human being can.

By 115 or so, the human body, any human body, has reached its ultimate limit. Humans, even Godless ones, have a form of immortality; the life of our genes, which live on down the generations. In geneticists' terms our bodies are merely disposable vehicles, carrying our genes from one generation to the next. The surprising thing about human beings is not that their life has a restricted term but that they live so long. Few animals outlive humans, many simply reproduce and die. Slow ageing and gradual decline does not occur in the animal world, only in ourselves.

The 'disposable soma' theory, is now accepted as the most promising solution to a problem that has dogged biology for ages; why do we die when we do? The theory is complex, but it states that our genes will not build a body which will live for centuries because this strategy will not work in evolutionary terms. The human organism has adopted a strategy that makes a major investment in repairing the damage the body takes as the decades go by. But this investment will not go to the extremes of repairing a body for centuries. The theory postulates that there comes a point at which repairing damage simply becomes too costly and could only be done at the expense of risking what is ultimately the *raison d'être* of life: passing on genes.

This theory sets a limit to what has been an extraordinary trend. A hundred years ago, a typical newborn baby in Britain could expect to live about 42 years. Now average life expectancy is 76.5 years for females and 71.5 for males. The improvement is entirely due to environmental factors: better diet, better housing, better medicine. But there is a point at which these environmental factors come up against the genetic barrier – the ultimate facts of life.

Physically and mentally we peak early, at about the time we are sexually most active, and from then on it's a downhill journey. We begin to feel the effects of our age: tiredness, lack of agility and so on. Our hearts, lungs, muscles and kidneys all gradually lose their function. This occurs because of what happens at the molecular level. The molecules of our cells are constantly being damaged. Repairing this wear and tear is costly. Our bodies spend a lot of energy doing it and this means there is less energy for that other vital ingredient of life: sex. Humans as a species have followed the strategy of repair at the expense of quick reproduction, which is why we live much longer than other comparable animals.

Two hundred years ago men lived longer than women because life was much harder for them than for men. The difference we see today, putting women ahead in the life expectancy stakes, is not because one is exposed to more wear and tear than the other. One of the geneticists' theories suggests that *Homo sapiens* lived in polygamous societies many hundreds of thousands of years ago; males mated with several females and therefore were following a mini-strategy of reproduction at the expense of repairing the wear and tear of the passing years. The fact that they passed their genes on so easily and fecundly left them with little reason for investing in the repair of their own bodies, unlike females. And so when the genes of males and females get transferred to a modern setting – where there are roughly equal environmental influences on both men and women – the result is a difference in life expectancy of roughly five years.

Recent research on fruit flies has lent experimental weight to the disposable soma theory. In fact, scientists who have painstakingly monitored the lives of a million flies living in a laboratory believe that if humans can survive the first 70 or so years of life, with all the dangers it contains, they are well on the way to living a good deal longer because they have proved they are blessed with the genes that could take them past the century.

But this does not mean that we can cheat on death itself. Mrs Hughes was luckier than most of us will be. The rest of us will have to be content with three score years and ten, plus a little more if we are lucky, depending on which sex we are.

*Steve Connor*

# Reflections

* Latest scientific theory suggests then that the body does wear out and that the human body does not have the capacity just to go on and on. The article also has some interesting facts about women's and men's lives through history.

Can you imagine what it would be like to live to 115? More and more people in our society are living longer, with all the questions about adequate resources for the old that accompany that fact. But to take the question further – would it be desirable for people to live to, say, 150, if scientists and doctors could make that possible? What would be the implications for our community?

Should we, on reflection, be content that thus far 'modern medicine has proved useless at giving us the secrets of immortality'? There is a key point to reflect on here: quality versus quantity. In the end, was Mrs Hughes *'luckier than most of us will be'*?

# 4 Communication

## Introduction

It is frequently observed these days that, on the one hand, technology has given us a whole new range of ways of communicating with each other; on the other, that very technology (e.g. the INTERNET, personal stereos) makes us all shut off in our own little worlds and less good at talking to one another.

Is that true? For all the BT messages of 'It's Good To Talk', do we always communicate properly with our family, our friends, our teachers, our employers?

Listen to these two poems on the subject.

## Reading

### Phone Booth

Someone is loose in Moscow who won't stop
Ringing my phone.
Whoever-it-is listens, then hangs up.
Dial tone.

What do you want? A bushel of rhymes or so?
An autograph? A bone?
Hello?
Dial tone.

Someone's lucky number, for all I know,
Is the same, worse luck, as my own.
Hello!
Dial tone.

Or perhaps it's an angel calling collect
To invite me to God's throne.
Damn, I've been disconnected.
Dial tone.

Or is it my old conscience, my power of choice
To which I've grown
A stranger, and which no longer knows my voice?
Dial tone.

Are you standing there in some subway station, stiff
And hatless in the cold,
With your finger stuck in the dial as if
In a ring of gold?

And is there, outside the booth, a desperate throng
Tapping its coins on the glass, chafing its hands,
Like a line of people who have been waiting long
To be measured for wedding-bands?

I hear you breathe and blow into some remote
Mouthpiece, and as you exhale
The lapels of my coat
Flutter like pennants in a gale.

Speak up, friend! Are you deaf and dumb as a stone?
Dial tone.

The planet's communications are broken.
I'm tired of saying hello.
My questions might as well be unspoken.
Into the void my answers go.

Thrown together, together
With you, with you unknown.
Hello. Hello. Hello there.
Dial tone. Dial tone. Dial tone.

*Andrei Voznesensky*

## The Wrong Number

One night I went through the telephone book name by name.
   I moved in alphabetical order through London
Plundering living-rooms, basements, attics,
   Brothels and embassies.
I phoned florists' shops and mortuaries,
   Politicians and criminals with a flair for crime;
At midnight I phoned butchers and haunted them with strange
      bleatings,
   I phoned prisons and zoos simultaneously,
I phoned eminent surgeons at exactly the wrong moment.
   Before I was half-way through the phone book
My finger was numb and bloody.
   Not satisfied with the answers I tried again.
Moving frantically from A to Z needing confirmation
   That I was not alone
I phoned grand arsonists who lived in the suburbs
   And rode bicycles made out of flames.
No doubt my calls disturbed people on their deathbeds,
   Their death rattles drowned by the constant ringing of
      telephones!
No doubt the various angels who stood beside them
   Thought me a complete nuisance.
I *was* a complete nuisance.
   I worried jealous husbands to distraction
And put various Casanovas off their stroke

And woke couples drugged on love.
I kept the entire London telephone system busy,
    Darting from phone booth to phone booth
The Metropolitan phone-squad always one call behind me.
    I sallied forth dressed in loneliness and paranoia –
The Phantom Connection.
    Moving from shadow to shadow,
Rushing from phone booth to phone booth till finally
    I sought out a forgotten number and dialled it.
A voice cackling with despair answered.
    I recognised my own voice and had nothing to say to it.

*Brian Patten*

# Reflections

* Have these two poets phoned each other?!
  If you reflect carefully on these poems you will detect a common theme –
  although telephones can put people in contact with one another they can also
  intensify feelings of loneliness and being isolated. If you think about it, there
  are not many sounds quite as depressing as the final click on a phone receiver
  – especially if someone has put the phone down in a mood of argument!
  The poems take us beyond telephones to communication more widely –
  through to computers, television, film, radio, newspapers. How do we manage our information-rich environment – are we servants or masters of this
  technology?

* And when it comes to communicating in person, how do we relate to people
  around us? Are we *careful* as opposed to *careless* in our conversations, faxes, e-
  mail? What distinguishes human beings from the rest of the animal kingdom
  is our capacity for advanced communication; we should not abuse it, nor
  allow fast-changing technology to replace the importance of personal contact.

* *Communication – a cautionary tale*

*Head to Deputy*: Tomorrow morning there will be an eclipse of the sun at 9
a.m. This is something we can't see every day. Let the pupils line up outside
in their best clothes to watch. To mark the occurrence of this rare phenomena
I will personally explain it to them. If it is raining we shall not be able to see it
very well and so the pupils should assemble in the hall.

*Deputy Head to Senior Teacher*: By order of the Head there will be a total eclipse
of the sun at 9 a.m. tomorrow. If it is raining we shall not be able to see very
well on sight, in our best clothes. In that case the disappearance of the sun will
be followed through in the hall. This is something that we can't see happen
every day.

*Senior Teacher to Head of Year*: By order of the Head we shall follow through, in
best clothes, the disappearance of the sun in the hall tomorrow morning at 9
a.m. The Head will tell us whether it is going to rain. This is something we
can't see happen every day.

*Head of Year to Form Tutor*: If it is raining in the hall tomorrow morning, which is something we can't see happen every day, the Head – in her best clothes – will disappear at 9 a.m.

*Form Tutor to Pupils*: Tomorrow at 9 a.m. the Head will disappear. It is a pity that we can not see this happen every day.

# 5 Silence

## Introduction

Would it be true to say that silence is something that has almost disappeared from our world? Is noise our master? When was the last time you heard real silence?

Let us begin this assembly with two minutes silence – just to *hear* silence!

Listen to the following commentary on the way society seems to have lost its capacity to enjoy and benefit from silence. It asks the central question: Why are we afraid of it? Why must we always be humans *doing* rather than, once in a while, humans quietly *being*?

## Reading

### Silence

Silence is almost an entirely alien concept in Britain today. It is a lost commodity in a world that knows the value of everything save a bit of peace and quiet.

It is, of course, a commonplace that modern life is everywhere beset by noise: the roar of traffic, the jabber of the radio, the clamour of the mobile phone. Today the automobile has even begun to answer back: *beep, beep, beep, this is a Securicor van, reversing, reversing, reversing.*

Once there were places of refuge; but now even the rhythmic peace of a long train journey is shattered by a succession of 'passenger service' announcements which add about as much to the quality of life as those pointless little stickers on supermarket apples. To the babbling of tongues in inane conversations is added the chirp of the cellphone and the tinnitus of alien earphones. The silent majority these days is far from aptly named.

Our only escape is to take refuge in our own noise. So we plug in our own Walkmans to block out the sound of others, even as 17th-century fops would clutch a nosegay to shut out the stench of the plague-ridden outside world. Either that or we indulge in a positive celebration of noise, turning the stereo up to full volume or peering in awe to the sky to watch Concorde, that great destroyer of tranquillity, screech over our homes with its magnificent total roar.

For silence is to be avoided at all costs. Think of those uneasy seconds at a public function when the official speaker has been applauded and no one knows whether they are yet allowed to recommence their chatter.

The minute's silence for the dead has long gone the way of standing for the national anthem. It lingers only at football matches where the Tannoy occasionally announces the death of some recently departed hero. And even that is often tainted by the usual contemporary oafishness, as when Leeds fans booed during a silent memorial for the former Man. United manager Matt Busby, on the grounds that their manager, Don Revie had not been accorded the same honour.

Silence is not just a lack of noise. It is not the nothingness of a vacuum or the eerie suppression of life in that stillness when thick fog descends. There can be the noise of nature – wind through the leaves, water over rocks, or the sound of wings around a dovecote – and we speak still of silence.

Silence is a lack of people noise. So there is no greater silence than that when many people are present. Listen to the silence among a people gathered in prayer.

Egyptian mystical devotees called their god 'the Lord of the Silent'. Augustine spoke of the still small voice of God. And monks such as the Cistercians, Carthusians and the Trappists practised it, often to excess. The Quakers, though lay people active in the world, made it the centre of their worship. Their founder George Fox, according to one 17th-century account, 'on one occasion sat in silence for some hours in order to famish the people from words' before beginning to preach.

The power of the Quaker silence was striking, as one contemporary account records:

'Sometimes when there is not a word in a meeting but all are silently waiting, if one come in that is rude and wicked, and in whom the power of darkness prevaileth much, perhaps with an intention to mock or do mischief, it will strike terror in such a one and he will find himself unable to resist'.

If such quietism is a preparation for the great silence of death it is not one that is limited to those of a religious disposition. Many secular folk have had the same sense of silence penetrating to the heart of the mysterium: 'Whereof one cannot speak, thereof one must be silent.' said Wittgenstein in one of the greatest philosophical truisms of all time.

* * *

So why the desperate attempt of modern men and women to do all they can to escape silence? In part it is simply a ratchet effect. Noise creates deafness – just as, to echo Bob Geldof's memorable observation, when everyone stands up at a rock concert, everyone ends up with no better a view than they would have had if they had all remained seated.

Noise is also addictive. There are many who cannot go from room to room in the house without flicking on a radio. The answer of the Paris Communards to such dictatorship was to destroy; they smashed all the public clocks they could see in rebellion against the tyranny of time. Noise, like time, may have become a master rather than a servant, but is that any more of a solution than equipping environmental health officers with decibel meters is the real answer to noisy neighbours? Or merely banning from public places the mobile phone – the nearest thing to a perpetual motion machine that modern society has come close to perfecting:

'Hello, I'm on the mobile … No, it's cutting in and out … Hello … yes, that's better. I'm on the mobile. I'm on the train … it's late. We're just at Putney. So I'll probably be 10 minutes late into Waterloo. Can you tell them I'll be ten minutes late …'

Such prattle often seems to serve no purpose beyond reassuring the speaker that he is still alive: I din therefore I am. The noise is a comfort which tells us that we are not alone.

Or is it the opposite? Perhaps the babel is something behind which we hide. What is it that we fear in silence? In the quiet comes the sound of truth; in the lonely darkness of the small hours we are each forced to face up to the question of our own integrity.

There is a story that in the 1970s a Dominican monk attempted to include a minute's silence in his *Thought For The Day* slot on Radio 4. Such quiet could only be a mistake in the modern world, so some automatic BBC device cut in to fill the gap.

Eventually, of course, the church decreed that Quietism – the belief that you can be at peace with God only by withdrawing from the world – was a heresy. But who is talking about withdrawing from the world? I only want the world to withdraw a little from me so that I might reclaim my right to silence. There are those who have suggested that the whole of society would benefit. As Thomas Carlyle put it:

'Silence is the element in which great things fashion themselves together; that at length they may emerge, full-formed and majestic, into the daylight of Life, which they are henceforth to rule ... Do thou thyself but hold thy tongue for one day; on the morrow, how much clearer are thy purposes and duties; what wreck and rubbish have those mute workmen within thee swept away when intrusive noises were shut out! Speech is too often not, as the Frenchman defined it, the art of concealing Thought; but of quite stifling and suspending Thought, so that there is none to conceal. Thought will not work except in Silence ... The great silent men! ... A country which has none of these is in a bad way. Like a forest that has no roots, which had all turned into leaves and boughs, which must soon wither and be no forest.'

It may be that even this is not enough. Perhaps the noise of words inside the head is just as corrosive. True silence may consist of emptying the mind and rediscovering the ability to exist without searching after meanings or somesuch, to re-become a human being rather than a human doing.

*Paul Vallely*

# Reflections

\* The story of the BBC programme *Thought For The Day* and how it immediately filled with sound what was meant to be a minute's silence is somehow a symptom of our age. Can you think of a public place where silence is not filled in some way by piped music – superstores, airports, restaurants, even some museums and libraries!

Occasionally, we hold a national minute or two of silence to remember an event in history, for example those who died in the two world wars. Sometimes at football matches there is a minute's silence, though some people (as the passage mentions) find even that difficult. If you think about it, those occasional silences in large gatherings are powerful emotional moments – they do cause us to stand back briefly from the noise and bustle of our daily lives.

\*    It is worth reflecting: speech can stifle thought, as in the phrase 'think before you speak'. Sometimes silence really is golden and not something to run away from or fill with embarrassed giggles.

'I din therefore I am.'

'In the quiet comes the sound of truth.'

# 6 Love

## Introduction

The Christian Bible writes of faith, hope and love – and the greatest of these is love. Love in all its dimensions is a critically powerful force in human lives. Of course, with love sometimes goes hate – extremes produce extremes. And often love is very difficult to understand, particularly love in families where emotions are strong and complex. Yet our lives are spent living in families and it is important that we seek to understand the nature of love between parents and children, brothers and sisters.

The following passage comes from the final pages of a short novel (also a film) titled *A River Runs through It*. The novel is set in the beautiful countryside of Montana in the United States and is about the great love and friendship in one family. The two brothers and the father are united in their love of fishing; Paul is a gifted fisherman but there is a dark side to his character which others in the family never come to understand. The river is a potent presence in the family's life history, and at the start of this passage the sons are in their twenties.

## Reading

### A River Runs through It

A river, though, has so many things to say that it is hard to know what it says to each of us. As we were packing our tackle and fish in the car, Paul repeated, 'Just give me three more years.' At the time, I was surprised at the repetition, but later I realized that the river somewhere, sometime, must have told me, too, that he would receive no such gift. For, when the police sergeant early next May wakened me before daybreak, I rose and asked no questions. Together we drove across the Continental Divide and down the length of the Big Blackfoot River over forest floors yellow and sometimes white with glacier lilies to tell my father and mother that my brother had been beaten to death by the butt of a revolver and his body dumped in an alley.

My mother turned and went to her bedroom where, in a house full of men and rods and rifles, she had faced most of her great problems alone. She was never to ask me a question about the man she loved most and understood least. Perhaps she knew enough to know that for her it was enough to have loved him. He was probably the only man in the world who had held her in his arms and leaned back and laughed.

When I finished talking to my father, he asked, 'Is there anything else you can tell me?'

Finally, I said, 'Nearly all the bones in his hand were broken.'

He almost reached the door and then turned back for reassurance. 'Are you sure that the bones in his hand were broken?' he asked. I repeated, 'Nearly all the bones in his hand were broken.' 'In which hand?' he asked. 'In his right hand,' I answered

After my brother's death, my father never walked very well again. He had to struggle to lift his feet, and, when he did get them up, they came down slightly out of control. From time to time Paul's right hand had to be reaffirmed; then my father would shuffle away again. He could not shuffle in a straight line from trying to lift his feet. Like many Scottish ministers before him, he had to derive what comfort he could from the faith that his son had died fighting.

For some time, though, he struggled for more to hold on to. 'Are you sure you have told me everything you know about his death?' he asked. I said, 'Everything.' 'It's not much, is it?' 'No,' I replied, 'but you can love completely without complete understanding.' 'That I have known and preached,' my father said.

Once my father came back with another question. 'Do you think I could have helped him?' he asked. Even if I might have thought longer, I would have made the same answer. 'Do you think I could have helped him?' I answered. We stood waiting in deference to each other. How can a question be answered that asks a lifetime of questions?

After a long time he came with something he must have wanted to ask from the first. 'Do you think it was just a stick-up and foolishly he tried to fight his way out? You know what, I mean – that it wasn't connected with anything in his past.'

'The police don't know,' I said.

'But do you?' he asked, and I felt the implication.

'I've said I've told you all I know. If you push me far enough, all I really know is that he was a fine fisherman.'

'You know more than that,' my father said. He was beautiful.'

'Yes,' I said, 'he was beautiful. He should have been – you taught him.'

My father looked at me for a long time – he just looked at me. So this was the last he and I ever said to each other about Paul's death.

Indirectly, though, he was present in many of our conversations. Once, for instance, my father asked me a series of questions that suddenly made me wonder whether I understood even my father whom I felt closer to than any man I have ever known. 'You like to tell true stories, don't you?' he asked, and I answered. 'Yes, I like to tell stories that are true.'

Then he asked, 'After you have finished your true stories sometime, why don't you make up a story and the people to go with it?

'Only then will you understand what happened and why.'

'It is those we live with and love and should know who elude us.'

Now nearly all those I loved and did not understand when I was young are dead, but I still reach out to them.

Of course, now I am too old to be much of a fisherman, and now of course I usually fish the big waters alone, although some friends think I shouldn't. Like many fly fishermen in western Montana where the summer days are almost

Arctic in length, I often do not start fishing until the cool of the evening. Then in the Arctic half-light of the canyon, all existence fades to a being with my soul and memories and the sounds of the Big Blackfoot River and a four-count rhythm and the hope that a fish will rise.

Eventually, all things merge into one, and a river runs through it. The river was cut by the world's great flood and runs over rocks from the basement of time. On some of the rocks are timeless raindrops. Under the rocks are the words, and some of the words are theirs.

I am haunted by waters.

*Norman Maclean*

## Reflections

* The narrator is – as an old man – looking back on his family's life and, in particular, on the death of his brother who turned out to be a gambler heavily in debt and thus was killed. But the very loving family cannot help him. The father makes two very telling observations:

'You can love completely without complete understanding.'

'It is those we live with and love and should know who elude us.'

Our own families are always a great source of strength and support to us. Sometimes we have differences of views and – given the nature of love – these differences can lead to intense feelings and arguments. But we should try to understand those we love and offer them help when they need it, recognising that we might find it difficult to sympathise with their actions.

# 7 Friends and enemies

## Introduction

War is all about pitting one group of people against another. It is about anger, hate, destruction and death. Sometimes human beings justify its necessity but there is no disguising the ultimate horror of war.

But it can also bring together people on opposing sides, so that they see each other not as enemies but as ordinary people caught up in the war game. What we then understand by the term 'friend' or 'enemy' takes on a different meaning.

The first reading is from First World War (1914–1918) poet Wilfred Owen. The second is a light-hearted picture of the Vietnam War of the 1960s.

## Reading

*Strange Meeting*

It seemed that out of battle I escaped
Down some profound dull tunnel, long since scooped

Through granites which titanic wars had groined.
Yet also there encumbered sleepers groaned,
Too fast in thought or death to be bestirred.
Then, as I probed them, one sprang up, and stared
With piteous recognition in fixed eyes,
Lifting distressful hands as if to bless.
And by his smile, I knew that sullen hall,
By his dead smile I knew we stood in Hell.
With a thousand pains that vision's face was grained;
Yet no blood reached there from the upper ground,
And no guns thumped, or down the flues made moan.
'Strange friend,' I said, 'here is no cause to mourn.'
'None,' said the other, 'save the undone years,
The hopelessness. Whatever hope is yours,
Was my life also; I went hunting wild
After the wildest beauty in the world,
Which lies not calm in eyes, or braided hair,
But mocks the steady running of the hour,
And if it grieves, grieves richlier than here.
For by my glee might many men have laughed,
And of my weeping something had been left,
Which must die now. I mean the truth untold,
The pity of war, the pity war distilled.
Now men will go content with what we spoiled.
Or, discontent, boil body, and be spilled,
They will be swift with swiftness of the tigress,
None will break ranks, though nations trek from progress.
Courage was mine, and I had mystery,
Wisdom was mine, and I had mastery;
To miss the march of this retreating world
Into vain citadels that are not walled.
Then, when much blood had clogged their chariot-wheels
I would go up and wash them from sweet wells,
Even with truths that lie too deep for taint.
I would have poured my spirit without stint
But not through wounds; not on the cess of war.
Foreheads of men have bled where no wounds were.
I am the enemy you killed, my friend.
I knew you in this dark; for so you frowned
Yesterday through me as you jabbed and killed.
I parried; but my hands were loath and cold.
Let us sleep now …

*Wilfred Owen*

## The Vietnam War

*In mid-1966 the US inaugurated 'pacification' campaigns, isolating villages to protect them from guerrillas, and spraying vast areas to defoliate trees that might provide cover for the Vietcong.*

When Sergeant Melvin Murrell and his company of United States Marines drop by helicopter into the village of Tuylon, west of Danang, with orders to sell 'the basic liberties as outlined on page 233 of the Pacification Programme Handbook' and at the same time win the hearts and minds of the people (see same handbook, page 86 under WHAM) they see no one: not a child or a chicken. The population has watched them come out of the sky, and most of them have retired to the paddies or stand silent in the shadows of their houses.

'Come on out, we're your friends,' Sergeant Murrell shouts through a loud-hailer, in English.

'Come on out, everybody, we got rice and candy and toothbrushes to give you,' he coos in the hot silence.

'Listen, either you gooks come out from wherever you are or we're going to come in there and get you,' he jokes, as soldiers at war are given to joke.

So the people of Tuylon come out from wherever they are and queue to receive packets of bulk supplies of US 'miracle rice', Uncle Ben's brand, and Hershey chocolate bars and 7000 toothbrushes, which come in four colours, and comics for the children – *Superman*, etc. – and in a separate, almost touching little ceremony, the district chief is presented with four yellow, portable, battery-operated flush lavatories.

'If these are right for your requirements, says Sergeant Murrell, 'there will be more where they came from.' And when it is all over and the children cheer on cue, Sergeant Murrell notes in his log of the day: 'At first, they did not appear to understand that we had come to help them. However, they were persuaded other-wise, and at this time they are secured and on our side. I believe they respect our posture of strength and humanity. I believe the colonel will be pleased.'

The Marines with whom I have come to Tuylon are called a CAC unit, which stands for Combined Action Company, which means their role is both military and civil. First, a CAC unit moves into a village and 'protects' it – whether or not the villagers have asked to be protected – with trenches and booby traps and barbed wire. Then they declare the village 'friendly' and set about selling 'the basic liberties as outlined on page 233 of the Pacification Programme Handbook' to old men and young men, women and children.

There is, however, a problem. The United States Marines would rather fight the Vietnamese than sell them the basic liberties and win their hearts and minds. 'I'll say this for these people,' says Murrell, 'they do what they're told. I guess it's like I always say: whoever's got the guns calls the tune.'

Tuylon, one week later:

Colonel Richard Trueball has arrived. 'Well, slap my mouth, it sure is good to see you, sir!' says Sergeant Murrell.

'How is everything here, Murrell? How is the hygiene programme coming along? Toothbrushes, toilets cause an impact?'

'Yes indeedie, sir. Toothbrushes went down a dandy but as for gettin' them to go to the bathroom and all that – well, I'm afraid these people been doin' it other ways for thousands of years and they seem to like it that way.'

The colonel thinks.

'Never say die, Murrell. I'll send you in a portable shower unit on Thursday.'

'Yes, *sir*!'

*John Pilger*

# Reflections

* Wilfred Owen movingly brings together two soldiers from the trenches – after they've been killed. In death they are strangely united; where once they were enemies, now they can be friends. The futility and pity of war shine through this celebrated poem from the Great War.

  By way of contrast, John Pilger discovers American soldiers trying to win over the enemy with gifts – seeking to win hearts and minds with gifts of comics and portable showers! What we mean by real friendship is worth reflecting on here. The tragi-comedy of the situation does not escape his keen journalist's eye.

* In different ways these writers make us think about the personal values of friendship. 'Friends and enemies' are often meaningless terms. 'Hearts and minds', however, offers an alternative perspective on what it is that unites and divides us from time to time.

  (See also **Friendship**, p. 227)

# 8 What is a community?

## Introduction

The word 'community' is defined in various ways in the dictionary:

- the people living in one locality

- the locality in which they live

- a group of people having cultural, religious, ethnic or other characteristics in common

- a group of nations having certain interests in common

- (ecology) a group of interdependent plants and animals inhabiting the same region.

Having something 'in common' unites these definitions, a reflection of the Latin origin of the word.

It is fair to say that we frequently use the word today to promote a positive image – the community school; community spirit; community action groups; a community of scholars. But there is a view that, while we say it, we may not actually mean it.

The following article challenges some of our assumptions about the word community. It is intriguingly titled: 'It sounds nice, but we don't want to live there'.

## Reading

*It sounds nice, but we don't want to live there*

'Community' is in danger of becoming the ruling banality of our times.

Politicians linger on it, roll it round their tongues and repeat it with a reverent relish, as if they thought it could turn any phrase from dross to gold. And, up to a point, it can; cosy, nostalgic and vaguely moral, it strikes a chord in most of us. It has survived, untouched, the ambiguities of 'community care' and 'community policing'. Whatever community is, we all want some of that stuff.

It is a strong word, despite its overuse, because it is associated with a golden memory of the Fifties, or even earlier, when we were a kinder, more united country.

Like freedom, the political buzzword, community is vague enough to allow rival parties to wrestle over it.

At its most trivial, community has come to mean a modest amount of social co-operation, epitomised perhaps by suburban Neighbourhood Watch schemes. A willingness to take one's garbage to the recycling station and stand as a governor for the local school are extensions of this. Worthy, yes, and even useful – but still light years away from the deeper involvement with neighbours that previous generations would have taken for granted. Instead of peeking round their curtains at shadowy figures trying car handles, they might have known the youths and confronted them, or indeed their parents. Instead of phoning neighbours to lobby for school elections, they would have been standing on doorsteps, gossiping.

For most people, that way of life has been ended forever by affluence and technology. We should, anyway, be cautious about any definition of community that reduces itself to the self-protection of social islands. It leads to those rich people's compounds surrounded by electric fences and security guards – which, in the United States, also call themselves 'communities'.

The difficulty is that a more generous definition of community, including a belief in social cohesion as a better way of living, involves sacrifices many people would now reject out of hand, even as they yearn for 'a sense of community'. If everyone sent their child to the local schools, Britain would be more communal. If petrol prices were much higher, so that we had to travel more by public transport, ditto. If there were no subsidies for private health care, ditto. If more families kept their old folk with them until death, ditto. If local authorities were stronger, ditto.

But, given the cash, individual parents, drivers, employees, families and voters have made different choices. Particularly in the suburbs of the South and Midlands. So it is fair to ask whether the whole community thing is mostly an exercise in the higher hypocrisy – or at least in wolfing our cake, and then whining about its disappearance. How much do most voters really want a greater sense of community along with the lifestyle changes they would have to make in return? Were the British ever particularly communal, or was it only poverty that made us so? In all affluent societies greater wealth has been used to buy *less* community and more privacy.

It is just possible that the consequences of social atomisation – in crime, congestion, urban loneliness and even the inner unhappiness of a social animal changing its ways – are such that millions of people are rethinking, at some deep level, the pay-off between individualism and community. It is conceivable that a revolution in attitudes has begun, and that politicians are picking it up.

But if so, where is the political programme? If politicians are giving us the rhetoric of a return to community values, while fighting shy of the substance, then perhaps they are shrewd judges of the national character. For too many

Britons, a community is something we would like to live in, but not something we want to be part of. We all want more grass round our houses.

*Andrew Marr*

## Reflections

* The argument of this article is, in essence, that society today increasingly has values which focus on the individual, rather than on what is communal. When the writer concludes, 'we all want more grass round our houses' he is indicating that selfishness is more powerful than altruism – thinking of the good of others.

  But if greater material wealth moves us towards more privacy and less community, it is all the more important that in schools and the workplace we promote communal values and beliefs. We are all dependent for example, on one another's respect for law and order if our local community is to be a positive one. It is appropriate to celebrate certain human activities together rather than separately.

  A British politician once claimed, 'there is no such thing as society, only the individual.' A successful school, hospital, factory, orchestra, sports team, or whatever is living proof that individuals cannot thrive as islands. We need to steer our politicians away from misusing the important word 'community'.

# 9 Brain sex

## Introduction

Do you think that women and men experience the world in very different ways? Do we learn in the same way, males and females? Do we feel equal opportunity exists in our society?

And what are the arguments for educating girls and boys in separate classes or separate schools?

Should we acknowledge that women are better at some things, men at others?

The following reading is from the introduction to a book titled *Brain Sex*. The authors argue a case with which you may or may not agree.

## Reading

*Brain sex*

Men are different from women. They are equal only in their common membership of the same species, humankind. To maintain that they are the same in aptitude, skill or behaviour is to build a society based on a biological and scientific lie.

The sexes are different because their brains are different. The brain, the chief administrative and emotional organ of life, is differently constructed in men and in women; it processes information in a different way, which results in different perceptions, priorities and behaviour.

In the past ten years there has been an explosion of scientific research into what makes the sexes different. Doctors, scientists, psychologists and sociologists, working apart, have produced a body of findings which, taken together, paints a remarkably consistent picture. And the picture is one of startling sexual asymmetry.

At last there is an answer to the exasperated lament 'Why *can't* a woman be more like a man?'; it is time to explode the social myth that men and women are virtually interchangeable, all things being equal. All things are not equal.

Until recently, behavioural differences between the sexes have been explained away by social conditioning – the expectations of parents, whose own attitudes, in turn, reflect the expectations of society; little boys are told that they shouldn't cry, and that the way to the top depends on masculine assertion and aggression. Scant attention was paid to the biological view that we may be what we are because of the way we are made. Today, there is too much new biological evidence for the sociological argument to prevail. The argument of biology at last provides a comprehensive, and scientifically probable framework within which we can begin to understand why we are who we are.

If the social explanation is inadequate, the biochemical argument seems more plausible – that it is our hormones which make us behave in specific, stereotypical ways. But, as we will discover, hormones alone do not provide the whole answer; what makes the difference is the interplay between those hormones and the male or female brains, pre-wired specifically to react with them.

What you will read in this book about the differences between men and women may make both sexes angry or smug. Both reactions are wrong. If women have reason to rage, it is not because science has set at naught their hard-won struggle towards equality; their wrath should rather be directed at those who have sought to misdirect and deny them their very essence. Many women in the last thirty or forty years have been brought up to believe that they are, or should be, 'as good as the next man', and in the process they have endured acute and unnecessary pain, frustration and disappointment. They were led to believe that once they had shaken off the shackles of male prejudice and oppression – the supposed source of their second-class status – the gates of the promised land of equal achievement would be thrown open; women would be free at last to scale and conquer the commanding heights of the professions.

Instead, in spite of greater emancipation in terms of education, opportunity, and social attitudes, women are not noticeably 'doing better' than they were thirty years ago. There were more women in the British Cabinet in the 1930s than there are at present. There has been no significant increase in the number of female MPs over the past three decades. Some women, seeing how far their sex has fallen short of the supposed ideal of power-sharing, feel that they have failed. But they have only failed to be like men.

Men, on the other hand, should find no cause for complacent celebration, although some will inevitably find ammunition for their bar-room prejudices: it is, for instance, true that most women cannot read a map as well as a man. But women can read a character better. And people are more important than maps. (The male mind, at this point, will immediately think of exceptions to this.)

Some researchers have been frankly dismayed at what they have discovered. Some of their findings have been, if not suppressed, at least quietly shelved because of their potential social impact. But it is usually better to act on the basis of what is true, rather than to maintain, with the best will in the world, that what is true has no right to be so.

Better, too, to welcome and exploit the complementary differences between men and women. Women should contribute their specific female gifts rather than waste their energies in the pursuit of a sort of surrogate masculinity. A woman's greater imagination can solve intractable problems – be they professional or domestic – at one apparently intuitive stroke.

The best argument for the acknowledgement of differences is that doing so would probably make us happier. The appreciation, for instance, that sex has different origins, motives, and significance in the context of the male and female brains, that marriage is profoundly unnatural to the biology of the male, might make us better and more considerate husbands and wives. The understanding that the roles of father and mother are not interchangeable might make us better parents.

The biggest behavioural difference between men and women is the natural, innate aggression of men, which explains to a large degree their historical dominance of the species. Men didn't learn aggression as one of the tactics of the sex war. We do not teach our boy children to be aggressive – indeed, we try vainly to unteach it. Even researchers most hostile to the acknowledgement of sex differences agree that this is a male feature, and one which cannot be explained by social conditioning.

We are an arrogant species. Our superiority to other animals, in terms of our capacity to reason and discriminate, has been said to put us closer to the angels than to the chimpanzees. Perhaps that makes us, thinking of ourselves as masters of our destinies, ignore the notion that we are still subject to the biological imperatives of our bodies. We forget that, ultimately, like other animals, what we are and how we live is largely dictated by the messages that mould and inform our brains.

Men and women could live more happily, understand and love each other better, organise the world to better effect, if we acknowledged our differences. We could then build our lives on the twin pillars of our distinct sexual identities. It is time to cease the vain contention that men and women are created the same. They were not, and no amount of idealism or Utopian fantasy can alter the fact. It can only strain the relationship between the sexes.

*Anne Moir and David Jessel*

# Reflections

* Arguments continue to rage about equality between the sexes. These writers argue that society should not try to encourage women to be like men; women and men should recognise they have different strengths – arising out of biology and what they call their 'brain sex' – and build on them accordingly. Of course, there are other writers and thinkers who believe that differences should not be underlined, that biology does not divide the sexes significantly, and that women have historically been put in their place by a male-dominated set of social rules.

You will have your own views on this subject. It remains a difficult one for parents and teachers who want to offer equality of opportunity and *access* to that opportunity to boys and girls alike.

There are certainly issues raised in the passage about innate female and male qualities that we should reflect on. For example, innate male aggression versus the female's greater imagination?

Would the world be a better place if, as these writers suggest, 'we acknowledged our differences?'

# 10 Intelligences

## Introduction

A quick observation of any group of people immediately tells you that some are better at some things than others. But one of the problems of our society is that it tends to recognise and value certain kinds of intelligence at the expense of others. Imagine, for a moment, that our society valued practical intelligence above factual intelligence: how we teach in schools and universities would be rather different, and maybe governments wouldn't only be in the hands of people with academic degrees?

Various writers have tried to define intelligences; some have done it more narrowly than others. The following list comes from a writer called Charles Handy who suggests that you can be as bright as a button in one and a dunce in another. You can shine in five or only in two. Here are his nine different forms of intelligence, with personal comments.

## Reading

### The intelligence investment

*Factual Intelligence*: the sort of walking encyclopaedia who wins the mastermind competitions in Britain, who knows the answer to every question in Trivial Pursuit and can give an impromptu lecture on the state of the Romanian economy over dinner. We are envious but often bored.

*Analytical intelligence*: the person who loves intellectual problems, crosswords and puzzles. Such people delight in reducing complex data to more simple formulations. Strategic consultants, scientists and academics are strong in this type of intelligence. When this intelligence is combined with factual intelligence, examinations come easy. When we describe someone as an intellectual it is often this combination which we have in mind.

*Linguistic intelligence*: the one who speaks seven languages and can pick up another within a month. I envy such people, since I don't have this facility myself, but we have to remember that it is not necessarily connected with the first two intelligences.

*Spatial intelligence*: the intelligence which sees patterns in things. Artists have it, as do mathematicians and systems-designers. Entrepreneurs have it in dollops, but without necessarily having the other intelligences, which explains why many an entrepreneur failed at school and would never go near a business school.

*Musical intelligence*: the sort that gave Mozart his genius, but which also drives pop stars and their bands, many of whom would never have a chance of going to college, because their scores on the first two intelligences would have been too low.

*Practical intelligence*: the intelligence which allows young kids to take a motorbike apart and put it together again, although they might not be able to explain how in words. Many 'intellectuals', intelligent in the first two senses of the word, are notoriously impractical and unworldly.

*Physical intelligence*: the intelligence, or talent, which we can see in sport stars, which enables some to hit balls much better than others, to ski better, dance better and generally co-ordinate mind and muscle in ways that defeat me.

*Intuitive intelligence*: the gift which some have of seeing things which others can't, even if they cannot explain why or wherefore. It is said that women have this intelligence to a greater degree than men, which may be why men often disparage it.

*Interpersonal intelligence*: the wit and the ability to get things done with and through other people. Notoriously, this intelligence often does not go with analytical or information intelligence. 'Too clever by half' – the jibe aimed at the Conservative politician Ian Macleod in years gone by, to explain why he would never be the great leader he could have been, applies to others as well. Without this form of intelligence, great minds can be wasted.

*Charles Handy*

# Reflections

* Which of these do you think you possess more or less of? 'Know Yourself' – the words inscribed on the ancient temple of Delphi – are words important to us as we develop and make decisions about our future: that may be deciding which subjects to study at school or college; it may be deciding what to specialise in when thinking about certain employment.

  The challenge for teachers and parents is to ensure that individual intelligences are spotted and developed, so that potential is harnessed. A healthy and wealthy society of the future needs to make sure that human intelligences which were often neglected in the past are celebrated for the good of all.

* Beware: 'He that is good with a hammer tends to think everything is a nail.'

# School Matters

## Teamwork

*There are four people named Everybody, Somebody, Anybody and Nobody. There was an important job to be done and Everybody was asked to do it. Everybody was sure Somebody would do it. Anybody could have done it, but Nobody did it. Somebody got angry about that, because it was Everybody's job. Everybody thought Anybody could do it but Nobody realized that Everybody wouldn't do it. It ended up that Everybody blamed Somebody when Nobody did what Anybody could have done.*

*Dear Mummy & Daddy*

*I have to tell you that I have ended up – unexpectedly – in hospital, with both legs broken. I have also fallen in love with an American nurse – in fact, we are going to get married and I am about to have his baby.*

*None of the above is true, but I have just failed my final exams, and I thought you ought to put things in perspective.*

Letter from an 18-year-old girl, away at boarding-school.

# 1 Reading books is not worth the effort

## Introduction

We are urged by parents and teachers alike to apply ourselves to studying at school. At the heart of study is reading – the exploration of books. But has a time come when books are no longer the attraction they were for previous generations?

A sixteen-year-old girl explains here why her generation prefers to watch a flickering screen rather than plough through a book.

## Reading

### Reading books is not worth the effort

A recent survey enthused that people are reading more than ever. I would like to know, first, what it is they are reading, and, second, who exactly these avid readers are. I have seen no reference in this survey to teenage readers. Is this because we do not exist? I can tell you only what I see every day at school. A teenager who reads is a rarity.

Our school library has been recently and beautifully refurbished and now boasts a catalogue ranging from Austen to Zola (before then I think it started with Kingsley Amis and stopped at Martin Amis because there was no more shelf-space). And while the computer room is packed every lunch hour, the turn-out in the library is sparse at best. Occasionally people come to stick discarded bubblegum on the radiator.

Possibly the non-visitors find the studious atmosphere intimidating, but I think it is simpler than that. Reading is hard work. For a long time children believed their parents when they were told that something which took effort was more worthwhile than instant gratification, that hard work is eventually pleasurable: 'Taking time to clean and boil spinach, good. Using finger to eat peanut butter out of a jar, bad.'

It seems that mine is the first generation to reject this theory. My mother was genuinely surprised when she asked if I didn't feel better for having cleaned my room and I said no. Why should I feel better? I stubbed my toe on the Hoover and it ate into time I could have used to watch pop videos on MTV.

When Marshall McLuhan prophesied in the 1960s that people would eventually stop reading and communicate instead through the electronic media, his work was considered as subversive as Darwin's. The notion that the printed word might be made obsolete terrified a generation of liberal intellectuals, whose status within society was testimony to the importance of literacy.

Looking back we can see that McLuhan's chant 'the medium is the message' was the original soundbite. I am assured that hardly anyone actually read his work. Today his books are largely out of print. But it seems his prophecies might be worth re-reading. When he wrote *Understanding Media – The Extensions of Man*, he was dealing with the radio, telephone and television. With microwaves, satellite dishes and fax machines to back us up, we seem to have proof that gratification must always be provided instantly. Because I and all the other children of the 1980s never knew a time when things took effort, we have a different slant on reading. Times may be hard but living is still meant to be easy. It is screens and sounds that link us and give us our identity.

Even the cult literature of angry young men (now dead or, worse, old) fails to persuade us that reading is worth the effort. What use is Jack Kerouac's *On The Road* when we have no desire to venture beyond the boundaries of our bedrooms with their view of the world via satellite? Which of us can relate to the teenage trauma of *The Catcher in the Rye* when the cast of *Beverly Hills 90210* tell us everything we need to know?

These rebellious books, besides, are now on the school syllabus, immediately labelling them as duty and hard work. It is difficult to find personal pleasure in *The Catcher in the Rye* after you have had to write a 2,000-word essay analysing its use of slang. Books enjoyed by my parents' generation as subversive tales of adolescents battling against the Establishment have been adopted by the Establishment and I resent it.

Constant testing at school leaves us with no desire for anything that resembles effort when we get home. As the GCSE exams are based on course work, there is pressure all year round. So now, more than ever before, we want to tune out in front of a television screen once we stagger home.

I can sit all day watching MTV, eating Pop Tarts heated in the microwave, drinking lo-cal, nutrient-free Diet Pepsi, listening to electronic music created by people taking smart drugs. Sometimes it all makes me feel a bit queasy. It is then that I find myself tentatively reaching for a book to accompany my Pop Tarts. But much as I may enjoy a few stolen hours with black on white, I do not talk about my reading at school. It would be like saying I occasionally get the urge to sleep with fish under my pillow.

On the one hand, my school friends' uncompromising rejection of literature and reading disturbs me; but, on the other, I identify with it. Not reading is our way of alerting the intellectual establishment that we have moved on. 'Unliteracy' is our unique contribution to modern culture.

*Emma Forrest*

# Reflections

* Has this generation rejected the theory that something which takes effort is more worthwhile than instant gratification?

  Do you agree with Emma Forrest's view that 'It is screens and sounds that link us and give us our identity'?

  Is it true that 'unliteracy' is the present generation's contribution to modern culture?

  Her views in this article might well be supported by many young people; equally there would be those who would hotly oppose her. We are probably led to ask the question: does it have to be *either* books *or* MTV? Can the two not flourish side by side?

* Our school libraries are increasingly including CD Rom and other electronic

data, but books remain at the core of a vibrant library. And if teachers and parents want to encourage children to read, they could do worse than grant them the following adult rights:

- the right not to read
- the right to skip pages
- the right not to finish a book
- the right to re-read
- the right to read anything
- the right to read anywhere
- the right to browse
- the right to read out loud
- the right to remain silent.

# 2 Projects: 'Tarzan's easy'

## Introduction

Project-work is a mainstay of most school subjects. What is important about projects is that – at their best – we learn the important skills of research, planning, drafting and redrafting, and final presentation; and these apply equally to Geography, Design Technology, Music, whatever.

Of course, there are always short-cuts, as the following extract from Jan Mark's novel *Thunder and Lightenings* amusingly reveals.

## Reading

*'Tarzan's easy'*

'You're the new boy, are you?' said someone beside him. 'I'm Miss Beale, who are you?'

'I'm Mitchell,' said Andrew. 'Andrew Mitchell, Miss.' It sounded like a silly sort of tongue twister.

'How do you like it here?' said Miss Beale. Andrew didn't intend to be side-tracked.

'What are we supposed to be doing?' he asked.

'That rather depends on you,' said Miss Beale. 'In General Studies you can choose your own subject and follow it through. You'll be rather behind the others but you can start on a project now and work on it through the holidays. That's what most of the others will do, if they haven't finished by next week.'

Andrew found this hard to believe.

'What are you interested in?' asked Miss Beale.

'Motor racing, guinea-pigs,' said Andrew.

'Well, either of those would do for a start,' said Miss Beale. 'Perhaps Victor would show you round so that you can see how the others set about it.' Andrew thought she wanted to be rid of him and when he turned round he found that a restive queue had formed behind him. Miss Beale directed him to Victor. He was the very fat boy with the very thin face.

Andrew was reluctant to go any closer. How could he stroll up and hold a normal conversation with anyone so deformed? He picked up his satchel and walked casually round the fat boy's desk as though he just happened to be passing it. When he got close, Andrew realized that Victor was not fat at all. On the contrary, he was exceptionally thin; all of him, not just his head and legs. The fat part was made up of clothes. Andrew could see a white T-shirt, a red shirt, a blue sweater and a red sweater. Further down he wore a pair of black jeans with orange patches sewn over the knees and yellow patches on the hip pockets. Over it all he had an anorak so covered in badges and buttons that it was difficult to tell what colour it was.

In fact, he was not so much dressed as camouflaged. Even his hair seemed to be some part of a disguise, more like a wig than live hair, dusty black as if it had been kicked round the floor before being put on. It was so long at the front that Victor was actually looking through it. His ears stuck out cheerfully, like a Radar device.

'Miss Beale said you would show me round, to look at the projects,' said Andrew.

'Why, do you want to copy one?' asked Victor, lifting a strand of hair and exposing one eye. 'You could copy mine, only someone might recognize it. I've done that three times already.'

'Whatever for?' said Andrew. 'Don't you get tired of it?'

Victor shook his head and his hair.

'That's only once a year. I did that two times at the junior school and now I'm doing that again,' he said. 'I do fish, every time. Fish are easy. They're all the same shape.'

'No, they're not,' said Andrew.

'They are when I do them,' said Victor. He spun his book round, with one finger, to show Andrew the drawings. His fish were not only all the same shape, they were all the shame shape as slugs. Underneath each drawing was a printed heading: BREAM; TENSH; CARP; STIKLBAK; SHARK. It was the only way of telling them apart. The shark and the bream were identical, except that the shark had a row of teeth like tank traps.

'Isn't there a "c" in stickleback?' said Andrew. Victor looked at his work.

'You're right.' He crossed out both 'k's, substituted 'c's and pushed the book away, the better to study it. 'I got that wrong last year.'

Andrew flipped over a few pages. There were more slugs: PLACE; COD; SAWFISH; and a stingy thing with a frill round its neck: EEL.

'Don't you have to write anything?' asked Andrew.

'Yes, look. I wrote a bit back here. About every four pages will do, said Victor. 'Miss Beale, she keep saying I ought to write more but she's glad when I don't. She's got to read it. Nobody can read my writing.

Andrew was not surprised. Victor's writing was a sort of code to deceive the enemy, with punctuation marks in unlikely places to confuse anyone who came too close to cracking the code. He watched Andrew counting the full stops in one sentence and said, 'I put those in while I think about the next word. I like doing question marks better.' He pointed out two or three specimens, independent question marks, without questions. They looked like curled feathers out of a pillow. One had a face.

'Do you put a question mark in every sentence?' said Andrew.

'Oh, yes. I know you don't actually need them,' said Victor, 'but they're nice to do.'

Andrew turned to the last page of the book. There was a drawing of a whale.

'Whales aren't fish,' said Andrew.

'Aren't they?' said Victor. 'Are you sure? I always put a whale in.'

'Whales are mammals.'

'What's a mammal?' said Victor. He wrote 'This.is.not.a.fish?' under his whale and closed the book. 'Come and see the others.'

'Mammals don't lay eggs,' said Andrew, as they set off round the room.

'That's a pity,' said Victor. 'I'd like to see a whale's egg. Big as a bath, wouldn't that be?' He stopped by the boy in the pink shirt. 'Let's have a look at your project, Tim.'

Andrew thought he had seen most of Tim's project before. It featured a man in a tree, knotty with muscles and wearing a leopard skin.

'Tarzan,' said Tim.

'Why do a project about Tarzan?' said Andrew.

'Tarzan's easy,' said Tim. 'You just cut him out and stick him in.'

'Fish are easier,' said Victor.

'Why not do worms then?' said Andrew. 'Nothing could be easier than worms. Wiggle-wiggle-wiggle: all over in a second. Page one, worms are long and thin. Page two, worms are round.'

Victor began to grin but Tim sat down to give the idea serious consideration.

Victor's grin became wider, revealing teeth like Stonehenge.

'I reckon you're catching on,' he said. 'Why don't you do worms?'

'I want to do something interesting,' said Andrew.

'Ho,' said Victor. 'You'll come to a bad end, you will.'

They went on round the room. Andrew noticed that nearly all the boys were doing a project on fish or fishing. The girls tended to specialize in horses except for Jeannette Butler, who wouldn't let them see hers.

'Why don't you go and stand in the road and catch cars?' said Jeannette, giving them a hefty shove when they tried to look.

'Give us a kiss,' said Victor and got a poke in the chest instead.

'I think I'll do motor racing,' said Andrew when they got back to Victor's desk. ' I know a bit about that, already. Me and my Dad used to go to Brand's Hatch a lot, when we lived in Kent.'

'Where's Kent?' said Victor. 'Down at the bottom somewhere, isn't it?'

'Some of it is,' said Andrew. 'We were further up, near London.' Andrew fetched a piece of drawing paper and sat down to draw a Formula One racing car. Victor drew some scales on his whale and broadcast punctuation marks throughout the book, letting them fall wherever he fancied.

*Jan Mark*

# Reflections

\* Well, apart from the quality of punctuation mentioned, there are some serious points to be made about how *not* to approach project-work: fish, worms and Tarzan might be three words to remind you next time you embark on a school project that it is not about copying out a previous one, nor is it choosing a subject that you can't find out much about.

To produce a History project that is going to attract good marks demands the same sort of thoughtful preparation that any professional writer needs before starting work. Writing a full plan; thinking about resources you'll need; researching in the appropriate places; compiling notes in rough; ordering those notes; preparing a first draft; asking someone to check that through; a final write-up, including a list of sources used – these are the skills needed to move beyond Tim's 'man in a tree, knotty with muscles and wearing a leopard skin'.

# 3 Reputations

## Introduction

The reputation of any organisation depends on how the members of that organisation conduct themselves. In the case of a hospital it will be the professional expertise of doctors that counts but, crucially, it will also be how nurses, physiotherapists, telephonists, porters, pharmacists treat patients – in other words, a team approach.

In a school context the quality of teaching and learning is a key to the school's reputation; but so too is the way staff and pupils alike present themselves in the local community.

And what is always true about reputation is that it can take a long time to build a good one, but it can be damaged quickly by the thoughtless actions of one or two individuals.

Listen to the following accounts of a fight which took place outside a school. There are five perspectives, which, as you'll see, don't necessarily paint the same picture.

## Reading

### The fight

*Old lady*

I was walking home and I just got opposite the school – Devenport Comprehensive – you know it. Anyway, I was practically pushed into the traffic by this crowd of teenage thugs milling about, swearing – I think the language of these kids today is dreadful. One of them was shoving another one in the chest and yelling at him – something about a girl. The others were all egging them on. One of them was actually waving a penknife around. It's a wonder nobody was hurt. Luckily the police arrived in a van and started breaking it up. I know what I'd do to them if I was in charge. What they need is a good hiding. I think the police have a very hard job these days coping with that sort of thing. Still, they soon pushed them along and got rid of them.

*Window cleaner – on the opposite side of the street*

I didn't see much – just the usual group of kids all trying to push on to the bus. Seemed a bit more rowdy than usual, though. I think one of them was from another school – had a different uniform anyway. He was looking for a fight – all mouthy. You know how kids are. The girls are just as bad – yelling their heads off. One of them was crying and shrieking, hysterical. The funny part was the way some old dear laid into them with her handbag. Anyway, the police roared up, late as usual in a white Rover. It was all over by then, really.

*Headteacher*

This is most unfortunate. One of our pupils was involved in an altercation with a lad from another school. It was connected with a dispute about a girlfriend. I am proud of my school and am sure this incident was exceptional. Many of our senior pupils are involved in community work and we enjoy a good reputation in the area. The notion that people are terrorized by our pupils is a gross exaggeration. I dealt with the boy the following morning. I talked it over with him and have imposed a week's detention plus the loss of certain privileges. His parents have been contacted and agree with me that the matter should now be forgotten. I have no idea who called the police. Certainly no member of my staff would overreact in such a way.

*Anna*

It was all Wayne's fault. He goes to St Jacobs round the corner. Anyway I gave him up two weeks ago and he's been going about threatening my current boyfriend. He was waiting outside the school and he called me a name and I got annoyed. He's a loud-mouthed bully – he is always involved in some aggro or other, him and his mates. My boyfriend gave him a mouthful and they had a go at each other. I could have killed him. All I had on me was a metal comb but I had a few jabs at him. I don't know what the fuss is all about. There's often a bit of bullying and fighting outside the school. The police pushed everybody about and we all went home.

*Local radio news item*

And now a disturbing report from one of the town's largest comprehensive schools – Devenport. Several pupils and members of the public were injured in an incident outside the school in Sidmouth Street. We go over now to our reporter on the scene ...

Only a few hours ago this whole area was the scene of one of the most violent clashes we have seen in recent years involving pupils at the strife-torn Devenport Comprehensive. Members of staff refused to comment but Mr John Hurtson, the headteacher, issued a statement in which he claimed that 'the incident was exceptional' and that the pupils would be 'talked to' and 'the parents contacted'. Mr Hurtson maintained he was 'proud of the school', a view not shared by an elderly lady who was physically assaulted in the incident, which apparently involved a row over a fifth former's girlfriend. A local resident, Mrs Avely, saw a crowd of teenage thugs milling about and swearing. What made the fight particularly grave was the evidence of the weapons used. 'One of them was waving a penknife ... it's a wonder nobody was hurt.' Another witness stated that 'the girls were just as bad – yelling their heads off ... shrieking and hysterical'.

Luckily on this occasion the police arrived promptly and were able to subdue the crowd and limit the damage. One of the pupils of the school said a group of fifth years were 'always involved in some aggro or other'. She stated that there was 'often ... bullying and fighting outside the school'.

Police are pursuing their enquiries but as yet no arrests have been made. In the meantime, local residents are asking is this what we must learn to expect from today's young people?

## Reflections

* A not untypical set of statements! Of course they highlight how different people can see what is apparently just one set of events so differently. But they also remind us how, despite the Headteacher's defence of the students, people in a local community – particularly the press looking for news, not facts – can be quick to judge a whole school on one isolated incident. The fact that Devenport School might have outstanding sporting or musical achievements is at once forgotten by the local radio station.

We all need to guard and promote the reputation of our school by the way we conduct ourselves in the local community.

# 4 Stereotypes

## Introduction

It is a rare person who doesn't have any prejudices or doesn't occasionally fall into stereotyping someone else or a group of people. By its very nature, prejudice is about pre-judging; stereotyping can have its comic side but it can also be destructive.

The following story by Alice Walker offers a thoughtful commentary on how one young girl seeks to combat prejudice and possible stereotyping.

## Reading

### Elethia

A certain perverse experience shaped Elethia's life, and made it possible for it to be true that she carried with her at all times a small apothecary jar of ashes.

There was in the town where she was born a man whose ancestors had owned a large plantation on which everything under the sun was made or grown. There had been many slaves, and though slavery no longer existed, this grandson of former slaveowners held a quaint proprietary point of view where colored people were concerned. He adored them, of course. Not in the present – it went without saying – but at that time, stopped, just on the outskirts of his memory: his grandfather's time.

This man, whom Elethia never saw, opened a locally famous restaurant on a busy street near the center of town. He called it 'Old Uncle Albert's'. In the window of the restaurant was a stuffed likeness of Uncle Albert himself, a small brown dummy of waxen skin and glittery black eyes. His lips were intensely smiling and his false teeth shone. He carried a covered tray in one hand, raised level with his shoulder, and over his other arm was draped a white napkin.

Black people could not eat at Uncle Albert's, though they worked, of course, in the kitchen. But on Saturday afternoons a crowd of them would gather to look at 'Uncle Albert' and discuss how near to the real person the dummy looked. Only the very old people remembered Albert Porter, and their eyesight was no better than their memory. Still there was a comfort somehow in knowing that Albert's likeness was here before them daily and that if he smiled as a dummy in a fashion he was not known to do as a man, well, perhaps both memory and eyesight were wrong.

The old people appeared grateful to the rich man who owned the restaurant for giving them a taste of vicarious fame. They could pass by the gleaming window where Uncle Albert stood, seemingly in the act of sprinting forward with his tray, and know that though niggers were not allowed in the front door, ole Albert was already inside, and looking mighty pleased about it, too.

For Elethia the fascination was in Uncle Albert's fingernails. She wondered how his creator had got them on. She wondered also about the white hair that shone so brightly under the lights. One summer she worked as a salad girl in the restaurant's kitchen, and it was she who discovered the truth about Uncle Albert. He was not a dummy; he was stuffed. Like a bird, like a moose's head, like a giant bass. He was stuffed.

One night after the restaurant was closed someone broke in and stole nothing but Uncle Albert. It was Elethia and her friends, boys who were in her class and who called her 'Thia'. Boys who brought Thunderbird and shared it with her. Boys who laughed at her jokes so much they hardly remembered she was also cute. Her tight buddies. They carefully burned Uncle Albert to ashes in the incinerator of their high school, and each of them kept a bottle of his ashes. And for each of them what they knew and their reaction to what they knew was profound.

The experience undercut whatever solid foundation Elethia had assumed she had. She became secretive, wary, looking over her shoulder at the slightest noise. She haunted the museums of any city in which she found herself, looking, usually, at the remains of Indians, for they were plentiful everywhere she went. She discovered some of the Indian warriors and maidens in the museums were also real, stuffed people, painted and wigged and robed, like figures in the Rue Morgue. There were so many, in fact, that she could not possibly steal and burn them all. Besides, she did not know if these figures – with their valiant glass eyes – would wish to be burned.

About Uncle Albert she felt she knew.

What kind of man was Uncle Albert?

Well, the old folks said, he wasn't nobody's uncle and wouldn't sit still for nobody to call him that, either.

Why, said another old-timer, I recalls the time they hung a boy's privates on a post at the end of the street where all the black folks shopped, just to scare us all, you understand, and Albert Porter was the one took 'em down and buried 'em. Us never did find the rest of the boy though. It was just like always – they would throw you in the river with a big old green log tied to you, and down to the bottom you sunk.

He continued:

Albert was born in slavery and he remembered that his mama and daddy didn't know nothing about slavery'd done ended for near 'bout ten years, the boss man kept them so ignorant of the law, you understand. So he was a mad so-an'-so when he found out. They used to beat him *severe* trying to make him forget the past and grin and act like a nigger. (Whenever you saw somebody acting like a nigger, Albert said, you could be sure he seriously disremembered his past.) But he never would. Never would work in the big house as head servant, neither – always broke up stuff. The master at that time was always going around pinching him too. Looks like he hated Albert more than anything – but he never would let him get a job anywhere else. And Albert never would leave home. Too stubborn.

Stubborn, yes. My land, another one said. That's why it do seem strange to see that dummy that sposed to be ole Albert with his mouth open. All them teeth. Hell, all Albert's teeth was knocked out before he was grown.

Elethia went away to college and her friends went into the army because they were poor and that was the way things were. They discovered Uncle Alberts all over the world. Elethia was especially disheartened to find Uncle Alberts in her textbooks, in the newspapers and on TV.

Everywhere she looked there was an Uncle Albert (and many Aunt Albertas, it goes without saying).

But she had her jar of ashes, the old-timers' memories written down, and her friends who wrote that in the army they were learning skills that would get them through more than a plate glass window.

And she was careful that, no matter how compelling the hype, Uncle Alberts, in her own mind, were not permitted to exist.

*Alice Walker*

# Reflections

* Growing up as a young black girl, the Uncle Albert of the story symbolises for Elethia the way black people had been treated as slaves through the generations. She is keen to challenge stereotypes she sees around her, wherever she goes – thus her jar of ashes is very precious to her, a reminder that stereotypes that are destructive need to be countered: 'Uncle Alberts, in her own mind, were not permitted to exist'.

* Elethia's story is a reminder to us that in our school or local community it is vital to see differences as positive aspects of being human. We should be quick to counter those who seek to display prejudices towards others because of their creed, their language, their skin colour, their physical presence, their family background.

The values of a thriving, purposeful community celebrate choice and diversity; they challenge prejudice and injustice; they seek to promote a sense of sharing so that individuals can come together with their differences at least tolerated and, at best, understood.

# 5  Value-added

## Introduction

How do we judge whether the nation's schools are doing for children and students what they should be doing? How do we judge whether our own school is being successful as a place of learning? One of the phrases that is often used when assessing a school's performance is 'measuring the value-added'. In other words between the ages of, say, 11 and 16, what value has the school added to a child's learning? Has, for example, the pupil's reading age increased, or their test scores in Maths improved?

But there are questions that need asking about how and what we measure, before we can come to a true picture of a school's success or otherwise. Listen carefully to the following short paragraph.

## Reading

'The first step is to measure whatever can be easily measured. This is OK as far as it goes. The second step is to disregard that which can't be easily measured or to give it an arbitrary quantitative value. This is artificial and misleading. The third step is to presume that what can't be measured easily really isn't important. This is blindness. The fourth step is to say that what can't be easily measured really doesn't exist. This is suicide.'

(*Read twice*)

## Reflections

*   There are always some things that can be easily measured; equally, there are other achievements that are more difficult to measure. But should we then in schools fall into the trap of saying 'what does not get counted does not count'?

    In looking thoughtfully at the idea of value-added we might come up with two separate lists – one which lists those things which are measurable; and another which lists those things we value but which are not easily counted.

*   *What do we measure?*

    Examination performance
    Reading ages
    Attendance/lateness
    Drug misuse
    Racist incidents
    Social Services referrals

Library book usage
Numbers attending:
   IT club
   orchestra/choir
   field trips/visits/sports practices
Number of outside speakers
Numbers learning a musical instrument
Number of school teams
Loss of textbooks
Cost of vandalism
Work experience placements

\*   *What do we wish to value?*

Leadership skills
Spiritual development
Honesty and integrity
Interpersonal skills
Codes of conduct
Tolerance and respect
Excellence vs mediocrity
Community involvement
Pupil self-assessment
National Record of Achievement

In coming to judgements about a school's success we need to ensure that we look at *everything* that the school community values, and not just those things that fall neatly into league tables. We might indeed conclude that this subject is as much about *values*-added as it is about *value*-added.

# 6  God in a test-tube

## Introduction

A writer called C. P. Snow once observed (in 1959) that our society was split into two cultures – 'the arts' and 'the sciences'. He went on to say that society's major problem was that people who inhabited one camp didn't understand anything about the other; the example he gave in particular was that the group of university teachers who knew the plays of Shakespeare knew nothing of the second law of thermodynamics (heat transfer) – and vice versa.

The following article by scientist Richard Dawkins challenges us to think about the place of science within religious education. He poses some thought-provoking questions.

## Reading

### God in a test tube

When it is put to me, as it often is, that science, or some particular part of science such as evolutionary theory, is just a religion like any other, I usually respond with indignant denial. Perhaps this is the wrong tactic. Maybe I should accept the charge gratefully and demand equal time for science on the religious education syllabus. And, indeed, an excellent case could be made.

One of the recognised aims of religious education is to encourage pupils to reflect on the deep questions of existence: to invite children to rise above the humdrum preoccupations of ordinary life and think *sub specie aeternitatis*. Science can offer a vision of life and the universe which, for humbling poetic inspiration, far outclasses any of the mutually contradictory faiths and disappointingly recent 'traditions' admitted by the agreed syllabus.

What religion teacher could remain disillusioned if challenged to convey to children some inkling of the age and size of the universe? Suppose that, at the moment of Christ's death, the news had started travelling at the maximum possible speed around the universe. How far would the terrible tidings have travelled by now? The answer is that the news could not, under any circumstances whatever, have reached more than one-fiftieth of the way across one paltry galaxy, not one-thousandth of the way to our nearest neighbour in the 100-million-galaxy-strong universe. The universe at large could not be anything other than indifferent to Christ, his birth and his passion. Even such momentous news as the origin of life could only just have travelled across our little local cluster of galaxies. Yet so ancient was this event, that, if you span its age with your open arms, the whole of human history would fall in the dust from your fingertip at a single stroke of the nail file.

The argument from design and the spell-binding wonders of the living kingdoms cannot be ignored. Our model religion classes would certainly consider Darwinism alongside the creationist alternatives and the children would easily make up their own minds which they found most convincing. It would also be interesting to study the historic derivations of the various origin myths and the arbitrary accident of which particular tradition a given child happens to be brought up in.

More sophisticated arguments from design suggest that the laws of physics and the fundamental constants of the universe are too good – as if set up deliberately to make evolution possible. One can argue over whether the laws of the universe *could* have been different, or whether they all depend upon some yet more fundamental principles yet to be discovered. Some might say that the 'put-up job' argument depends trivially upon the fact that it is we, here, making the observations. A controversial but intriguing speculation is that there is a kind of Darwinian selection among universes, with sentient creatures in a position to ask questions only about those universes whose laws fostered their evolution.

So much for Genesis, we could say to the children. How about the prophets? Halley's Comet will return, without fail, in 2062. Did any child in the class see it in 1986 when it was last here? In that case, you are one of those rare people with a good chance of seeing it twice. I shan't because I shall be dead by 2062. In the past, comets have often been taken as portents of disaster. By what physical route could the alleged influence on human affairs travel?

Astrology has played an important part in various religious traditions, including Hinduism. The three wise men are said to have been led to Jesus by a star. Horoscopes purport to predict, but do they get it right any more frequently than you'd expect by chance? How do we know what to expect by chance? One simple class exercise would be to remove the star sign labels from all the horoscopes, then let everybody state which one most closely matches their own experience.

We'd expect one in 12 of the children to pick their own horoscope by chance. Is the actual figure noticeably higher? Contrast astrological predictions with astronomical. The arrival of Shoemaker-Levy on Jupiter was forecast to the minute. What do you think would happen if astrologers and seers had to put their (often very plentiful) money where their mouth is?

When the religion class turned to ethics, science would, in my model syllabus, give way to rational moral philosophy. Do the members of the class think there are absolute standards of right and wrong, or are there just working principles like 'do as you would be done by' and 'the greatest happiness of the greatest number'?

In any case, in our evolutionary view of life, it is a rewarding question to ask where our feelings of right and wrong come from. The 'right to life' lobby is wholly preoccupied with *human* life, but what is so special about human life, given that we are close cousins of other apes and more distant cousins of all animals and plants? Should we value the life of a human foetus with the faculties of a worm over that of a fully thinking and feeling chimpanzee or whale?

Coming finally to *eschatology [*eschatology means theology concerned with the end of the world], we know from the second law of thermodynamics that all complexity and all life, all laughter and all sorrow, are hell bent on levelling themselves out into cold nothingness. They, and we, can never be more than local and temporary buckings of the great universal slide into the abyss of uniformity. We know that the universe is expanding and that it probably will expand forever (though the end of this world is nigh, in a mere 60 million centuries when the sun engulfs it). A possible alternative Last Thing is the Big Crunch, in which all the matter in the universe collapses again into its starting point and time comes to an end. Time does locally come to an end in miniature crunches called black holes. The laws of the universe seem to be true all over it, but they might change in these 'crunches'. To be really speculative, time could begin again with new laws and new physical constants. It has even been suggested that there could be many universes, each one isolated so utterly that, for it, the others do not exist.

Science, then, could give a good account of itself in the religious education classroom. It wouldn't be enough, of course. Some familiarity with the King James Bible is important for anyone wanting to take their allusions in reading English literature. Together with the Book of Common Prayer, the Bible gets 58 pages in the Oxford Dictionary of Quotations. Only Shakespeare has more.

The Koran has zero quotations recorded, rather to my surprise. Obviously things would be different if we were dealing with Arabic literature, but we are concerned with English literature and our children need to understand the provenance of phrases like 'through a glass darkly', 'all flesh is grass', 'the race is not to the swift', 'crying in the wilderness', 'reap the whirlwind', 'amid the alien corn', 'eyeless in Gaza', 'Job's comforters' and 'the widow's mite'.

Moreover, there is much to be said for studying a wide diversity of religions. Children may then observe that the various religions contradict each other – a possibility that has already caused misgivings among apologists who fear that children will become 'confused'. Confused is right!

*Richard Dawkins*

## Reflections

\*    Richard Dawkins is a professor of science at Oxford and has made his name studying and developing the work of Charles Darwin. He has regularly argued for a coming together of 'arts' and 'sciences'. His point is an important one because too often, from quite an early age in Britain, we specialise as students of one or the other. Knowledge doesn't divide out neatly – as his article shows. Why then should our education system not develop scientific historians, religious geographers, mathematical musicians or literary economists?

It is probably fair to say that what C. P. Snow identified as two cultures in the 1950s is still with us today, although perhaps in a less divisive way. The National Curriculum means that all students cover similar ground up to the age of 16 in both the arts and sciences. Post-16 is another story.

In choosing which subjects to study at sixth-form or college level, it may well be worth reflecting on Richard Dawkins's image of God in a test-tube.

# 7  Looking back

## Introduction

We probably take for granted the institution called school. The law of the land demands that everyone between the ages of 5 and 16 goes to school. The government has the duty to provide adequate places, resources and trained teachers; parents then have the legal duty to ensure their children attend.

But if we look back in our history – say 150 years – to when schools were first establishing themselves as a place for all children rather than a privileged few, we realise they were not organised and resourced as we know them today.

Here is an extract from *The History of Tackley School*; Tackley is a small village in north Oxfordshire.

## Reading

*The History of Tackley School*

Punishments are recorded in the log books, mostly of boys, without giving names but usually noting the misdemeanour:

12th June 1863 'Punished 3 boys for coming late'.

23rd June 1863 'Punished 2 children for getting on the school wall'.

13th July 1863 'Kept 3 boys in from play for being late'.

Lucy Turner, the third mistress to be in charge of the school in 1863 set about enforcing discipline in her first two weeks by punishing four boys for lateness, one for not speaking the truth, three boys for climbing the trees, and two girls for bad behaviour. More seriously a boy was punished for 'stealing and then telling a lie' on 13th November, 1863.

Little can be discerned of what was taught – the school log book reports 'ordinary progress and duties' for most days of the early years and later comments were weekly rather than daily. Highlights appear as 'The 3rd class read from books for the first time' (2nd June, 1863), 'Taught the children a new Hymn' (20th June, 1863), 'Taught the 2nd class a new rule in Arithmetic' (16th July 1863). Often the teaching of reading, arithmetic and learning hymns was recorded.

The monitors and pupil teachers are interesting in that they were youngsters from the village and can therefore be identified in other contexts. The first references to monitors were in the log book recording that 'The Monitor (A. Toms)' was taken ill on 31st October, 1865. The next day several children were ill with scarlet fever, and a week later Ellen Gibbs (Monitor) died after a week's illness. She was 11 years old. Two days later the school closed early to attend her funeral. The next week Elizabeth Bloomfield was buried. She was three years old. Five Tackley children were buried that November after no other burials of children since 1848. Anne Toms did not resume her duties as monitor until 12th February 1866 after 14 weeks illness. In August 1867 Anne was left in charge of the school for an entire week. She was then 13 years old. She was the oldest child of William Toms, publican, and his wife Sarah of Nethercott. She married Richard Toms Patrick, in 1880, the same year her grandmother died at the grand age of 100.

After 1862 a government grant was paid to schools dependent on the results attained at an annual inspection. There was a fixed sum for children under six years, with older children tested in reading, writing and arithmetic, the 'three Rs' in each of six standards. The school received 2s. 8d (i.e. 13p) for each R passed plus four shillings for satisfactory attendance making a total of twelve shillings (60p) for each successful good attender aged 6 upwards. In 1863–4 subscriptions, mostly local, brought in about half the income (£24), with the capitation grant (£7–15s–0d) and school pence (£18–6s–4d) providing the remainder.

Her Majesty's Inspectors visited Tackley School each year and wrote reports on what they found. Following a creditable report in 1863, there was a fair report in 1864 and 1866, whereas in 1865 the report was poor and one tenth of the grant was deducted. In 1867, however, although the report was poor, no deduction was made because, as the inspector states in beautiful handwriting, 'The school has suffered severely from measles which have prevailed in the Parish for more than two months. More than half the children have been afflicted. Five have died'. The Parish Burial Records show that more villagers died in 1867 than in any year since 1837, seven of them in March. The Inspection was on 8th April, and the epidemic built up in March so five of the six children recorded as dying in March died of measles. These were: Mary Kilby (aged 7), Edith Elizabeth Gibbs (2), Sarah Jane Skidmore (5 months), Elizabeth Jane Willet (1), Jason Kilby (1). Another two toddlers died in April. The School log book records the build up of the epidemic. On 11th February: 'six children absent through illness', by the 14th and 15th eight children were 'absent from sickness'. On Monday the 18th, nineteen children were absent from sickness, and the next day it simply reports 'many children absent'. By the 25th 'More children ill with the measles only 37 in school'. The next day 'two more children ill' and by the 28th 'only 26 present'. On 1st March Miss Tyrer notes that 'M. A. Kilby one of the school children died after a week's illness'. The attendance hovered between 23 and 35 for the next two weeks, and in the third week of March which was 'very snowy' many children were still ill. Only on the 26th March could she report that 'several children returned to school after being ill with the measles'. It was June before attendance returned to 67, close to its maximum for that year.

In 1868 the Inspector reported that discipline and reading were much improved but he was still not satisfied with the arithmetic or spelling. He noted that the mistress 'had taken great pains with her school'. In the same year a new subject crept into the school when 'The Rector gave the children a Geography lesson'. The next day the first class boys began to learn to make button holes! A century later 'progressive schools' were to re-introduce sewing for boys.

In 1869 the Inspector was less happy. He found that the reading was unskilfully taught, dull and monotonous. The spelling and arithmetic were very imperfect. He reduced the grant by one tenth 'for faults of Inspection' although the pupils attained more than the required two thirds of possible passes in the examinations. Following this poor report the visits by the Rector became more frequent and at the beginning of October Miss Tyrer was replaced by Emily Hall as a temporary arrangement until January 1870 when 'Maria Beesley from Fishponds took charge of the school'

Maria Beesley recorded the attendance for every session, indicating that attendance increased during the year from the fifties and sixties up to the seventies and as high as 86 for a few sessions. She lasted until Easter 1871 and had two assistants, one of them Susan Toms who was presumably the younger sister of Anne Toms and was recorded as Susannah in the parish register of baptisms. She was sixteen years old at this time. The Inspector brought bad news again in 1870: 'The attainments of the children are imperfect. No grant is payable for the period during which the school was without a certificated mistress. The grant is reduced by one tenth ... for faults of instruction'. The five month gap shows that Miss Tyrer departed a few weeks after the adverse report by the Inspector leaving the school with the Rector and his family in charge for a month before Emily Hall (uncertificated) took over. The school was inspected again on 21st February 1871. Maria Beesley left on March 31st before the Inspector's Report was received. The Inspector found the condition of the school to be 'very imperfect'. The examination results were even worse than in the previous year: only 3 of 35 children present passed in reading and nine in arithmetic. It seems likely that the results led to Maria Beesley's departure before the written report arrived.

*John Harding*

# Reflections

\* Some things don't change! But other features of school-life in the 1860s and 1870s do sound very different:

- the 13 year-old Monitor in charge of the school for a week
- the sad deaths because of scarlet fever
- the funding of the school being dependent on its results
- the introduction of a new subject, Geography
- the departure of the headmistress *before* the Inspector's written report!

This log comes from the early, imperfect days of public education. The resources we now enjoy in schools offer wealth beyond the dreams of those

Oxfordshire children in the 1860s. But do we always value those resources? Do we value our right to a free education?

The United Nations Declaration of Human Rights (shaped in 1948) proclaims free education as a common birthright for the world's children. Still, in our world today, millions of children don't have access to even the basics of teaching and learning. In our own advanced technological society we should not take education for granted. We all have a responsibility to ensure that educational resources are well used.

# 8 Competition or co-operation?

## Introduction

Do you think you learn more in a situation of competition or co-operation with fellow students? Where should the emphasis be in schools?

Listen carefully to the following account of how a group of sixth-formers learned a little about team skills. The exercise they took part in – 'the red–blue game' – was organised by a management training consultancy.

## Reading

### *May the nice guys win*

Eleven sixth-formers are divided into two groups and placed in separate classrooms. They are told they will be asked to make a series of 10 decisions about whether to play red or blue. Neither group will know what the other has decided until it has made up its own mind.

If both groups play red, each scores three points. If one plays red and the other blue, the red players lose six points and the blue players gain six. If both play blue, each loses three points. The groups are allowed to confer after the fourth round and the eighth.

The pupils are told that their group's principal objective is to end up with a positive score. They are also asked to contribute 10p each to a kitty, which will go to the team with the highest score.

In the first round, Rachel's group – five girls, one boy – plays red. This is said to demonstrate trust, the message being, 'I can help you'. However, it is also a high-risk strategy because the trust may turn out to be misplaced.

Alexis's group – three boys, two girls – plays blue. This is described as a minimum-risk but short-sighted strategy: either your group wins or both groups lose. The message is, 'I can hurt you'.

After the fourth round – both groups having played blue consistently – Rachel's score is –15, Alexis's –3. Rachel's group asks for a meeting but Alexis's, which thinks it is winning, refuses. They do not know it, but the odds now are that neither group will end up with a positive score.

By the end of the eighth round, Rachel's score is –21, Alexis's –9. Both are in trouble; both want to meet. They rapidly agree to play red from then on, assuring each other it is what they should have done from the beginning.

Returning to their classrooms, both teams promptly play blue.

The final scores – the tariff being doubled for the last two rounds – is –**33** and –**21**.

* * *

On such texts are sermons preached. If each group had considered the needs of the other ... if both had remembered their mutual long-term objective ... if only, understanding where power truly lay, they had co-operated rather than competed ...

As it was, confrontation – as, say, between government and government, employer and employees, husband and wife – led inevitably to mutual destruction.

Powerful though the lesson was, it was only a subsidiary theme of a workshop run by a training consultancy employed mainly by multinationals such as IBM, Kodak, Volvo and Mercury.

At the heart of the one-day course was a technique for analysing the way people behave in meetings and helping them to perform more effectively – the starting point being that, on average, we spend 75 per cent of our time at work talking to others.

Also, as organisations 'flatten' their management structures, all the emphasis is on working co-operatively, being a 'team player'. Indeed, employers' most common complaint about the school leavers and graduates they recruit is their lack of 'inter-personal skills', their inability to work in teams.

Where better, then, to start teaching such skills than in schools, before behaviour patterns become ingrained?

The method involves breaking down verbal behaviour into 11 categories that can be used to record accurately and objectively what happens when people meet. First come the initiating behaviours: proposing ('Let's go to the pub') and building ('Yeah, I'll borrow my Mum's car').

Next are the reacting behaviours: supporting ('That's a great idea'); disagreeing ('No, I don't want to go'); and attacking ('How typical of you to suggest such a thing').

Stage three are the clarifying behaviours: testing understanding ('Why are you against going to the pub?'); summarising; and seeking and giving information. Finally, there are two 'control' behaviours: shutting out (interrupting, talking over) and bringing in (encouraging others to participate).

During the red–blue game and other similar exercises, observers noted each contribution every participant made and placed it in one of the 11 categories.

For some, the resulting profile was sobering: few ideas, too much attacking and – for nearly all, especially in the red–blue game – a huge amount of 'shutting out'. Conversely, those who were good at 'building', 'supporting' and 'bringing in' were a select few.

* * *

Applied to the meetings as a whole, the technique pinpointed which were successful and which were not: too many proposals and the result was confusion, too few and everyone was bored; too much reaction and people became over-excited, too little and the meeting seemed stilted; too much clarification and the participants felt they were swimming in treacle, too little and no one was sure what had been agreed. The trick was to find the right balance.

'Laying on the course for pupils was an experiment', the course director explained. 'So many of the adults we work with have told us they wished they'd learnt the technique 20 years ago.

'Also, I'd heard that schools had changed – become less competitive, more co-operative. I thought the youngsters would be more flexible than adults.'

He could not have been more wrong. Asked what they had got out of the day, some pupils said dutifully they had learnt the importance of working in teams, being ready to compromise, showing consideration and so on.

But the bolder among them – including Rachel and Alexis – said what they had learnt was how to 'manipulate others without them realising it', 'control a meeting to get what you want', and 'recognise when others are trying to manipulate you' – skills, in other words, of competition not co-operation.

The course director seemed nonplussed. 'They're so adversarial – just like managers in industry,' he said.

'Our observation records show they were constantly talking across and shutting each other out. It's obviously going to be a while before they learn the lessons of the red–blue game.'

*John Clare*

## Reflections

* The red–blue game is worth playing.
  What is revealed in this account is that the sixth-formers were not naturally strong on trust and, as the course director commented, 'They're so adversarial – just like managers in industry.'
  There are also some interesting findings about how our behaviour comes through in language: testing understanding; seeking information; bringing in and shutting out others.

* There are some areas of learning and many aspects of school-life where competition with others is vital if we are to achieve high standards. Equally – as the red–blue game reveals – when a team or group approach to learning is needed, co-operation is critical or progress cannot be made. Think of working on a Design brief, for example.
  And if we extend the idea to our dealings with other people generally, confrontation can so often lead to mutual destruction. Whereas both parties feel better and empowered if there is mutual trust and co-operation.

# 9 Passing exams: here are the answers

## Introduction

How best can you prepare for exams and turn in your top performance? Everyone's preparation for examinations will be slightly different; the important point is to adopt a plan of campaign which works for *you* – and don't be worried if a friend has a slightly different way of handling things.

Here are some DOs and DON'Ts from two sources: one, a Chief Examinations Officer; two, an alternative!

# Reading

*Passing exams: here are the answers*

1. PLAN REVISION

- Do not pretend that everything can be done in a rush the night before an exam.

- Work out how long you have to revise before exams and plan how to use that time.

2. BE PREPARED

- Make sure you know what will be examined in each subject, and the way in which the questions will be asked. Have a look at the syllabus for this year's exams and at past examination papers.

- Make sure you know what equipment you will need for each exam (such as pens, calculator, spare batteries), what is provided for you, and what you must provide yourself.

- Make sure you know where and when your exams are to be held. Every year students fail because they go to the wrong place, or the right place at the wrong time.

- Make sure you don't have two exams at the same time. Alternative arrangements need to be made. Check this now.

- Make sure you know the rules for each exam. Never be tempted to break them. If you do, you could be disqualified from all of your exams – or even arrested.

- Don't try to learn anything new the night before an exam. Try to relax. Check your equipment and the details of where the exam is to be held, and when it starts.

- Have a leisurely breakfast and walk to school, if possible. Be there in good time. Get an earlier bus or train, if necessary.

- Avoid friends outside the exam room. They could confuse you. Keep your thoughts to yourself and concentrate on the exam.

- Make sure you are comfortable before going into an exam – go to the lavatory, wear comfortable clothes if your school allows this.

3. IN THE EXAM ROOM

- Take six deep breaths, ignore the other students around you, and concentrate solely on what you have to do.

- Have a piece of chocolate, or some other sweet, to boost your energy – but don't crunch or eat sweets with wrappers, which might disturb other students.

- Read the instructions on the exam papers carefully – do the appropriate number of questions from the right sections, and answer compulsory questions.

- Make sure you know how many marks each question carries – don't spend too long on any one. Use the number of marks as a guide. A question with 20 per cent of the marks for a particular paper deserves only 20 per cent of the time available.

- If you run out of time, complete your remaining answers in outline only. In mathematics, for example, you could indicate how you would solve the problem by stating the formulae you would use, and indicating where and how you would calculate missing values.

- Those who start working straight away, without reading the exam papers carefully, are either very stupid or very bright. Not so many of us are that bright.

- Read questions carefully before you write anything – not halfway through your answer. The examiners allow time for you to read the paper when they plan the exam, so don't think you are wasting time. Use that time to choose the questions you are going to do, and write notes on the question paper.

- Answer the questions set, not the ones you hoped for. However good your work, you will get no marks if you don't answer the examiner's questions.

- Make sure your answers are carefully presented – write clearly and label diagrams, for example, if this helps.

- Let the supervisor know if anything is disturbing you – other people tapping nervously with a pencil, noise outside the exam room, or even the supervisor's squeaky shoes.

4. After the exam

- Don't worry about the one you have just taken; you can't do anything about it now. Concentrate instead on the next one. You *can* do something about that.

- Tell your school straight away about illness or other circumstances that might have affected your performance.

5. Don't panic

- Exams are not designed to catch you out.

- Being calm and thoughtful will help you to get the most out of your preparation.

- And if all else fails, remember that there are more millionaires without GCSE and A-level qualifications than there are with.

Good luck.

*George Turnbull*

\* \* \*

## It's never too late to mug up on excuses

For those who are new to the world of revision, here are 20 excuses that you can cut out and stick on your wall next to the Nirvana poster.

1. You know the subject so well that further study is unnecessary. In fact, consulting a reference book would merely cause confusion, thus causing you to drop a grade or two.
2. You are so ignorant of the subject that the paper in question has become a lost cause. Further consideration of it would be throwing good money after bad, which would hinder you from steaming ahead with your strong subjects (assuming you have any).
3. It is too early to start revising. No one wants to peak too soon. You are quite old enough to know when the vibes are right to really go for it.
4. It is too late to start revising. Why did no one – parents, teachers, education pages of newspapers – tell you to get your academic act together? You are too young to handle this trip by yourself.
5. Relax. The important thing at this stage is not to become bogged down in detail, but to keep your mind clear. The inside of your mind is, in fact, so clear that it contains vast spaces of emptiness uncorrupted by information.
6. There now, look what they've done. Your parents, teachers and education correspondents have nagged so much you're far too worried to concentrate. It's their fault you will get an E instead of a C.
7. Exams are irrelevant anyway. When Winston Churchill took the Harrow entrance paper, all he could write down was his name; still, he got that right and didn't he do well? No one wants to know your history marks when you go for a decent job, such as stand-in Midnite Hour DJ on Radio Essex.
8. Exams are irrelevant (Part II). Life is more a matter of continuous assessment than examinations. Preferably, it is a matter of no assessment at all. The only people who need qualifications are hospital doctors, who take so many exams they practically have to answer a paper on 'Retirement Studies' before they can hang up their stethoscopes for good. No one is bothered by an N in Economics A-level when you are applying to be deputy fashion editor on *Scallywag* magazine.
9. Exams are irrelevant (Part III). Knowledge is something you dial up, not lumber your own brain cells with. Think information technology. Should you need to know the foreign policy of Louis XIV, you can call it up on a CD-Rom disc or virtual reality headset. Not that you will need to know anyway, when you are assistant PR person for the chief hairdresser of *The Word*. The day they start a GCSE on the guitar solos of Primal Scream will be the day you run happily into an examination room.
10. Your notes are so good you have it all wrapped up. No more work is necessary. You have written on one page of A4 all the crucial points, each of which is the trigger for a stylish dissertation on whatever the examiner throws at you.
11. Your notes are so hopeless that there is no point in revising at all. They are either a jungle of scribbles, or have been distilled so much that, instead of containing the essence of the subject, they state merely 'Ammonia – not to be sniffed at,' or 'Modern politics – a lot of it about'.

*Apology. I was supposed to provide 20 excuses, but this is as far as I got in the time. Also, I lost my notes. And I never did my homework in the first place.*

*Jonathan Sale*

## Reflections

* Lots to digest here!
  A reminder that you need a plan that works for you personally, not one that your friends find useful. And make a point of reminding your family – including noisy brothers and sisters – that you are taking your exams seriously and need a bit of hush …

* BTBYCB = Be The Best You Can Be!

# 10 The best years of their lives

## Introduction

The cliché is: 'the best years of your life'. Here are the thoughts of students from a variety of schools as they reflect on their last days at school and what the future might bring.

## Reading

### The best years of their lives

I always swore that I'd never cry when I left here. Now I think I will but honestly not because I'm leaving school, I'm happy to be leaving the institution and the restrictions. It's just really sad to leave all the people who know exactly what you like doing and how they can cope with you. Now you have to start again.

In leavers' books I've written stuff like 'Live your life. Be free. Long live insanity and the Scots'. In my book people have written 'Goodbye, you little Scottish Haggis. Carry on drinking the beer'.

*Philippa Tattersall*

The atmosphere today is a mixture between people who are slightly stressed and a bit snappy, and others getting sentimental and emotional. Some of us are excited that this is it, and we've got our futures ahead of us. Other people are pondering over the fact that we're never going to see each other again in this kind of environment. For me, it's the great unknown. I don't know whether to be looking forward to it or dreading it.

I've just been writing cards to all my old staff, and I was really close to tears. We've had the chance to become independent here: you cook for yourself and do your washing and you think, this is what it's going to be like when you leave. But just now I'm thinking, the staff understand my character, they've known me since I was nine, which you won't get at university, where there's thousands of people.

There's a tradition that 6-2 does something to mark their leaving. Sometimes people go too far – one year they bricked up the door to the main entrance, another year they stuck a really huge 'For Sale' sign between the two bell towers, which was very funny, but they could have killed themselves climbing up on the roof.

*Naomi Bull*

What I'll miss most is the laughs in class; being sent to the headmaster and saying I've been sent out, sir. I used to get into a lot of trouble at school. I did a lot of fighting – mostly outside the school, but they always found out.

I was looking forward to leaving, but now I've left I want to go back. It was a laugh at school – at work you have to get on and get the job finished. The best thing about work is you get some money in your back pocket to spend. Most of my friends haven't got jobs. I feel different from them.

It wasn't easy to find a job. I'd like to do demolition, like my dad, but you have to be 18. When study leave started I'd go out looking for work then come back to school and do some exams.

*David Munday*

Everything's ending. I don't know what to do with myself now. I'm lost. At school you knew what you were going to do. It's boring just sitting at home.

I want to get a job to get some money. I've applied for a couple, but I haven't got anything to go to yet. I'm a bit up in the air. As soon as I get a job or a college place I can start planning.

*Jamie Hall*

I was having a cigarette just now and the headmaster walked by – we're out of school so it doesn't matter, but I still thought, Oh no, he's caught us smoking.

I'm doing voluntary work on the Bristol Playbus, subsidised by working as a part-time receptionist. The main thing I'm looking forward to is doing exactly what I want when I want, not being patronised and not having to go for registration every morning. But I'm a bit nervous of it, too. After being in the school system for 13 years, it's a bit daunting to leave it – the security of being able to muck about and get away with it. We could usually argue our way out of whatever trouble we got into, whether it was bunking off General Studies, playing cards, water fights or smoking in the toilets.

*Angela Hunt*

You've closed off a whole section of your life; you're an adult now. I'm looking forward to that, although the prospect of university is a bit nerve-racking – coping without your family and friends near you.

*Dawn Crook*

You reach a stage when you've had enough of school. Your time's come to an end. But I miss the security, the routine. It used to be get up at 8, go to school, get back at 4 and that took care of the day. Now I'm working part-time in the pub, and there's no routine – they just ring me when they want me.

I'd like to get a job, but all the news about jobs being hard to come by worries me, I know people who haven't got a job even after a couple of years' training.

*Chris Newport*

I've heard of people who've come out of university and been unable to get jobs – so I want some experience. That's why I'm getting a job (working for an accountant).

For my parents the most important thing about school is getting good grades. For me it's the people. You want to say things to people who've meant a lot to you – just 'It's been great being friends with you.' I get on really well with this boy who's going away to university, so I told him I fancied him. Things like that come out, things you wouldn't normally talk about because you're frightened you might not see people again.

*Sarah Naish*

By the end of this evening everyone will be drunk and dancing, claiming undying love for everyone else and hugging and getting off with each other. There'll be gossip. And we'll all be in tears.

*Kay*

It's so much part of your life. Your parents have much less effect on who you turn out to be than school does. The worst thing is, this place doesn't feel like our own any more. Everybody else seems to own it, whereas we used to. This is the last day we can strut in the place as if it's ours. When we come back the only people we'll be able to talk to are the teachers; no one else will remember us.

*Anthony Dakin*

# Reflections

*   What will be your abiding memories of school?
    Do you think of these years already as 'the best days' – or will that view take some time to come?

*   What has been the purpose of school:

    – to impart knowledge
    – to teach skills
    – to foster character
    – to inculcate beliefs
    – to turn out employees for commerce and industry
    – to establish habits of courteous behaviour
    – to kindle patriotism
    – to promote an international outlook?

Each person will have her or his own answer. Let us hope school has given an academically worthwhile experience *and* helped develop a set of values which will serve you through life as international 21st century citizens, and parents in your turn.

# Moral Mazes

*If you can keep your head*
*when all about you are losing theirs,*
*it may just be you haven't quite*
*grasped what's going on.*


*If you must come up and spout, expect a few harpoons.*

The Whale Principle

# 1 Storytelling

## Introduction

Storytelling is as ancient as humankind itself. We all tell stories as part of every-day life, whether it's a summary of what happened at school today, a description of a football match, a retelling of a soap opera episode, an eye-witness account of an accident – all of these are different kinds of story.

But do we always tell the truth? Or do we tell the truth as we *think* it is? Listen to the following two extracts from writer Tim O'Brien. He was a soldier in the 1960s Vietnam War; he witnessed some horrific scenes, and raises in his book *The Things They Carried* some interesting questions about the truth as it really happened and the truth as we later want to remember it.

## Reading

*Storytelling*

It's time to be blunt.

I'm forty-three years old, true, and I'm a writer now, and a long time ago I walked through Quang Ngai Province as a foot soldier.

Almost everything else is invented.

But it's not a game. It's a form. Right here, now, as I invent myself, I'm think-ing of all I want to tell you about why this book is written as it is. For instance, I want to tell you this: twenty years ago I watched a man die on a trail near the vil-lage of My Khe. I did not kill him. But I was present, you see, and my presence was guilt enough. I remember his face, which was not a pretty face, because his jaw was in his throat, and I remember feeling the burden of responsibility and grief. I blamed myself. And rightly so, because I was present.

But listen. Even *that* story is made up.

I want you to feel what I felt. I want you to know why story-truth is truer sometimes than happening-truth.

Here is the happening-truth. I was once a soldier. There were many bodies, real bodies with real faces, but I was young then and I was afraid to look. And now, twenty years later, I'm left with faceless responsibility and faceless grief.

Here is the story-truth. He was a slim, dead, almost dainty young man of about twenty. He lay in the center of a red clay trail near the village of My Khe. His jaw was in his throat. His one eye was shut, the other eye was a star-shaped hole. I killed him.

What stories can do, I guess, is make things present.

I can look at things I never looked at. I can attach faces to grief and love and pity and God. I can be brave. I can make myself feel again.

'Daddy, tell the truth,' Kathleen can say, 'did you ever kill anybody?' And I can say, honestly, 'Of course not.'

Or I can say, honestly, 'Yes.'

\* \* \*

The dead guy's name was Curt Lemon. What happened was, we crossed a muddy river and marched west into the mountains, and on the third day we took a break along a trail junction in deep jungle. Right away, Lemon and Rat Kiley started goofing. They didn't understand about the spookiness. They were kids; they just didn't know. A nature hike, they thought, not even a war, so they went off into the shade of some giant trees – quadruple canopy, no sunlight at all – and they were giggling and calling each other yellow mother and playing a silly game they'd invented. The game involved smoke grenades, which were harmless unless you did stupid things, and what they did was pull out the pin and stand a few feet apart and play catch under the shade of those huge trees. Whoever chickened out was a yellow mother. And if nobody chickened out, the grenade would make a light popping sound and they'd be covered with smoke and they'd laugh and dance around and then do it again.

It's all exactly true.

It happened, to *me*, nearly twenty years ago, and I still remember that trail junction and those giant trees and a soft dripping sound somewhere beyond the trees. I remember the smell of moss. Up in the canopy there were tiny white blossoms, but no sunlight at all, and I remember the shadows spreading out under the trees where Curt Lemon and Rat Kiley were playing catch with smoke grenades. Mitchell Sanders sat flipping his yo-yo. Norman Bowker and Kiowa and Dave Jensen were dozing, or half dozing, and all around us were those ragged green mountains.

Except for the laughter things were quiet.

At one point, I remember, Mitchell Sanders turned and looked at me, not quite nodding, as if to warn me about something, as if he already *knew*, then after a while he rolled up his yo-yo and moved away.

It's hard to tell you what happened next.

They were just goofing. There was a noise, I suppose, which must've been the detonator, so I glanced behind me and watched Lemon step from the shade into bright sunlight. His face was suddenly brown and shining. A handsome kid, really. Sharp gray eyes, lean and narrow-waisted, and when he died it was almost beautiful, the way the sunlight came around him and lifted him up and sucked him high into a tree full of moss and vines and white blossoms.

\* \* \*

In any war story, but especially a true one, it's difficult to separate what happened from what seemed to happen. What seems to happen becomes its own happening and has to be told that way. The angles of vision are skewed. When a booby trap explodes, you close your eyes and duck and float outside yourself. When a guy dies, like Curt Lemon, you look away and then look back for a moment and then look away again. The pictures get jumbled; you tend to miss a lot. And then afterward, when you go to tell about it, there is always that surreal seemingness, which makes the story seem untrue, but which in fact represents the hard and exact truth as it *seemed*.

*Tim O'Brien*

# Reflections

* Descriptions here of death in war, remembered and written down years later by the writer. Note his words:

'I want you to know why story-truth is truer sometimes than happening-truth.'

'In any war story, but especially a true one, it's difficult to separate what happened from what seemed to happen.'

We find ourselves in situations from time to time where we do something or see someone else doing something which we are later asked to account for. We have to tell a story – to a friend, a parent, a teacher, perhaps a police officer. In these circumstances, do we end up giving 'story-truth' or 'happening-truth'?

\* And are there situations when, if we think the truth will hurt someone, we lie, we tell a 'story-truth'? Are lies justified in certain situations: to spare someone's feelings, to make excuses, to buy time?
What about the following excuses given to the police by speeding motorists?

– 'I had just washed my car and was driving fast to dry it off.'

– 'There was a warning light on my dashboard. I needed to get to the garage.'

– 'My car's an automatic, it doesn't go that slow.'

– 'I'm so glad you stopped me. I knew something must be wrong, because drivers coming towards me were flashing their lights and waving at me.'

Which do *we* use? 'Story-truth' or 'happening-truth'?

(See also **Being certain**, p. 242)


# 2  Death came to my front door

## Introduction

Life can suddenly present us with events which cause us to look back on our previous actions and reflect on whether decisions we made were the right ones or not. In a sense, we come face to face with our past, with the moral choices we have made.

In the following piece, a war photographer talks about just such a moment in his life.

## Reading

*Death came to my front door*

We were separated, and I was living with somebody who had my child and everything was rosy; I had a little baby, two years old of age, and I was the happiest man.

And then one day I got this phone call from my daughter. My wife, ex-wife, had a brain tumour. I was in my darkroom at the time and I threw all the cameras away, made some tea, and I felt pain and panic all over.

I thought, hang on, you survived 20 years of warfare with men dying next to you in battles, do not panic. This was always my golden rule in war: never panic – I'd seen so many men who'd died because they were shot in the back running away from a battle. It was a great test for me. For the first time in my life the test came to my front door – normally it was on somebody else's battlefields, I was always looking at somebody else cradling the dead child, grieving for a husband or son.

It's amazing, the importance of that past history, even if you've left a wife for somebody else. It was three years since I'd left, but I'd been suffering enormous guilt for having done that to the family.

And when she deteriorated, as she did, the whole family was drawn into this tragedy, and it spared nobody; her illness raked its way right through the whole family. And it started affecting my relationship with the person I lived with, because I felt that my priorities lay with the woman I had left.

I went into the ward, a dreary ward at Bart's hospital in London, and I saw her sitting on the edge of her bed, and I thought, this is the beautiful young girl I married 20 years ago. And she said: 'I hate to ask you this, but I want to go to the ladies.'

I said: 'Well, I'll wait.'

'No, no, she said, 'I can't walk.'

So she took my arm, and suddenly I was going down this corridor with a woman who was walking like a spastic sufferer, and I thought, my God, what's going on? And I'd seen it all by then, I'd seen everything in human suffering you could ever dream of, and suddenly I was trying to cope with something I wasn't capable of coping with.

We passed a room, an isolation ward, and there was a child sitting there in a cot, he was about three years of age. She said: 'He's had radiation, poor little thing.'

And I could only see half of him, and I looked in, and as he turned around he revealed an eye that was cancerous, it was the most horrendous thing, the eye was completely opaque. I thought it amazing that she noticed another sufferer and somehow gave more emphasis to his suffering than her own.

I waited outside the loo, took her back, and she sat on the bed with her head bowed. And I felt, this is going to be a bad journey.

There was no treatment for the brain tumour, they went straight for the knife.

I had to go on assignment to an extremely remote area of Indonesia called the Mentawai islands, off the coast of Sumatra. As soon as I finished my work I went straight back to England, to the hospital. All her hair had gone, and I saw what I thought was a little old lady lying in the bed – she reminded me of my grandmother, actually. I touched her hand, and her eyes opened up, and we made kind of small talk, then I left.

A few weeks went by and they let her out, but she wasn't well at all, we took her back to Bart's and she had another scan, and they said they had found another tumour, in the neck this time. We were sitting in the doctor's room and as he spelt out the death sentence, she threw up, and I got one of the doctor's files and put it under her mouth so it didn't hit her clothes, and she collapsed.

She eventually left the hospital, but she was having relapse after relapse.

My son Paul came back from Australia with the girl he was going to marry; we planned to have the wedding right away at her home so she could see it. And she bought a new dress, new shoes, new handbag, the works.

I slept on the floor in the hall because there was no room in the house, it's only a little house, and in the morning I went upstairs and she was dead, she didn't make it.

We had the wedding, would you believe that? We had what you might call a rather subdued wedding, and I was the photographer.

I tell you, that was a really tough thing to get through, having your wife, ex-wife, dying on your son's wedding morning and seeing the morticians dragging her body down the stairs in a bag that you'd first discovered in Vietnam. I used to see those body bags in Vietnam, I used to look at them with some disgust, a lot of disgust, and suddenly I had a Vietnam here in my wife's little parlour.

I was at that stage pretty mad, I was like gelignite that shouldn't be handled; it's just that you can only take so much, and I felt as if I'd been kicked from one street to another. I've always thought myself to be a strong character, but things crept in and took my legs away. It started killing me a bit. I felt drink might help; it didn't, it made it worse.

I went down to my house in Somerset and took it out on the landscape. I photographed what looked like the end of the world, I turned sunny days into war, and I printed as dark as I could.

I've met an awful lot of people in this world, really nice people, and some murderers and mercenaries and things like that. I don't think there is anybody who could hold a candle to her, her qualities of being a very decent person who never said a bad word about anybody. She was an amazingly nice person, that's why I married her in the first place; loyal, nice and feminine.

You might ask, then, why did I leave her? The answer is that I was weak, and I was beguiled by this strikingly beautiful woman who came along, so you know, I have strengths and weaknesses, some people don't have either.

I lost a lot. I lost a great companion, and at the same time I lost the woman I lived with and my little boy. A great chunk of me was cast away. It's as if someone took some ochre powder and just threw it in the wind. And I see the future with some concern really, because I'm 56 now, and I've started feeling my age.

Death has been a very close companion of mine for the past 20 years. I've seen more of it than most. Once it comes to your front door it's a companion you want to disown, but it will come, and it's up to you to try to get through it.

*Don McCullin and Danny Danziger*

# Reflections

* He reveals, then, that despite having seen and photographed terrible scenes of war (the Vietnam body bags), it was only when death came to his own front door that its true impact was brought home to him.

    Clearly he wrestled with all kinds of emotions during the course of his former wife's terminal illness. The stages of that illness made him look searchingly at himself and his previous actions.

    Perhaps our very make-up as human beings – our innate selfishness and a natural feeling that we do things right – means that we only face up to ourselves, question ourselves honestly when presented with extreme experiences – in this example, the death of a wife.

# 3 Friendship

## Introduction

We've probably all had the experience of not quite telling the whole truth in order to spare someone's feelings. Perhaps a friend has saved up for months to buy clothes which they really like; we don't like the clothes at all but make pleasant comments so as not to put down a friend.

In contrast, we may have had the other experience of having to be cruel to be kind – for example with a younger brother's or sister's personal safety or behaviour in the home, and talking to parents about it.

But can you imagine the moral dilemma faced by a man who knows his friend has murdered a woman? What should he do to protect his friend from being hunted down by the dead woman's husband? The following extract comes from the closing pages of the celebrated novel by John Steinbeck *Of Mice and Men.* Lennie is a big, simple man who does things – some very serious – that he cannot help. Throughout the novel his friend George has rescued him from trouble; but time has run out.

## Reading

*Friendship*

The little evening breeze blew over the clearing and the leaves rustled and the wind waves flowed up the green pool. And the shouts of men sounded again, this time much closer than before.

George took off his hat. He said shakily: 'Take off your hat, Lennie. The air feels fine.'

Lennie removed his hat dutifully and laid it on the ground in front of him. The shadow in the valley was bluer, and the evening came fast. On the wind the sound of crashing in the brush came to them.

Lennie said: 'Tell how it's gonna be.'

George had been listening to the distant sounds. For a moment he was business-like. 'Look acrost the river, Lennie, an' I'll tell you so you can almost see it.'

Lennie turned his head and looked off across the pool and up the darkening slopes of the Gabilans. 'We gonna get a little place,' George began. He reached in his side pocket and brought out Carlson's Luger; he snapped off the safety, and the hand and gun lay on the ground behind Lennie's back. He looked at the back of Lennie's head, at the place where the spine and skull were joined.

A man's voice called from up the river, and another man answered.

'Go on,' said Lennie.

George raised the gun and his hand shook, and he dropped his hand to the ground again.

'Go on,' said Lennie. 'How's it gonna be. We gonna get a little place.'

'We'll have a cow,' said George, 'An' we'll have maybe a pig an' chickens …

an' down the flat we'll have a … little piece alfalfa …'

'For the rabbits,' Lennie shouted.

'For the rabbits,' George repeated.

'And I get to tend the rabbits,'

'An' you get to tend the rabbits.'

Lennie giggled with happiness. 'An' live on the fatta the lan.'

'Yes.'

Lennie turned his head.

'No, Lennie. Look down there across the river, like you can almost see the place.'

Lennie obeyed him. George looked down at the gun.

There were crashing footsteps in the brush now. George turned and looked toward them.

'Go on, George. When we gonna do it?'

'Gonna do it soon.'

'Me an' you.'

'You … an' me. Ever'body gonna be nice to you. Ain't gonna be no more trouble. Nobody gonna hurt nobody nor steal from 'em.'

Lennie said: 'I thought you was mad at me, George.'

'No,' said George. 'No, Lennie. I ain't mad. I never been mad, an' I ain't now. That's a thing I want ya to know.'

The voices came close now. George raised the gun and listened to the voices.

Lennie begged: 'Le's do it now. Le's get that place now.'

'Sure, right now. I gotta. We gotta.'

And George raised the gun and steadied it, and he brought the muzzle of it close to the back of Lennie's head. The hand shook violently, but his face set and his hand steadied. He pulled the trigger. The crash of the shot rolled up the hills and rolled down again. Lennie jarred, and then settled slowly forward to the sand, and he lay without quivering.

George shivered and looked at the gun, and then he threw it from him, back up on the bank, near the pile of old ashes.

The brush seemed filled with cries and with the sound of running feet. Slim's voice shouted: 'George. Where you at, George?'

But George sat stiffly on the bank and looked at his right hand that had thrown the gun away. The group burst into the clearing, and Curley was ahead. He saw Lennie lying on the sand. 'Got him, by God.' He went over and looked down at Lennie, and then he looked back at George. 'Right in the back of the head,' he said softly.

Slim came directly to George and sat down beside him, sat very close to him. 'Never you mind,' said Slim. 'A guy got to sometimes.'

But Carlson was standing over George. 'How'd you do it?' he asked.

'I just done it,' George said tiredly.

'Did he have my gun?'

'Yeah. He had your gun.'

'An' you got it away from him and you took it an' you killed him?'

'Yeah. Tha's how.' George's voice was almost a whisper. He looked steadily at his right hand that had held the gun.

Slim twitched George's elbow. 'Come on, George. Me an' you'll go in an' get a drink.'

George let himself be helped to his feet. 'Yah, a drink.'

Slim said: 'You hadda, George. I swear you hadda. Come on with me.' He led George into the entrance of the trail and up toward the highway.

Curley and Carlson looked after them. And Carlson said:

'Now what the hell ya suppose is eatin' them two guys?'

*John Steinbeck*

## Reflections

* After rehearsing once again the dream of these two migrant farm-workers – the dream of having their own farm – George puts a bullet through his friend's head to save him from the anger of the gang of men.

This, of course, is an extreme example of a difficult moral dilemma within friendship.

Friendship is important to all of us; we often have to work hard at our friendships so we are loathe to do anything that might damage them. But occasionally we do find ourselves in a situation of having to 'tell' on a friend, of having to be cruel to be kind because that is the honest action to take. No-one pretends this is easy. And, as in George's killing of Lennie, we may also have to live with the fact that others around us haven't quite grasped the whole truth!

# 4 Revenge

## Introduction

It is a natural human reaction to want to get our own back when we feel we've been hurt – physically or emotionally – by someone else. The Christian Bible tells us in such situations both 'to turn the other cheek' and to 'take an eye for an eye, a tooth for a tooth.'

Which is right? What is your natural reaction?

Listen to this gripping story of revenge by the French author Maupassant.

## Reading

### Vendetta

Paolo Saverini's widow dwelt alone with her son in a small, mean house on the rampart of Bonifacio. Built on a spur of the mountain and in places actually overhanging the sea, the town looks across the rockstrewn straits to the low-lying coast of Sardinia. On the other side, girdling it almost completely, there is a fissure in the cliff, like an immense corridor, which serves as a port, and down this long channel, as far as the first houses, sail the small Italian and Sardinian fishing boats, and once a fortnight the broken-winded old steamer from Ajaccio. Clustered together on the white hill-side, the houses form a patch of even more dazzling whiteness. Clinging to the rock, gazing down upon those deadly straits where scarcely a ship ventures, they look like the nests of birds of prey. The sea and the barren coast, stripped of all but a scanty covering of grass, are for ever harassed by a restless wind, which sweeps along the narrow funnel, ravaging the banks on either side. In all directions the black points of innumerable rocks jut out from the water, with trails of white foam streaming from them, like torn shreds of linen, floating and fluttering on the surface of the waves.

The widow Saverini's house was planted on the very edge of the cliff, and its three windows opened upon this wild and dreary prospect. She lived there with her son Antoine and their dog Sémillante, a great gaunt brute of the sheep-dog variety, with a long, rough coat, which the young man took with him when he went out shooting.

One evening, after a quarrel, Antoine Saverini was treacherously stabbed by Nicolas Ravolati, who escaped that same night to Sardinia.

At the sight of the body, which was brought home by passersby, the old mother shed no tears, but she gazed long and silently at her dead son. Then, laying her wrinkled hand upon the corpse, she promised him the vendetta. She would not allow any one to remain with her, and shut herself up with the dead body. The dog Sémillante, who remained with her, stood at the foot of the bed and howled, with her head stretched out towards her master and her tail between her legs. Neither of them stirred, neither the dog nor the old mother, who was now leaning over the body, gazing at it fixedly, and silently shedding great tears. Still wearing his rough jacket, which was pierced and torn at the breast, the boy lay on his back as if asleep, but there was blood all about him, on his shirt, which had been stripped off in order to expose the wound, on his waistcoat and his trousers, face and hands. His beard and hair were matted with clots of blood.

The old mother began to talk to him, and at the sound of her voice the dog stopped howling.

'Never fear, never fear, you shall be avenged, my son, my little son, my poor child. You may sleep in peace. You shall be avenged, I tell you. You have your mother's word, and your know she never breaks it.'

Slowly she bent down and pressed her cold lips to the dead lips of her son.

Sémillante resumed her howling, uttering a monotonous, long-drawn wail, heart-rending and terrible. And thus the two remained, the woman and the dog, till morning.

The next day Antoine Saverini was buried, and soon his name ceased to be mentioned in Bonifacio.

He had no brother, nor any near male relation. There was no man in the family who could take up the vendetta. Only his mother, his old mother, brooded over it.

From morning till night she could see, just across the straits, a white speck upon the coast. This was the little Sardinian village of Longosardo, where the Corsican bandits took refuge whenever the hunt for them grew too hot. They formed almost the entire population of the hamlet. In full view of their native shores they waited for a chance to return home and take to the 'marquis' again. She knew that Nicolas Ravolati had sought shelter in that village.

All day long she sat alone at her window gazing at the opposite coast and thinking of her revenge, but what was she to do with no one to help her, and she herself so feeble and near her end? But she had promised; she had sworn by the dead body of her son; she could not forget, and she dared not delay. What was she to do? She could not sleep at night, she knew not a moment of rest or peace, but racked her brains unceasingly. Sémillante, asleep at her feet, would now and then raise her head and emit a piercing howl. Since her master had disappeared, this had become a habit; it was as if she were calling him, as if she too, were inconsolable and preserved in her canine soul an indelible memory of the dead.

One night, when Sémillante began to whine, the old mother had an inspiration of savage, vindictive ferocity. She thought about it till morning. At daybreak she rose and went to church. Kneeling on the stone floor, humbling herself before God, she begged Him to aid and support her, to lend to her poor, wornout body the strength she needed to avenge her son.

Then she returned home. In the yard stood an old barrel with one end knocked in, which caught the rainwater from the eaves. She turned it over, emptied it, and fixed it to the ground with stakes and stones. Then she chained up Sémillante to this kennel and went into the house.

With her eyes fixed on the Sardinian coast, she walked restlessly up and down her room. He was over there, the murderer.

The dog howled all day and night. The next morning the old woman brought her a bowl of water, but no food, neither soup nor bread. Another day passed. Sémillante was worn out and slept. The next morning her eyes were gleaming, and her coat dulled, and she tugged frantically at her chain. And again the old woman gave her nothing to eat. Maddened with hunger Sémillante barked hoarsely. Another night went by.

At daybreak, the widow went to a neighbour and begged for two trusses of straw. She took some old clothes that had belonged to her husband, stuffed them with straw to represent a human figure, and made a head out of a bundle of old rags. Then, in front of Sémillante's kennel, she fixed a stake in the ground and fastened the dummy to it in an upright position.

The dog looked at the straw figure in surprise and, although she was famished, stopped howling.

The old woman went to the pork butcher and bought a long piece of black blood pudding. When she came home she lit a wood fire in the yard, close to the kennel, and fried the black pudding. Sémillante bounded up and down in a frenzy, foaming at the mouth, her eyes fixed on the pan with its maddening smell of meat.

Her mistress took the steaming pudding and wound it like a cravat round the dummy's neck. She fastened it on tightly with string as if to force it inwards. When she had finished, she unchained the dog.

With one ferocious leap, Sémillante flew at the dummy's throat and, with her paws on its shoulders, began to tear it. She fell back with a portion of her prey between her jaws, sprang at it again, slashing at the string with her fangs, tore away some scraps of food, dropped for a moment, and hurled herself at it in renewed fury. She tore away the whole face and reduced the neck to shreds.

Motionless and silent, with burning eyes, the old woman looked on. Presently she chained the dog up again. She starved her another two days, and then put her through the same strange performance. For three months she accustomed her to this method of attack, and to tear her meals away with her fangs. She was no longer kept on the chain. At a sign from her mistress, the dog would fly at the dummy's throat.

She learned to tear it to pieces even when no food was concealed about its throat. Afterwards as a reward she was always given the black pudding her mistress had cooked for her.

As soon as she caught sight of the dummy, Sémillante quivered with excitement and looked at her mistress, who would raise her finger and cry in a shrill voice, 'Tear him!'

One Sunday morning when she thought the time had come, the widow Saverini went to confession and communion, in an ecstasy of devotion. Then she disguised herself like a tattered old beggar man, and struck a bargain with a Sardinian fisherman, who took her and her dog across to the opposite shore.

She carried a large piece of black pudding wrapped in a cloth bag. Sémillante had been starved for two days, and her mistress kept exciting her by letting her smell the savoury food.

The pair entered the village of Longosardo. The old women hobbled along to a baker and asked for the house of Nicolas Ravolati. He had resumed his former occupation, which was that of a joiner, and he was working alone in the back of his shop.

The old woman threw open the door and called:

'Nicolas! Nicolas!'

He turned round. Slipping the dog's lead, she cried:

'Tear him! Tear him!'

The maddened animal flew at his throat. The man flung out his arms and grappled with the brute, and they rolled on the ground together. For some moments he struggled, kicking the floor with his feet. Then he lay still, while Sémillante tore his throat to shreds.

Two neighbours, seated at their doors, remembered seeing an old beggar man emerge from the house and, at his heels, a lean black dog, which was eating, as it went along, some brown substance that its master was giving it.

By the evening the old woman had reached home again.

That night she slept well.

*Guy de Maupassant*

# Reflections

*   A very neat, bloody and satisfying tale of revenge set on the Mediterranean island of Corsica. Would you say the woman was justified in her actions? So much for fiction!

    The tale raises an important moral question – how do we respond when we (or our family/friends) are attacked in some way? It may be a question of pride being hurt, or, more seriously, of physical or mental bullying.

    We all have a duty to ensure that, if possible, wrongful treatment of others doesn't occur in the first place. When it does we have an equally strong obligation in a school community *not* to take the law into our own hands (that is the stuff of Maupassant's fiction) but to help friends and adults resolve problems in a *peaceful* and *enduring* way.

    Revenge has no place in a tolerant and civilised community, no matter how strongly we might feel at the time of an incident of physical or mental intimidation. Solutions have to be found that satisfy our natural human desire for justice and fairness, and which seek to ensure no repetition of wrongdoing.

# 5 Addictions

## Introduction

Modern society is often said to be a society of addictions – addictions to TV soap opera, golf, football, the car, fashion; most of us could probably be classed as addicts in some way if we spend a lot of time interested in one particular thing. But, of course, the subject of addiction has a serious side when it comes to the use and abuse of alcohol, soft and hard drugs.

What should be our reaction and response to friends misusing drugs? This presents us with a difficult moral and legal question.

Listen to the following article about a young man called Julian Rossiter and his experimentation with the drug 'E' – Ecstasy.

## Reading

*He was mad, like an aeroplane, then he crashed*

Julian Rossiter hadn't intended going out that night. It was the end of his second week as a shop assistant in a DIY store and he was tired from the long hours he had worked that Saturday. As he didn't get paid until the next week, he couldn't afford to go out, although his friends did their best to persuade him. They had all bought tickets for the concert at Elland Road football ground the coming week, and wanted to 'get in training'.

Eventually Julian, 24, gave in and borrowed £15 from his parents. It was the same £15 that he used to buy the tablet that nearly killed him.

The lads bought their supplies at about 8 o'clock in the local pub where they all met up. Each of the four bought and took one Ecstasy tablet and £5-worth of speed. Usually, they would take half an 'E' and a £5 wrap of speed, but this was, after all, a practice run for the gig. They took the speed at about 9.30pm, had a few soft drinks, then made their way to the nightclub.

That night, the club was packed solid and the low ceilings dripped with condensed perspiration. Julian took his tablet of 'E' at 10 o'clock. It took about 40 minutes for the drug to begin to work, though he was already buzzing on the amphetamine he had taken earlier. 'I was having a great time,' he says. 'My "E" came on and I felt great. I was dancing like mad, and I just felt wonderful.'

Julian's friends also saw little cause for concern. One of them said: 'He seemed fine. He was dancing like mad, but we all dance like that. That's what it's all about.'

Another friend, Paul, did notice something unusual. 'We're all mad dancers, but Julian … Julian was really mad. He was like an aeroplane – arms out wide, flying all over the club. Everywhere I looked, Julian was there. People were beginning to get a bit pissed off with him. Then around 1.00am, all of a sudden, he collapsed.'

Although Julian remembers little of what happened that night, he believes he recalls the sequence of events that happened next. Suddenly, he developed tunnel vision and the room began to go wobbly. He thought he was about to 'take the knock' (faint) and headed for the door. As he staggered across the dance floor, other clubbers mistook him for a 'beer monster', and some dancers lashed out at him, angry at what they assumed to be his drunken state.

'I began to get really paranoid,' he says. 'It was as though everybody in the club was following me. I'd go to one corner, start to dance, then I'd notice that everybody had followed me over there, so I'd have to move somewhere else. Then, I couldn't take any more so I left the club and walked as far as the garage, but realised that everybody had followed me out. They were all laughing at me on the street, so I turned around and walked back inside.

'I can remember it all as clearly as I can see you. I stopped someone on the way back to the club and asked them, 'Is it still open?', but all my mates say I never left the club. Mind you, I didn't have any money so I couldn't have got back in, but it's so clear in my mind, I'd swear it all happened.'

Back on the dance floor, Julian had the first in a series of seizures that lasted for more than four hours. Club bouncers carried him outside and for some time he lay in the street comatose, until a female employee insisted on calling an ambulance. Paul went with him to the hospital, and while still high on the drug himself, had to call Julian's parents.

'It was terrible,' Paul says. 'Have you seen the advert where the kids take their mate to the hospital? "But he's our friend!" It was just like that. The nurses gave me a really hard time, and my eyes were still out on stalks with the "E".'

Yet Julian probably owes his life to Paul. By accompanying Julian to the hospital and telling medical staff what he had taken, Paul gave the intensive care team a head start. Nevertheless, his friend was extremely lucky to survive. After several hours of fits, Julian went into a coma that lasted four days. A priest was twice called to administer the last rites.

When Julian's parents had arrived at the hospital, his mother asked staff if there was an animal on the premises. It was Julian, making a sound she describes as a cross between a baby crying and a wild animal howling. His convulsions were so intense that his heels were almost touching the back of his head. It reminded his mother of the transformation scene in a horror film, when the man turns into a werewolf.

A single Ecstasy table had brought on an extreme reaction, virtually unknown until 1989, when the drug began to be widely used on the UK club scene. Last year, at least six young people died from the same symptoms. It may be that the circumstances in which 'E' is being taken – in hot, overcrowded environments where frenetic dancing can bring on rapid dehydration – are increasing the drug's capacity to kill.

The reaction closely resembles heatstroke. It begins with collapse or convulsions, and the body heats up to between 40 °C and 42 °C. At some point, the victim begins to bleed internally. Such bleeding causes a range of complications, including respiratory and kidney failure, liver and neurological damage, and possibly death.

This was the course that Julian's reaction followed that night. At first, staff doubted that they could save his life. Even if he did pull through, they warned his parents, he might have severe brain damage. His survival is probably largely thanks to the anaesthetist's decision to use haemofiltration, a technique that filtered the remnants of the drug from his blood.

When he recovered consciousness, Julian was astonished that one Ecstasy tablet could have such an impact. His first question was: 'Does that mean I can't take it any more?'

Yet his near-death did not seem to deter his friends from using 'E'. One of them thought hard about it, but at the concert the next week went ahead and took two tablets. 'The doctors said it was a toxic reaction but I don't believe them. We all had the same tablets and I had a great time,' he says.

'I said at the time, that isn't poisoning, it's dehydration or heat exhaustion. I've worked as a fireman and I've seen it before. The only difference between me and Julian that night was that every half-hour, I'd go to the toilets and drink a pint of water, then throw a few more pints over my head to cool me down. Julian just kept going for it.

'Besides, when your time is up, your time is up.'

Julian has now returned to work, in a new job as a building labourer, but he finds the physical exertion hard. Eleven months on, he still feels weak, and complains of continuous exhaustion. More worrying is his loss of memory: 'I have real trouble remembering things.'

He also complains of a speech defect, a tendency to get the beginnings of words jumbled up. Whether this is a result of brain damage, it is too early to say.

Experts are still at a loss to explain why Ecstasy affects certain people this way. Some medical specialists believe it should be enough simply to warn people that the drug can kill. This is the attitude that Dr John Henry, director of the national poisons unit, based at Guy's Hospital in London, seems to have taken in the past. In recent months, though, he has favoured an explanation that takes into account the environment in which the drug is taken.

As yet, nobody has examined together the medical histories of the six who have died and others who have been hospitalised. Julian's mother has suggested that the casualties may all share a predisposition to this unusual reaction.

She explains: 'When Julian was little, this type of thing would often happen. If he got a cold, his temperature would shoot right up to 103 or 104. If he was running around on a sunny day, he would sometimes collapse and suffer from hallucinations. But he's 24 now, he isn't going to do what we say any more. He's a man and he'll make his own way in the world, regardless of what we tell him.'

*Peter McDermott*

# Reflections

* This account reveals that the actions of Julian's friend Paul were decisive, telling medical staff what he had taken. Though, as we also hear, Julian's near-death didn't seem to deter some of his other friends from using 'E'. While his mother concludes:

'He's a man and he'll make his own way in the world, regardless of what we tell him.'

Her resignation is perhaps understandable. But what responsibility do friends who mix together every day have towards one another in the area of drug taking? Peer group pressure to join in is always very strong; but equally strong should be the loyalty to protect one another from doing something that can be dangerous and life-threatening if done to excess.

'Think first, act later' may sound predictable, boring advice – but it has merit. And it may just offer time for friends to consider their moral responsibilities to each other.

# 6 Time

## Introduction

'Look at your watch; the hands are going round in circles. If you've got a digital watch then the numbers are too. We all are. Everything is. If you hurry you'll only arrive faster at the place where you started.'

How can we come to terms with this particular moral maze? If the above is true, why *do* people hurry everywhere in today's society?

The following article has some provocative thought on how we can come to terms with time past, time passing and time to come.

## Reading

### Time

The wristwatch is a symbol of death. Most of us wear one. We look at it constantly and see the minutes of our lives ticking away. We are constantly measuring our lives in days on the calendar, in the lines round our eyes, in birthdays and coffee spoons. And the truth is that all this measuring achieves very little, except maybe to make our lives shorter.

Awareness of time, and the influence of this on your health, became a popular notion in the Seventies after two American researchers described the increased susceptibility of so-called Type A individuals to heart disease. Type A individuals are goal-orientated, aggressive and ambitious, continually striving for the next deadline and in the process pushing up their blood pressure, their heart rate and their gastric acid secretion. As a result Type A individuals die earlier. They are, as it were, hurrying towards an early grave.

But Type A people are usually described as achievers, and it's my belief that most of us see ourselves as non-achievers. We're not driven to succeed, we just fear being stuck and being left behind by our peers. At times we feel so acutely that life is rushing past us that the sense of panic becomes in itself a major impediment to progress. At this point – and the feeling besets all of us at some point to the greater or lesser degree – life becomes coloured by the perceived failure to excel, to breed, to earn, to achieve certain arbitrary goals within the timescale set by those in colour magazines.

The first, indeed the only medical reference to this state of mind that I've come across is in a book called *Time, Space and Medicine* (Shambala Press, 1982). In it, Dr Larry Dossey, a Californian physician, describes what he calls time sickness or fear of time. He likens it to claustrophobia – the irrational fear of enclosed spaces. Time sick people feel walled in by encroaching time. And the resulting panic attacks can render them incapable of achieving anything.

I know what Larry Dossey is talking about. And I agree with him that the fear of time is a very real but largely undocumented neurosis which we should take just as seriously as all the other phobias, and treat in the same way.

There are two basic approaches to the treatment of phobias: cognitive therapy, where you teach people to see around their problem, and behavioural therapy, in which people learn through action.

If you take the cognitive approach to time sickness you have to teach yourself that time is less important than you think it is. Time is a human construct. We invented it, as the saying goes, to stop everything happening at once. It is not of paramount importance. More time is not better. Workaholics who are terrified of losing time believe that if they work a 12-hour day they'll achieve more than they will in four hours, but this is not true. It depends entirely on the quality and the relevance of the work.

I can spend three days writing one of these articles or I can spend three hours. Annoyingly, the one I write quicker is quite likely to be better. For the same reasons, a long life is not necessarily better than a short one. Early achievement has no more value than late achievement. Time being happy is not time wasted. Time, when you analyse it, is unrelated to happiness or worth or achievement or anything else.

That's the cognitive approach to time sickness. You might think it's baloney. You might find behavioural therapy more useful.

The standard behaviour therapy for any phobia is to expose sufferers to the feared object until they become aware of its harmlessness. But how do you expose someone to time? Western medicine has never tackled this one, but other civilisations have grappled with the problem and prescribed meditation, in which, commonly, a mantra or a devotional act is repeated over and over until time itself becomes immaterial. Which mantra doesn't really matter. It's the repetition that's important.

I've always been fascinated by the lure of repetition. It's interesting that in this respect many forms of recreation – fishing, knitting, cricket – have in common the satisfaction of a single action repetitively performed. Each cast of the fishing line, each stitch stitched and each ball bowled arrests your attention and simultaneously becomes a part of something far greater and more protracted; so that for a while time itself is held in check.

Eventually, every game, every fishing trip, every garment you knit becomes part of a much bigger pattern. Year after year the same problems and pleasures recur. Thus as you get older, I'm told, the urgent desperation of linear time, in which it seems that things happen once and are gone, is replaced by a cyclical image of time in which all things are seen to repeat, nothing is entirely lost and all opportunities will come around again. The seasons recur, you are reborn in your grandchildren and after you die the atoms of which you are composed will continue to exist in the changing forms of the cosmos.

Look at your watch again; the hands are going round in circles. If you've got a digital watch then the numbers are, too. We all are. Everything is. If you hurry, you'll only arrive faster at the place where you started.

*Dr John Collee*

# Reflections

\* Do you agree with any of the points Dr Collee is making here? Do you find his observations depressing?

Someone once wrote that you should *live* every day as if it were your last, and *work* every day as though you were going to live for ever. Certainly at all stages in our lives balancing 'work' and 'play' poses difficult decisions about how we organise our time. Time is probably the most precious gift we can give to family and friends but so often we do find ourselves hurrying on to something else saying, 'catch up with you later'!

* A successful company wanted to see its senior executives work even harder and spend less time with their families. They came up with the slogan 'The slower day *is* coming.' That made the executives give even more time to the company in the belief that eventually the slower day would come and give them time with their friends and families. The illusion won them over.

Time management remains a personal challenge to us all our lives. Learning to live with time racing by is a particular challenge the older you get!

# 7 Underclass or just unfortunates?

## Introduction

We are all aware that in our community there are differences and divisions of all kinds. Differences of language, religion, family background, interests, talents – these we celebrate and build on as part of the richness of a thriving community. Divisions are something else: prejudices, poverty, ill-treatment – these we seek to combat.

Poverty in our society continues to exist. What, though, can we do to remove it? Do we, for example, only encourage beggars if we give them money? The following article asks some searching questions about society's underclass.

## Reading

### Underclass or just unfortunates?

Coming up the stairs from a London Underground ticket hall I encountered, standing on the pavement, one of those people who hawk *The Big Issue*. This is a magazine sold on the capital's streets by homeless men and women. Sellers keep a proportion of the price, and provide a service.

The magazine is good value: 60p and unglossy. Many respected British writers contribute articles free. The young magazine seller was calling out *'Big Issue! Big Issue!'* in a not-too-confident voice as I emerged into the spring sunlight. He was standing by the pedestrian railings. I had time to look at him carefully before going over to proffer my money.

He was an undernourished spotty youth in ill-fitting clothes, trousers an inch too short. His arms and wrists were painfully thin, his neck so thin it looked as if one sharp blow would knock his head off. His eyes were watery blue, and his pale, knotted face bore an expression of permanent anxiety, old before his time.

His hair, ill-cut as though by a friend with scissors, was fair, lifeless, patchy: an unevenly sown lawn – lacking nutrients or sun, it had not properly taken. Unshaven there was nothing you could call a beard, just tufts. I sensed from his features, speech and movements that he was a bit simple: part of that pitiful band on the margins of viability 'in the community', without any community, in London.

He could have been anything between 18 and 25, one of those youths that have never had a youth, but moved from a neglected, abused childhood into some wretched travesty of independence as an adult.

He just looked completely bashed-about. But not as a fighter looks. He was anything but a survivor, not canny, not cunning: no warrior from that hardbitten, street-fighting tribe that cities also produce, well able to take care of themselves and winners in their way. This was just a loser. He looked only confused. You need to be so quick in London, and he was not quick. He was like some broken-winged chick that the fox hasn't found yet.

I went up and handed him a £1 coin. With jerky movements he gave me my *Big Issue* and tried to work out the change. I said 'Keep the change.' He said, 'Thank you, fellow.' He said 'fellow', I think, out of some desire to answer a friendly approach, but not quite getting it right. Perhaps someone had told him he shouldn't say 'sir' and someone else had told him it's rude to say 'mate'.

I said 'all the best then', and moved off. 'It's a nice day, isn't it, fellow?' he called to my departing back.

And I felt so completely, dejectedly, sorry for him. What hope, what possible hope, did he have, finished before he's ever started, in London? Manual labour, you say? No, he was not very strong at all. Don't kid yourself that this was some young innocent who only needed a bit of kindness and a break to kick-start him into a self-respecting job. It was far, far too late for that. He was broken: broken, probably, beyond retrieval by the time he was ten. I really don't believe in the possibilities of improving people once they have grown up. I wish I did, but I don't.

More than 70 years ago Margot Asquith wrote: 'If you think you are going to influence the kind of fellow who has "never had a chance, poor devil", you are profoundly mistaken. One can only influence the strong characters in life, not the weak; and it is the height of vanity to suppose that you can make an honest man of anyone.'

This youth was probably not an 'honest' or even potentially 'good' young man. He was a nothing young man. He looked like the kind of shoplifters who always get caught, the abject creatures you see cornered by the store detective or hand-cuffed by the police, a hopeless expression on their pinched faces; and, absurdly, you feel on their side and will them to make a run for it. They drift from institution to magistrates' court to hostel to council bedsit and back to court. They cost millions, yet always as an irritant, never as a threat.

We have talked such gibberish about the underclass. We have exaggerated it and thus mis-diagnosed it. The problem about people in the underclass is not that they are a threat or that there are millions of them, but that they are no threat, and they are not very many This young man was no threat to anything.

*Matthew Parris*

# Reflections

* 'One can only influence the strong characters in life, not the weak; and it is the height of vanity to suppose that you can make an honest man of anyone.'

   'The problem with the underclass is that they are no threat.'

If we take this view of society we are really shrugging our shoulders in despair, aren't we? Is there not a moral responsibility on those who 'have' to shape a community where the numbers of 'have nots' are reduced? And just because they aren't a threat doesn't mean we should forget those who live in poverty, does it?

These are difficult moral, social and political questions. Most societies throughout history have had to face up to them. In our own school communities we need to continue to argue and educate against divisions. That is our moral duty. Schools cannot solve all society's problems but good education can make a difference, and perhaps help reduce the number of youths who end up broken and on the streets.

# 8 Who not to treat?

## Introduction

The advances of modern medical technology mean that many young children can now be kept alive in a way that would not have been scientifically possible even five years ago. But is it always right to keep someone alive if the quality of their life is such that there is no prospect of their ever getting better? The question of who our doctors should or should not treat is a moral and medical question that is now being asked more and more often.

In 1995 a boy named Thomas Creedon came into the news; here is how one newspaper presented his case.

## Reading

### *Should we feed Thomas Creedon?*

Thomas Creedon was brain-damaged in the womb. Now aged 22 months, he is blind and deaf, cannot talk and has no control over his limbs. He cries inconsolably. It is said that he cannot be cuddled properly because touching sends him into painful muscular spasms. He has fits and is fed through a hole in his stomach. Without a miracle, there will be no improvement: we cannot realistically hope for an operation that will make Thomas's life better.

His parents, Con and Fiona Creedon, are brave people. After much deliberation, they have sought permission from the courts that he should be allowed to die. They do not want him to suffer any more.

Hearing of these severe handicaps, many people would reluctantly agree with them. The Creedons have cared for Thomas throughout his life, as well as for their two other children. The NHS has provided a great deal of support, including respite care three days a week, but the emotional strain, never mind much of the physical nursing, inevitably falls on the Creedons. Surely, everyone, including the family, would be better off if this little boy slipped away peacefully.

Yet when Thomas appeared this week on the television, the issue suddenly did not seem so clear cut. This child is evidently not on the verge of death. He is not lying unconscious in a cot, with endless tubes connecting his body to a variety of life-support machines. He is simply fed through a tube.

Certainly, Thomas is appallingly handicapped. But on television, dressed in a

T-shirt, washed with his hair combed, his eyes were bright, he looked lively, responsive to his environment, sitting between parents who clearly love him. It was impossible not to think: how could it be right to end Thomas's life?

Nothing will be switched off. Thomas will die, like any other child of his age, if he is not fed. The artificial tube would have to be withdrawn. He would die from lack of fluids. Doctors would ensure that he died peacefully without pain. But this prospect is still hard to accept.

It is said that Thomas's situation is like the case of Tony Bland, a victim of the 1989 Hillsborough disaster, who was left brain-dead after being crushed. Mr Bland was unconscious, unaware of his surroundings, in what is known as a persistent vegetative state. In 1992 the House of Lords agreed that doctors should stop his artificial feeding and so he died. Since then, there have been five other similar decisions involving people in a persistent vegetative state.

But Thomas is different from Tony Bland. He is conscious, his brain is active. Indeed, the chief difference between him and other very severely handicapped people is that he is fed via a tube rather than by hand. So denying him food and water would represent a dramatic change in the law. In creating this precedent, it could affect the existing right to life of many disabled people, including the elderly, who cannot speak for themselves. Who are we to decide that, because of profound disability, they do not lead worthwhile lives and should be helped to die?

Most people will find it difficult to make up their minds in this case, which is fraught with complex moral issues and which breaks fresh legal ground. The judicial process is likely to take up to two years, during which time the question will be thoroughly debated. One can only feel immense sympathy for the Creedons. But given what we know so far, it would be wrong to let Thomas Creedon die from lack of nourishment. To stop feeding him would have implications too serious for thousands of vulnerable people whose lives may also seem marginal.

*Leading article, The Independent*

# Reflections

* The central moral question here is:

   'Who are we to decide that, because of profound disability, they do not lead worthwhile lives and should be helped to die?'

What is your own response? What will the courts decide eventually?

Such cases as Thomas Creedon's and Tony Bland's are also part of a wider debate that is taking place amongst doctors. That debate focuses on the cost of certain types of treatment if there is little prospect of a patient getting better. For example, at a time when the nation faces a higher and higher medical bill because we are all living longer, is it right to spend money operating on a patient who has cancer and refuses to stop smoking? If you have only limited resources, who do you *not* treat, and who makes that decision?

These perplexing and challenging moral questions are not going to go away. Society – in the shape of the law of the land – will have to make some judgments.

(See **Euthanasia**, p. 71)

# 9 Being certain

## Introduction

Can we really ever be *certain* of something – to the point of 'beyond reasonable doubt'?

We are witness to a road accident; we give evidence to the police; we tell the truth as we see it; then we find our own evidence doesn't match someone else's. No one has deliberately lied, but we come to realise events may not have been exactly as we remembered them. Can we be *certain*?

Listen to the following short story by Graham Greene, titled *The Case for the Defence*.

## Reading

### *The Case for the Defence*

It was the strangest murder trial I ever attended. The named it the Peckham murder in the headlines, though Northwood Street, where the old woman was found battered to death, was not strictly speaking in Peckham. This was not one of those cases of circumstantial evidence in which you feel the jurymen's anxiety – because mistakes *have* been made – like domes of silence muting the court. No, this murderer was all but found with the body; no one present when the crown counsel outlined his case believed that the man in the dock stood any chance at all.

He was a heavy stout man with bulging bloodshot eyes. All his muscles seemed to be in his thighs. Yes, an ugly customer, one you wouldn't forget in a hurry – and that was an important point because the Crown proposed to call four witnesses who hadn't forgotten him, who had seen him hurrying away from the little red villa in Northwood Street. The clock had just struck two in the morning.

Mrs Salmon in 15 Northwood Street had been unable to sleep; she heard a door click shut and thought it was her own gate. So she went to the window and saw Adams (that was his name) on the steps of Mrs Parker's house. He had just come out and he was wearing gloves. He had a hammer in his hand and she saw him drop it into the laurel bushes by the front gate. But before he moved away, he had looked up – at her window. The fatal instinct that tells a man when he is watched exposed him in the light of a street-lamp to her gaze – his eyes suffused with horrifying and brutal fear, like an animal's when you raise a whip. I talked afterwards to Mrs Salmon, who naturally after the astonishing verdict went in fear herself. As I imagine did all the witnesses – Henry MacDougall, who had been driving home from Benfleet late and nearly ran Adams down at the corner of Northwood Street. Adams was walking in the middle of the road looking dazed. And old Mr Wheeler, who lived next door to Mrs Parker, at No. 12, and was wakened by a noise – like a chair falling – through the thin-as-paper villa wall, and got up and looked out of the window, just as Mrs Salmon had done, saw Adam's back and, as he turned, those bulging eyes. In Laurel Avenue he had been seen by yet another witness – his luck was badly out; he might as well have committed the crime in broad daylight.

'I understand,' counsel said, 'that the defence proposes to plead mistaken iden-

tity. Adams's wife will tell you that he was with her at two in the morning on
February 14, but after you have heard the witnesses for the Crown and examined
carefully the features of the prisoner, I do not think you will be prepared to admit
the possibility of a mistake.'

It was all over, you would have said, but the hanging.

After the formal evidence had been given by the policeman who had found the
body and the surgeon who examined it, Mrs Salmon was called. She was the
ideal witness, with her slight Scotch accent and her expression of honesty, care
and kindness.

The counsel for the Crown brought the story gently out. She spoke very firmly.
There was no malice in her, and no sense of importance at standing there in the
Central Criminal Court with a judge in scarlet hanging on her words and the
reporters writing them down. Yes, she said, and then she had gone downstairs
and rung up the police station.

'And do you see the man here in court?'

She looked straight at the big man in the dock, who stared hard at her with
pekingese eyes without emotion.

'Yes,' she said, 'there he is.'

'You are quite certain?'

She said simply, 'I couldn't be mistaken, sir.'

It was all as easy as that.

'Thank you, Mrs Salmon.'

Counsel for the defence rose to cross-examine. If you had reported as many
murder trials as I have, you would have known beforehand what line he would
take. And I was right, up to a point.

'Now, Mrs Salmon, you must remember that a man's life may depend on your
evidence.'

'I do remember it, sir.'

'Is your eyesight good?'

'I have never had to wear spectacles, sir.'

'You are a woman of fifty-five?'

'Fifty-six, sir.'

'And the man you saw was on the other side of the road?'

'Yes, sir.'

'And it was two o'clock in the morning. You must have remarkable eyes, Mrs
Salmon?'

'No, sir. There was moonlight, and when the man looked up, he had the lamp-
light on his face.'

'And you have no doubt whatever that the man you saw is the prisoner?'

I couldn't make out what he was at. He couldn't have expected any other
answer than the one he got.

'None whatever, sir. It isn't a face one forgets.'

Counsel took a look round the court for a moment. Then he said, 'Do you
mind, Mrs Salmon, examining again the people in court? No, not the prisoner.
Stand up, please, Mr Adams,' and there at the back of the court with thick stout
body and muscular legs and a pair of bulging eyes, was the exact image of the
man in the dock. He was even dressed the same – tight blue suit and striped tie.

'Now think very carefully, Mrs Salmon. Can you still swear that the man you
saw drop the hammer in Mrs Parker's garden was the prisoner – and not this

man who is his twin brother?'

Of course she couldn't. She looked from one to the other and didn't say a word.

There the big brute sat in the dock with his legs crossed and there he stood too at the back of the court and they both stared at Mrs Salmon. She shook her head.

What we saw then was the end of the case. There wasn't a witness prepared to swear that it was the prisoner he'd seen. And the brother? He had his alibi too; he was with his wife.

And so the man was acquitted for lack of evidence. But whether – if he did the murder and not his brother – he was punished or not, I don't know. That extraordinary day had an extraordinary end. I followed Mrs Salmon out of court and we got wedged in the crowd who were waiting, of course, for the twins. The police tried to draw the crowd away, but all they could do was keep the roadway clear for traffic. I learned later that they tried to get the twins to leave by a back way, but they wouldn't. One of them – no one knew which – said, 'I've been acquitted, haven't I?' and they walked bang out of the front entrance. Then it happened. I don't know how, though I was only six feet away. The crowd moved and somehow one of the twins got pushed on the road right in front of a bus.

He gave a squeal like a rabbit and that was all; he was dead, his skull smashed just as Mrs Parker's had been. Divine vengeance? I wish I knew. There was the other Adams getting on his feet from beside the body and looking straight over at Mrs Salmon. He was crying, but whether he was the murderer or the innocent man nobody will ever be able to tell. But if you were Mrs Salmon, could you sleep at night?

*Graham Greene*

## Reflections

* Divine vengeance? Could *you* sleep at night?!

   A story which really does make us think twice about being certain of something we've witnessed. The phrase 'beyond reasonable doubt' is a helpful one with the legal process, and it should guide us in our own lives when we are called upon to give our version of particular events.

   Truthfulness must also be our watchword. In a school community there will be many occasions when the truthfulness of our words will be relied upon; we should never compromise our integrity when serious issues or incidents are under scrutiny.

# 10  Taking sides

## Introduction

We sometimes find ourselves in a position where we are moved to take sides. By definition, taking sides means supporting one viewpoint and opposing another. If we're debating a particular interpretation of history or exploring an environmental issue this is a vital aspect of intellectual discovery. On the other hand, we may be asked to take sides in order to support one person against another in an argument. And in doing so we probably think that 'right' is on our side!

The following song lyrics from the American song writer Bob Dylan cast an ironic comment on those who feel they always have their 'God on their side'. And even if they do, does it make them right?

# Reading

*With God on Our Side*

Oh my name it is nothin'
My age it means less
The country I come from
Is called the Midwest
I's taught and brought up there
The laws to abide
And that land that I live in
Has God on its side.

Oh the history books tell it
They tell it so well
The cavalries charged
The Indians fell
The cavalries charged
The Indians died
Oh the country was young
With God on its side.

Oh the Spanish-American
War had its day
And the Civil War too
Was soon laid away
And the names of the heroes
I's made to memorize
With guns in their hands
And God on their side.

Oh the First World War, boys
It closed out its fate
The reason for fighting
I never got straight
But I learned to accept it
Accept it with pride
For you don't count the dead
When God's on your side.

When the Second World War
Came to an end
We forgave the Germans
And we were friends
Though they murdered six million

In the ovens they fried
The Germans now too
Have God on their side.

I've learned to hate Russians
All through my whole life
If another war starts
It's them we must fight
To hate them and fear them
To run and to hide
And accept it all bravely
With God on my side.

But now we got weapons
Of the chemical dust
If fire them we're forced to
Then fire them we must
One push of the button
And a shot the world wide
And you never ask questions
When God's on your side.

In many a dark hour
I've been thinkin' about this
That Jesus Christ
Was betrayed by a kiss
But I can't think for you
You'll have to decide
Whether Judas Iscariot
Had God on his side.

So now as I'm leavin'
I'm weary as Hell
The confusion I'm feelin'
Ain't no tongue can tell
The words fill my head
And fall ta the floor
If God's on our side
He'll stop the next war.

*Bob Dylan*

# Reflections

\* The writer throws down a provocative gauntlet:

'But I can't think for you
You'll have to decide
Whether Judas Iscariot
Had God on his side.'

In other words, did even the man who betrayed Jesus think he had God behind him?

In the final verse we are reminded that this protest song is actually against *all* wars; nations may go to war thinking their God is backing them, but would it not be better to think in terms of our different Gods working with us to prevent wars breaking out in the first place?

* When voting for something, you are by definition voting against something else. Taking sides in that way is part of the democratic process. But taking sides can be done in a less principled way when we feel we want to support someone against someone else. In the school community it is worth reflecting that often everyone enters an argument thinking they are right, God is on their side and that they can't possibly be wrong. The moral maze may just prompt us to question that certainty.

# Index of Authors

(* denotes author quoted in **Reflections**)

Adcock, John 99–101
Ahmed, Professor Akbar 65
American Indian Myth 66–8
Angelou, Maya 121–2
Anon 11–12, 52–4, 132–3
Auden, Wystan Hugh 75

Bainbridge, Beryl 48–50
Bannister, Roger 118–20
*Bible, The 51–2
Bradbury, Ray 104–7, 110–11
*Buddhism 55
*Burke, Edmund 15, 27
Byers, Jean 62–3

Chancellor, Alexander 162–4
Chief Seattle 32–5
Chladkova, Ludmila 155–7
Clare, John 211–13
Collee, Dr John 236–7
Conlon, Gerry 19–21
Connor, Steve 89–90, 108–9, 172–3

Danziger, Danny 224–6
Darke, Marjorie 45–8
Davies, Nick 166–8
Dawkins, Dr Richard 63, 205–7
de Bont, Ad 147–9
de Maupassant, Guy 229–32
Dickens, Charles 13–15
Dowsey, the Reverend Gary 64
Drabble, Margaret 64–5
Dylan, Bob 35–7, 245–6

Eliot, George 38–9
Elro 69–71

Fenton, James 75–6
Filipovic, Zlata 144–6
Forrest, Emma 194–5
Frost, Robert 11, 133–4

Gillmore, Andrew 78
Greene, Graham 242–4
Grisham, John 24–7

Hague, Douglas 97–8
Handy, Charles 190–1
Harding, John 208–10
Hesse, Herman 79–80
Hill, Paul 43–4
Hinds, Diana 59–61
Hughes, Ted 131–2
Hume, Cardinal Basil 81–3

Ignatieff, Michael 142–3

Jessel, David 187–9

Kantaris, Donna 77–8
Keenan, Brian 158–60
Keillor, Garrison 6–8
Kendall, Bridget 150–2
Kennedy, Ludovic 62
Kerr, Pat 16–18
*King, Martin Luther 28, 85, 165
Kinsman, Francis 50–1
Kipling, Rudyard 136

Lambert, Angela 140–1
Lochhead, Liz 134–5

Maclean, Norman 180–2
Mandela, Nelson 153–4
Mark, Jan 196–8
Marr, Andrew 185–7
*Mason, Sir John 99
McCullin, Don 224–6
McDermott, Peter 233–5
McEwan, Ian 22–3
McRae, Hamish 86–8, 95–6
Moir, Anne 187–9

Nellist, Dave 63–4

O'Brien, Tim 222–3
O'Connor, Joe 2–3
O'Flaherty, Liam 9–11
Okri, Ben 40–2
Orwell, George 169–71
Owen, Wilfred 182–3

Parris, Matthew 238–9
Patten, Brian 175–6
Pile, Stephen 114–15
Pilger, John 183–4
Pilley, Kevin 160–2

Redmond, Phil 30–1
Rogers, Richard 102–3

*Sachs, Rabbi Jonathan 113
Sale, Jonathan 216–17
*Shaw, George Bernard 165

Steinbeck, John 116–17, 227–9
Swenson, May 24

*Toffler, Alvin 108
Townsend, Sue 3–6
Turnbull, George 214–15

Udall, Elizabeth 72–4

Vallely, Paul 177–9
Voznesensky, Andrei 174–5

Waite, Terry 56–8
Walker, Alice 201–3
*Weldon, Fay 1
Wilkie, Tom 91–4
Wolfendale, Professor Arnold 65–6
*Wordsworth, William 40

*Yeats, William Butler 139

# Acknowledgements

The author would like to thank Cynthia Bartlett and David Birch for their ideas, and Janet Spencer and Sophie Goldsworthy for their editorial support.

The author and publishers would like to thank the following for permission to reproduce copyright material.

BBC Worldwide Ltd for an extract from Michael Ignatieff, *Blood and Belonging*, BBC Books, 1993; Curtis Brown on behalf of the author for Sue Townsend, 'Secret Passion Between the Covers', *The Times Saturday Review*, 29.8.92; Rosica Colin Ltd for an extract from Ad de Bont, *Mirad, A Boy from Bosnia*, trans. Marian Buijs, Longman, 1995. Copyright © Verlag der Autoren, D–Frankfurt am Main, 1994, © English translation Marian Buijs NL – Heemstede 1994; Faber and Faber Ltd for Ted Hughes, 'The Thought Fox' and extract from 'Capturing Animals' from *Poetry in the Making: An Anthology of Poems and Programmes from 'Listening and Writing'*, 1967; W H Auden, 'Twelve Songs IX' ('Stop all the clocks ...') from *Collected Poems*, ed. Edward Mendelson, 1994; and an extract from Garrison Keillor, 'Laying on Our Backs Looking Up at the Stars' from *We Are Still Married*, 1989; Guardian News Service Ltd for Richard Dawkins, 'God in a test tube', *The Guardian*, 8.8.94, Nick Davies, 'The breaking of Harry Roberts', *The Guardian*, 2.2.93, John Collee, 'The worst of times', *The Observer*, 1991 and Kevin Pilley, 'Barracuda Breakfast', *The Guardian*; HarperCollins Publishers for extracts from Tim O'Brien, *The Things They Carried*, 1991, and Ray Bradbury, 'A Sound of Thunder' from *The Stories of Ray Bradbury*, Grafton; A M Heath and Company on behalf of the Estate of the author for an extract from George Orwell, *1984*. Copyright © The Estate of the late Sonia Brownell and Martin Secker and Warburg Ltd; David Higham Associates on behalf of the authors for extracts from John Pilger, *Heroes*, Pan; Graham Greene, 'The Case for the Defence' from *Collected Stories*, Bodley Head; and Alice Walker, 'Elethia' from *You Can't Keep a Good Woman Down*, The Women's Press, 1982; The Independent for material from an editorial 'Should we feed Thomas Creedon?', *The Independent*, 2.8.95; Jonathan Sale, 'It's never too late to mug up on excuses', *The Independent*, 28.4.94; Paul Sieveking,